Death By Mustard Gas

How Military Secrecy and Lost Weapons can Kill

Other Books By Geoff Plunkett

Chemical Warfare in Australia

Let The Bums Burn

Death By Mustard Gas

Geoff Plunkett

International Edition

Published by LEECH CUP BOOKS
Berowra Heights, Sydney, Australia
International Edition - 2015
http://www.mustardgas.org

Printed by Lightning Source: Edited by Cathy McCullagh
Internal Design and Typsetting by Geoff Plunkett
Cover Design by Kim Gardner at Light Creative
Set in Minion Pro & Adobe Garamond Pro

National Library of Australia Cataloguing-in-Publication entry

Author: Plunkett, Geoff, author.
Title: Death by mustard gas : how military secrecy and lost weapons can kill / Geoff Plunkett.
Edition: International edition.
ISBN: 9780987427915 (paperback)
Series: Australian Army history collection.
Notes: Includes bibliographical references and index.
Subjects: 1. Australia. Royal Australian Air Force. 2. Royal Prince Alfred Hospital and Area Health Service (Sydney, N.S.W.). 3. Blue Funnel Line. 4. Chemical weapons--Australia--History. 5. Chemical agents (Munitions)--Toxicology. 6. Weapons of mass destruction. 7. Chemical weapons--Health aspects--Australia. 8. Chemical weapons--Southeast Asia--History. 9. World War, 1939-1945--Chemical warfare. 10. World War, 1914-1918--Chemical warfare. 11. Chemical weapons disposal--Australia--History. 12. Railroads and state--New South Wales--Blue Mountains (Mountains)--History. 13. Chemical weapons--Safety measures. 14. Stevedores. 15. Chemical warfare--Health aspects. 16. Chemical warfare--History--20th century. 17. Phosgene--Toxicology. 18. Mustard gas.
Authors: Australia. Department of Defence, author; Australia. Department of Defence. Army History Unit, author.
Dewey: 358.340994

Other Editions

Australian Edition: Big Sky Publishing   http://bigskypublishing.com.au
(Hardcover - ISBN 9781922132918)

Dedication

To All Those Involved

The Australian Army History Collection

PROTECTING ARMY HERITAGE

PROMOTING ARMY HISTORY

Winning with Intelligence
Judy Thomas

Duntroon
Darren Moore

The Warrior Poets
Robert Morrison

The History of the Royal
Australian Corps of
Transport 1973–2000
Albert Palazzo

Defenders of Australia
Albert Palazzo

The Fight Leaders
D. Butler, A. Argent and J. Shelton

Operation Orders
Pat Beale

Little by Little
Michael Tyquin

Red Coats to Cams
Ian Kuring

Bowler of Gallipoli
Frank Glen

Vets at War
Ian M. Parsonson

Only One River to Cross
A.M. Harris

The Fragile Forts
Peter Oppenheim

Hassett: Australian Leader
John Essex-Clark

Persian Expedition
Alan Stewart

The Chiefs of the Australian Army
James Wood

Never Late
Gordon Dickens

To Villers-Bretonneux
Peter Edgar

Madness and the Military
Michael Tyquin

The Battle of Anzac Ridge
25 April 1915
Peter D. Williams

Doves Over the Pacific
Reuben R.E. Bowd

The Lionheart
David Coombes

Battlefield Korea
Maurie Pears

Chemical Warfare in Australia
Geoff Plunkett

A Most Unusual Regiment
M.J. Ryan

Between Victor and Vanquished
Arthur Page

Country Victoria's Own
Neil Leckie

Surgeon and General
Ian Howie-Willis

Willingly into the Fray
Catherine McCullagh

Beyond Adversity
William Park

Crumps and Camouflets
Damien Finlayson

More than Bombs and Bandages
Kirsty Harris

The Last Knight
Robert Lowry

Forgotten Men
Michael Tyquin

Battle Scarred
Craig Deayton

Crossing the Wire
David Coombes

Do Unto Others
Alan H Smith

Fallen Sentinel
Peter Beale

Sir William Glasgow
Peter Edger

Training The Bodes
Terry Smith

Bully Beef and Balderdash
Graham Wilson

Fire Support Bases Vietnam
Bruce Picken

Toowoomba to Torokina
Bob Doneley

A Medical Emergency
Ian Howie-Willis

Dust, Donkeys and Delusions
Graham Wilson

The Backroom Boys
Graeme Sligo

Captains of the Soul
Michael Gladwin

Snowy to the Somme
Timothy J. Cook

Death by Mustard Gas
Geoff Plunkett

Mustard Gas - A Nasty Brew. Chemical Research Unit Mascot Card
Bowen Historical Society & Museum

Table of Contents

Foreword x
Author's Note xiv
Introduction xv
Chapter 1 – Group 13 Cargo 1
Chapter 2 – Worse than the Somme 15
Chapter 3 – The Devil's Hour 29
Chapter 4 – Green Vomit 39
Chapter 5 – A Fall 49
Chapter 6 – Hell Hold 62
Chapter 7 – The Tunnels 69
Chapter 8 – The Clean-up 79
Chapter 9 – Fall Guy 91
Chapter 10 – Aftermath 102
Chapter 11 – Security Reasons 109
Chapter 12 – Conclusion 125
Chapter 13 – Nandor Somogyi 139
Epilogue – *The Idomeneus* 170
Casualty Roll Call 172
Sources 175
Endnotes 180
List of Photographs and Maps 202
Acknowledgements 208
Index 209

Foreword

During the night of 12–13 July 1917, German forces bombarded the British 15th and 55th Divisions at Ypres with mustard shells for the first time. The British did not know they had actually been gassed, as the initial symptoms were mild and very different from the other gas shells being used at the time. The resulting delayed effects, particularly the blistering and conjunctivitis, resulted in many casualties. In the first three weeks of mustard shelling, the British had 14,276 casualties and between 21 July 1917 and the end of the war, British clearing stations admitted 160,970 gas casualties, with 77% of these due to mustard.[1]

Mustard had arrived as a new and devastating war weapon. Beyond its proven ability to produce casualties, mustard was tactically very useful because of its persistence in the environment, where it could go on affecting those who came in contact weeks and months later. Large areas could be made virtually impassable by heavy saturation with mustard, as was done by the Germans in Bourlon Wood in November 1917 and Armentières in April 1918.

Gassed World War I Australian Soldiers
Australian War Memorial

FOREWORD

The Germans were not to be the only users of mustard. The first Allied attacks, using captured German mustard shells, occurred at Cambrai in November 1917 and were followed by French mustard attacks against the *Seventh German Army* and *11th Bavarian Army* in June 1918 and British attacks in September 1918 during the breaking of the Hindenburg Line. Part of the Allies' delay in retaliating was the need by both the British and French to build specialist chemical plants to produce the agent. This was further exacerbated by the very toxic nature of the chemical processes, which produced many injuries in the various plants, with the British reporting 160 accidents and 1000 burns in one facility alone in a six-month period.

Mustard agents, particularly sulphur mustard, were probably initially synthesised in 1860 by Frederick Guthrie, who particularly noted its irritating effects, although there are claims that other French chemists may have produced it as early as 1822. Highly toxic, these agents had a delayed effect, producing conjunctivitis, respiratory effects and blistering after a delay of hours.

Post World War I, various attempts were made to ban the use of chemical weapons. This culminated in the signing of the Geneva Protocol in 1925 by 38 countries, including Germany, Japan, the British Empire and the United States, which banned the use of chemical and biological weapons. Ratification was another matter, however, with some countries not ratifying until the 1970s (Japan and the United States) or putting caveats on the Protocol, which effectively only made it a ban on the 'first use' of such weapons.[2]

By the late 1920s and despite the Protocol, production of mustard gas had recommenced in a number of countries, including Russia, Japan and Germany. Then, as the world moved towards another world war, the Italians used it in their invasion of Abyssinia in 1935 and 1936, using both aerial bombs and spraying, which caused massive suffering to the local inhabitants as well as killing or wounding 15,000 Abyssinian soldiers. The Japanese followed in 1937 with mustard attacks in China. While formal protests were made to the League of Nations, to little effect, other countries recommenced their own production of chemical weapons, with factories commencing production in England and France in 1936 and the United States in 1937. Preparations were increasingly put into place, including protecting civilians, to fight a full-out gas war, which fortunately never eventuated.

Despite plans and extensive preparations to use mustard in World War II, these agents were not to be used in anger, with the exception of China, where there was limited use until 1942. That is not to say they did not produce casualties, as was seen as a result of the sinking of the SS *John Harvey* in an air raid in Bari. Filled with over 2000 mustard bombs, the *John Harvey* sank on 2 December 1943, spewing mustard into the air and filling the surrounding waters with oil, with thousands of civilians and over 690 military killed or injured.[3]

In Australia, a range of Australian Army volunteers participated in exposure trials to mustard vapour in a tropical setting during 1943 and 1944 at field stations at both Innisfail and Proserpine. Preparations remained in place to react quickly to an emerging gas warfare situation, with shells moved to and from and around Australia in great secrecy.

This book dramatically highlights this movement of mustard agent and the cost in both lives and injuries that resulted from accidental releases of these agents. Unlike the Army volunteers in Innisfail, these

The Mustard Gas Disaster at Bari
Historic Wings

FOREWORD

men, both civilian and military alike, often had no or a very limited idea of what they were moving around, its potential uses or its possible medical effects. In a time of secrecy and Government denial, this was to prove seriously to their detriment. The author, Geoff Plunkett, has captured this period well — the secrecy, the misunderstandings, the limited technical knowledge, which persists even today, the largely useless medical treatments and the denials — to produce an enthralling, well-researched and very human story of the impact of mustard on unsuspecting civilians.

It would be heartening to be able to say that this was a very unfortunate time in our and the world's history, with mustard gas condemned to the historical scrapbooks of more than 65 years ago. Unfortunately, this was not to prove the case, with further probable use between 1963 and 1967 by the Egyptians in North Yemen, use by Iraq in the Iran-Iraq War between 1983 and 1988, and threatened use in the First Gulf War in 1990. While there have been no authenticated uses in the last 20 years, the spectre of mustard gas, its terrible injuries and the limited medical treatments remains. Claims by chemical warfare advocates after World War I that gas was the most 'humane' of weapons used are almost surreal given the subsequent history of mustard and other chemical agents.

Dr Andy Robertson, CSC, PSM
Deputy Chief Health Officer
Western Australian Department of Health

Author's Note

On 19 January 1943 a death notice appeared on page four of the 'Late Final Extra' edition of the Sydney tabloid *The Daily Mirror*. Entitled '50 Ft. Fall Kills Man', the short piece described how Andrew Williams, aged around 40, who was attempting to climb from his room at the Royal Prince Alfred Hospital, had lost his grip on a downpipe and crashed 50 feet to his death. The story stated that Williams, who was suffering hallucinations, had made previous attempts to leave the hospital where he had been an 'inmate' for more than 12 months.

The article contained numerous inaccuracies. Williams was, in fact, 63, he had made no previous attempts to leave the hospital and he had been a patient rather than an 'inmate' for some four days, a long way short of 12 months. But what is most revealing about this article is what was left unstated. One of Australia's greatest military secrets had held and would continue to do so for the next 70 years.

The reporter never discovered that Andrew Williams, a contented husband, father and grandfather, had had a catastrophic brain failure after having been severely poisoned by mustard gas. Royal Australian Air Force (RAAF) officers visited Andrew just prior to his death and warned him that he must never disclose the truth of his gassing.

I am bound by no such secrecy. Having discovered the truth behind the extraordinary events that led to Andrew Williams' death, the deceit practised by those determined to mask these events and the appalling and shameful treatment of the victim himself, I am determined to lay bare the facts. Andrew Williams' treatment was symptomatic of a callous disregard for the lives of men, justified at the time by the invocation of secrecy for the 'good of the nation'. We are now at peace and it is time for the veil of secrecy to be lifted and Andrew Williams and other victims of mustard gas to find peace also.

Introduction

In 2003, Australia went to war against Iraq. The primary reason for the invasion was the presence of chemical weapons and the threat they posed. An extensive search — conducted both before and after the military campaign — failed to find more than isolated remnants of chemical weapons.

It is ironic that the vast majority of Australians are completely unaware that 1,000,000 chemical weapons were landed on Australian soil during World War II. The idea that a man could have been gassed on a Sydney wharf by the same gas used as a weapon by the Germans in World War I sounds so fanciful as to be beyond belief.

It would be even more difficult for Australians to believe that mustard gas remains on the Australian mainland, in her oceans and along her coastal fringes, having been incompletely destroyed, buried or simply lost more than 70 years ago. But mustard gas containers are being

Australian Troops in Iraq
Defence

recovered even as this book goes to press. It was a discarded mustard gas container that killed an Australian resident as recently as 1964, almost 20 years after the end of World War II.

Australians know more of Iraq's chemical warfare history than their own. The events described in this book took place here in Australia and they concern so-called chemical weapons in general and devastating mustard gas in particular.

This book will examine how two men died of mustard gas poisoning as a result of the importation of chemical stocks during World War II. These deaths should never have occurred — but they did. The first was wharf labourer Andrew Williams, who was exposed to mustard gas in Sydney in 1943 while unloading drums from the carrier ship *Idomeneus*. He was poisoned despite the fact that the RAAF wing commander in charge of unloading the chemical warfare cargo knew 'in his heart' that other stevedores had been badly gassed only days before while undertaking the same operation. He allowed the exposure for security reasons — the top secret nature of the cargo gave precedence over all other matters, including the safety of the wharf labourers. Concern for military secrecy resulted in Williams tumbling out of a third storey hospital window; it resulted in another labourer dying of 'tuberculosis aggravated by mustard gas' and in many more being poisoned, the majority suffering permanent disability. Military secrecy has its place, but it must never result in the death or maiming of those who are simply doing their jobs.

A number of the chemical weapons that Williams and his colleagues were attempting to unload were subsequently buried at an Army base at Lithgow, just west of Sydney. In 2008 this burial site was identified and the weapons extracted, thankfully with no casualties. But in 1964 in the Northern Territory, the story was vastly different. An abandoned 6 lb bomb, full of mustard gas, was found by a hermit. In the most bizarre and unlikely death since the invention of chemical weapons, recluse Nandor Somogyi deliberately covered himself in the black oily substance, believing it to be a cure for arthritis. The dangers of leaving discarded chemical weapons exposed were further highlighted when a sample of the mustard gas was taken to the local school by a student who passed it among the staff in a vain attempt to identify it. All were burnt.

This story may appear to possess the hallmarks of fanciful fiction, but it is entirely factual. Abandoned, buried or incompletely destroyed

INTRODUCTION

Gas Cylinders Recovered from Talmoi, Queensland
Ernie Moore

chemical weapons pose a very real danger, even to today's Australians who live some 70 years after the end of the last war. Thankfully, in recent years, the Department of Defence has been active in identifying possible sites with residual chemical contamination or weapons and how these might be managed if they are identified

Mustard gas has had a long and deadly history. In its pure form, mustard gas is actually a liquid which vaporises easily, its destructive properties recognised as early as the nineteenth century. The Germans placed it in weapons in World War I, using it against the Russians in 1916 and, most infamously, against the British the following year at Ypres in Belgium. The devastating effects of the gas are legion — blisters, blindness and respiratory distress among the most common. The Allies recognised the efficacy of this weapon which, in maiming its victims, tied up vast numbers of medical staff in treating gassed soldiers. The British then produced their own chemical weapons and gave the Huns a taste of their own medicine. Inevitably other chemical weapons made an appearance, including phosgene, a lethal choking gas, extensively employed by the Australians during the Great War. Australian diggers would fire large quantities of phosgene towards the German enemy for three minutes in surprise attacks as it would kill men who were not wearing respirators. While Andrew Williams and his colleagues were being gassed on the *Idomeneus*, 3500 phosgene bombs lay in a nearby hold.

The effects of these weapons lingered long after the Great War. Stuart Glover, the radio officer on the ship *Idomeneus*, recalls a 1930s science master at his school in Britain — 'a nice and clever man' — who had been through the horrors of trench warfare and ended his soldier's experience by being gassed. The chemical which injured him was chlorine gas and it left him with dreadful respiratory problems, his lungs almost destroyed. He died from these disabilities after living with them, agonisingly, for almost 20 years. But, while chlorine gas was highly effective and lethal as a weapon, it was not in the same league as mustard gas which was to prove far more deadly.

Thousands of soldiers from both sides were gassed in World War I. Like the science master, many eventually returned to their families and civilian occupations. Their injuries were so horrifying that they caused a huge public outcry in condemnation of chemical weapons in Britain, Australia, the United States, Germany and everywhere where gas-injured soldiers attempted to make a life after the war. Public reaction

Phosgene Gas Venting from Cylinders at Talmoi
Chemical Warfare Armourers

INTRODUCTION

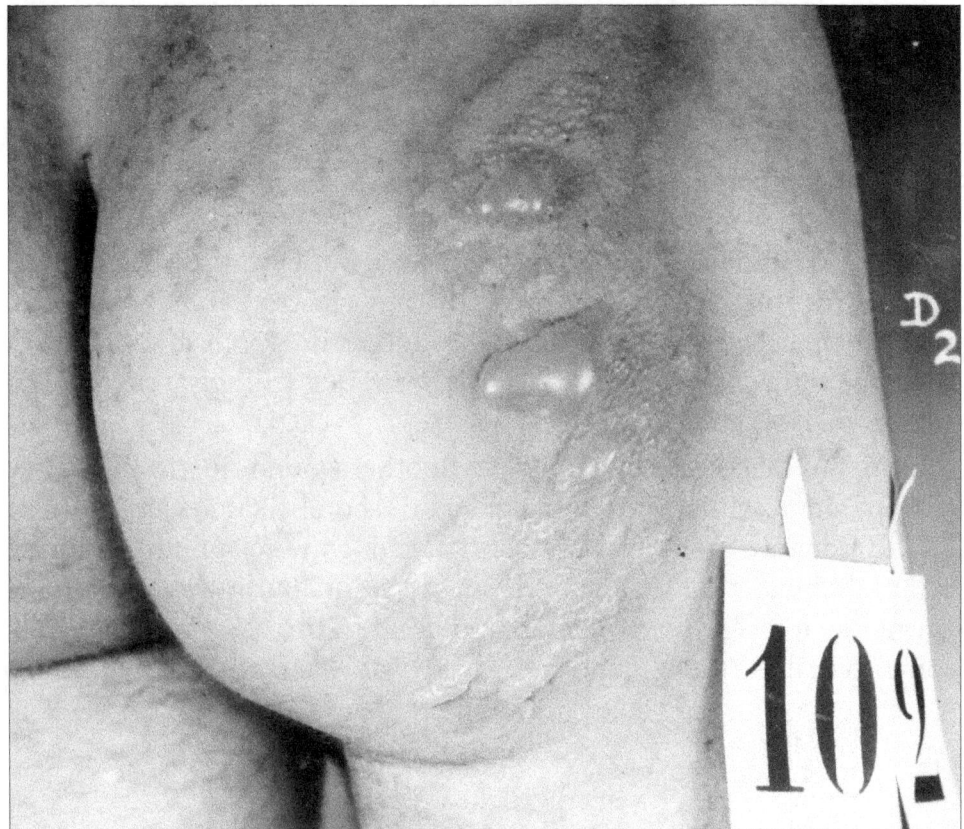

Typical Mustard Gas Blisters
Defence

was so strong and so universal that, in 1925 (seven years after the end of World War I), an international convention in Geneva 'prohibited the use in war of asphyxiating, poisonous or other gases and of all analogous liquids, materials or devices'.

Most nations signed up to this protocol, although some, including Britain and Australia, did so with conditions attached. The conditions referred to using chemical weapons in retaliation to any chemical attack by another nation. These nations also later pointed to the fact that, while the protocol clearly prohibits 'use of these weapons', it says nothing about their 'manufacture and storage … for retaliation'. Tellingly, neither the United States nor Japan ratified the protocol until several decades after World War II.

During the Sino-Japanese War which began in 1931, Japan deployed chemical weapons and responded to world condemnation by protesting that, 'not being a signatory to the Geneva Convention, Japan was not bound by its articles or intent'. Thus the use of poison gas in China was simply added to the long list of atrocities said to have been committed by Japan. By now both Britain and America had their well-established chemical weapons research and testing establishments. At the time there was little interest in investigating the reported use of chemical weapons against a nation (China) considered both primitive and of little consequence on the world stage. Clearly the writing was on the wall and, when chemical weapons were used in Ethiopia in 1935 by the Italians, a small measure of outraged protest was heard but, tellingly, provoked no action whatsoever.

In 1930s Britain, the possibility of another world war stirred a flurry of preparation. Military aircraft, fighters and bombers were designed and built. Ordnance factories were constructed, as were military training camps. Shipbuilding took on a new lease of life. But it was the issue of gas masks to every man, woman and child in the country that finally convinced the British population that war was imminent. Millions

Gas Drill, London
Life

INTRODUCTION

of respirators were manufactured. They were widely distributed and personally adjusted to fit each individual. At the same time (1937/1938) lists of chemical weapons were distributed suggesting that civilian populations could be bombed with poison gas. It was widely recognised that the Germans had been the first to deploy chemical weapons on the battlefield in the last war, so it was reasoned that they would do this again, this time against civilians in cities. But the Germans surprised their adversaries. They dropped plenty of high explosives and incendiary bombs on every conceivable target, but not a single chemical weapon. It was just as well. Britain had large stockpiles of these deadly weapons held in reserve for retaliatory strikes.

With the attacks on Pearl Harbor, the United States and Japan became opposing belligerents in the world war the European nations had been busily fighting for over two years. Japan's initial successes in the Pacific are legendary, but it was the fall of Singapore that was the game changer for Australia's military and its politicians. The fall of Singapore was clearly the catalyst for Australia's sudden move to formally request chemical warfare stocks from Britain. The idea behind the acquisition of chemical stocks, either through manufacture or importation, had been mooted many years before. But it was not just the Australian military driving the agenda. The Military Board, which comprised military representatives who provided policy advice to the government, was deliberately subject to the control of the Minister for Defence so that the military could not dictate policy. In 1938 the Board expressed grave concern that an enemy could use poison gas during an attack on Australia. By April 1939 further military analysis had demonstrated that mustard gas would have enormous defensive value against enemy raids and large-scale landings, particularly where troops were not available to mount a defence. The military and government were unanimous in their view that chemical weapons would be a determining factor in this next war.

On 16 March 1942, the day after Singapore fell, the Defence Committee argued that a formal arrangement should be made with Britain for the export of chemical weapons stocks to Australia. The request itself came three weeks later on 10 March 1942. The Australian Prime Minister received news on 24 March 1942 that immediate action was being taken to supply Australia's needs. The gas was on its way.

DEATH BY MUSTARD GAS

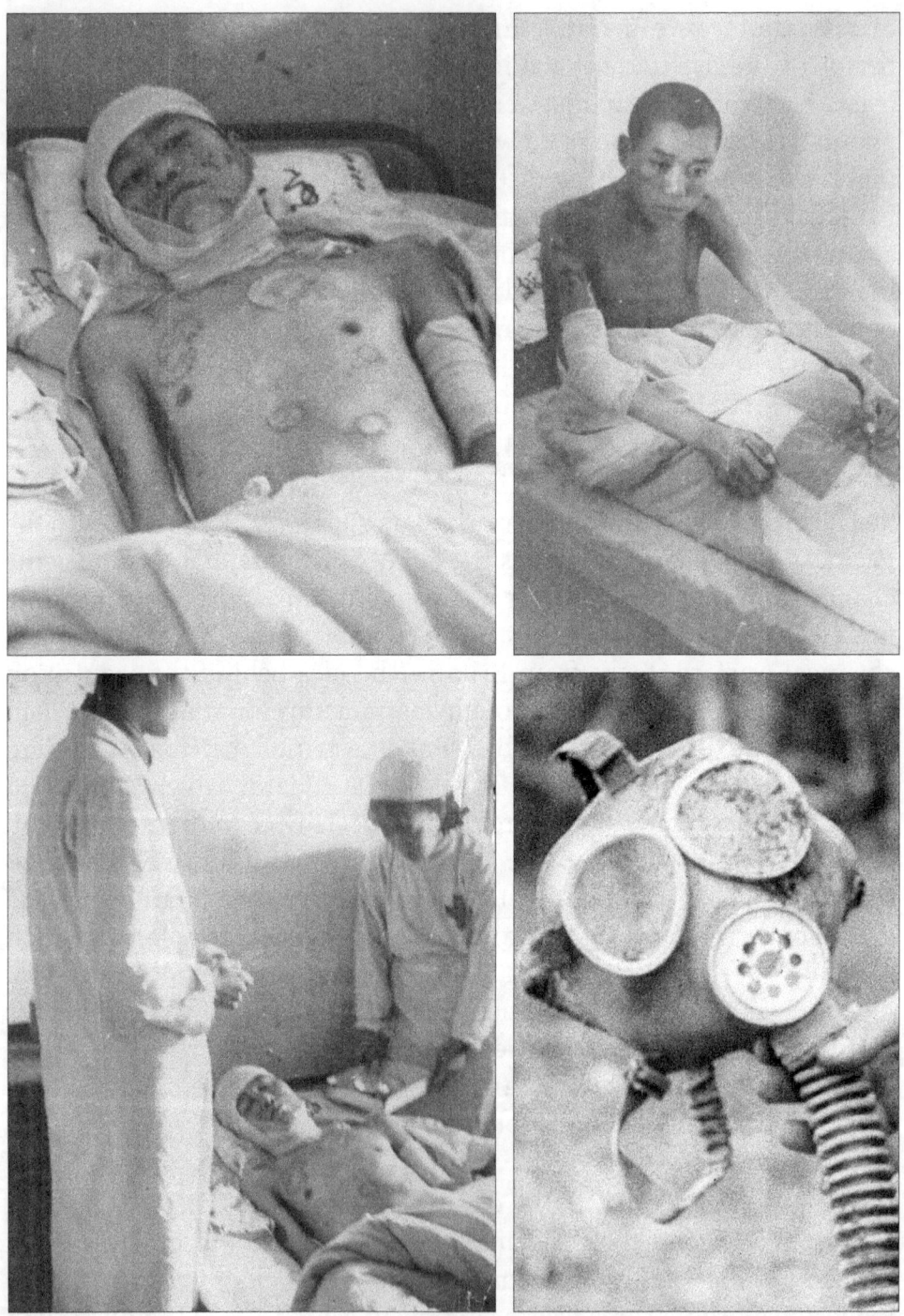

Intelligence Photos Showing Japanese Use of Chemical Weapons
Defence & Australian War Memorial

INTRODUCTION

By this time the Japanese were known to have six regiments of smoke or chemical warfare troops as Japanese chemical warfare munitions had been captured by the Allies and taken to Australia and elsewhere for analysis. Photographs of Chinese blister gas casualties were studied at Army Headquarters in Melbourne. Given their track record for using these gases, it took little to convince the Australian government that the Japanese threat was real and imminent, thus justifying the decision to import chemical stocks. This decision must be understood in the context of the time. The fear of a 'yellow peril' invasion was palpable. Military personnel in the north of Australia were known to keep their rifles close by at all times, even leaving them outside the shower — just in case.

The Australian government's intended use of chemical weapons was never an issue. It never wavered from its stance that chemical warfare agents were only to be used in retaliation, as permitted under the Geneva Protocol, and never as a first strike option. They were regarded as a retaliatory measure should Japan elect to use chemical weapons in its drive to invade this country.

Few national leaders who decide to stockpile toxic agents can have more than a vague inkling of the disasters they can potentially unleash or the corrupting influences they encourage. While the debate for chemical weapons stock had been in progress for some years, there was no parallel preparation of a trained group to handle this lethal material. Instead, unprotected and untrained wharf labourers were used, with deadly consequences.

The events of this narrative are shocking. Workers doing their best to support the war effort were exposed to mustard gas, not in error but in a deliberate act to ensure military secrecy. Andrew Williams was intimidated in hospital by military officials and told not to disclose the details of his contact with mustard gas. His death ensured that he kept his word. The irony is that Williams' death caused a number of people to ask questions and many subsequently discovered the existence of lethal gases in Australia. That these people never revealed the nature of their discoveries was a sure sign of the anxiety of the times given that Australia was at war. People took secrecy in the national interest very seriously indeed. Those involved in these events still do, maintaining that they signed a 50-year secrecy oath — or at least they thought they did.

There are two main protagonists in this story: Wing Commander Le Fèvre and Captain Dark. Le Fèvre was an academic turned military adviser while Dark was an experienced ship's captain. While there are similarities in their backgrounds, they chose a different path when confronted with the truth of a toxic cargo in the hold of a ship.

Captain Dark, who took the stain of the disaster to his grave, was exemplary in his actions, trying to enforce the use of gas masks despite being deliberately misinformed on the safety of his ship. Le Fèvre took the opposite tack. He lied. The question remains, however, why a man described by those who worked with him as compassionate and caring would mislead Dark, the stevedores and RAAF recruits, when the lives of men were at stake. This begs further investigation and is one of the enigmas of this story.

Thus it was that, in January 1943, as the chemical weapons carrier *Idomeneus* made its way to Australia, the stage was set for suffering and death by mustard gas and for years of secrecy and official lying which led to the denial of natural justice for the injured and innocent. This book represents my endeavours to seek the truth and, in some way, right these wrongs.

INTRODUCTION

Idomeneus
State Library of Victoria

Andrew Williams
Beryl Miller

Chapter 1

Group 13 Cargo

In early November 1942, ship's captain Walter Francis Dark strode into the oak-panelled offices of the Liverpool Holt Company. The elegant building that housed the offices was a conglomeration of two baronial mansions, numbers 52 and 54, which had been turned into shipping offices after the original Holt premises, known as the India Building, had been badly damaged in 1941. Liverpool had not been spared the blitz.

Shipping magnate Alfred Holt had founded his merchant line in 1866 and, by 1939, his shrewd investment had grown to become one of Britain's largest shipping fleets. Holt's fleet was nicknamed after the colour of its ships' towering blue funnel which was to become an emblem of its class. The ships were built to a specification superior to the still famous Lloyds A1 classification. On 3 September 1939, the first day of World War II, control of the proud fleet was placed in the hands of the government and its ships mobilised to support the war.[1]

Blue Funnel Line Postcard
The Ships List

Walter Dark was a Blue Funnel captain through and through. He had worked his way up from midshipman to mastering and, like many, was 'glad he had his war with Blue Funnel'.[2] Dark was born for the sea. His father was 'one of the most remarkable and well known sailors in North Devon.'

Three of his eight sons continued the family's maritime tradition, of whom Walter was the youngest. Walter was born in 1890 in the picturesque port town of Instow in North Devon and, as a boy, spent hours on the cliffs of tiny, windswept Lundy Island watching the tall ships passing in procession. He entered the Merchant Navy as an apprentice in 1906 and first went to sea in an iron three-masted, square-rigged vessel.[3] His love of the old sailing ships was reflected in the two-masted, square-rigged (brig) tattoo that adorned his right forearm.

Dark had captained a number of Blue Funnel ships during the war, proving both a capable captain and a courageous sailor. In 1940, when his ship the *Titan* was torpedoed by U Boat U-47 off Rockall Islet in the North Atlantic, he saved the life of an 'errant fireman' and was later awarded a medal for bravery.[4] It was not his first. He had previously been presented with a bronze medal for gallantry by King George V and had also been awarded the Lloyds War Medal for Bravery at Sea. These he added to what was a growing collection of awards for seamanship and exemplary service.

Stuart Glover, a radio officer who travelled with Captain Dark, remembers him as 'a hugely experienced and completely unafraid man who was liked and respected by junior officers'.[5] Captains who were popular with their juniors were something of a rarity.

Titan
New South Wales State Library

Walter Francis Dark
Jane Campbell Allan

Dark's temperament was grounded at least partly in the rather austere Protestant ethic in which he was raised and which predominated among the people who populated his childhood in the Instow area of North Devon. But he wasn't always serious and could also display a lighter side as the occasion demanded. He had a unique sense of humour, revealed mostly in the company of his family. He played the piano well and was known for his duets. Naturally, he was a regular church-goer.[6]

Ixion
New South Wales State Library

The Captain Dark who entered the Blue Funnel offices in late 1942 was in his fifties, multi-decorated and vastly experienced, having been at sea for some 36 years. He had survived at least two torpedo attacks, the most recent on board the Blue Funnel *Ixion*. On this chill November day, Captain Dark was heading to the Steam Ship Department where the officer crew had gathered. He had arrived for the customary interview with senior management to discuss his impending voyage. He was handed his essential instructions and informed that he had been assigned the Blue Funnel ship *Idomeneus* with a cargo bound for Australia. He sat for his customary cup of tea with Mr Calverly, the Day-to-Day Executive, and chatted with the Chief, Mr Cox, who always made a point of asking after his health and family and discussing his next assignment.[7] It was evidence of the very comfortable relationship that existed between the company and the crew.

But the briefing this day was slightly different. In wartime, sealed instructions such as those from the Ministry of War, were given directly to the captain and one was now placed in Dark's hand. He opened the single page of instructions and read them carefully. Signed by

GROUP 13 CARGO

the Explosives Officer commanding No. 3 Royal Air Force (RAF) Embarkation Unit, the letter began:

To the master S/S Idomeneus. 6 November 1942. It is requested that you would be kind enough to ensure that the following instructions are carried out when the ammunition carried on your vessel is discharged.[8]

The letter went on to inform him that the *Idomeneus* would be carrying chemical explosives and reassured him that, when he reached his destination, the cargo would be inspected by experts and unloaded. Dark often carried dangerous chemical explosives such as TNT, dynamite, cordite and nitroglycerin, so the letter came as no surprise. He knew he was not at liberty to decline the cargo; this was a government order. His task was simply to deliver a specified cargo from one point to another and that was what he would do.

But there was something different about the instructions outlined in the letter. At the bottom of the page there were two codes unfamiliar to him: Y3 (No. 1 hold) and G1 (No. 4 hold). Given his long experience of carrying dangerous cargo, Dark was well versed in the symbology used to describe the various toxic chemicals. But these were codes he didn't recognise. He was not meant to; these were top secret military codes known to very few. His only directions for the handling and storage of this 'Group 13 cargo' were contained in the handbooks *Dangerous Cargo carried in Merchant Ships* and *Dangerous Cargo* and *Explosives carried in Merchant Ships* to which he was referred in a note that told him that the two codes would be referenced there. He turned to the two handbooks which dealt with the safe stowage, handling and storage of dangerous items. But they did not and could not reveal the true nature of his top secret cargo. Dark was not surprised and had no real issue with such secrecy. He had carried everything imaginable in this war and in any case he was reassured by the presence of three specialist Royal Air Force (RAF) personnel. Two leading aircraftsmen and a flight sergeant had been officially assigned to the voyage to keep an experienced eye on the 577 tons of military weapons and, in particular, the mysterious Group 13 cargo.

The manifest also revealed that the *Idomeneus* was to carry other military equipment (non-Group 13) including mountings for guns, parts for a Matilda tank, ammunition, powder shot, mines, torpedoes, five Beaufighter aircraft and a Beaufighter fuselage, all amounting to another 285 tons. In total there were 861 tons of explosives. No. 1 hold also carried commercial cargoes including cottons, silks, earthenware, jute bags of soda ash, crates of crockery, drums of cable, box nails and machinery. In all, half the cargo was war munitions and the other half civilian cargo and the 1400-ton hold was close to capacity.

In a moment of black humour, Dark hoped that he wouldn't be torpedoed again as the holds contained enough explosives to blow up the entire convoy. All the general cargo in No. 1 hold was consigned to Sydney although, just prior to sailing, Dark was informed that some of the cargo in that hold would have to be discharged in Melbourne. There had been a mix-up. Some of the Melbourne cargo had been put in the wrong hold.

Stuart Glover
Stuart Glover

Stuart Glover was a tall, strapping lad who looked older than his 17 years. He had met a few Merchant Navy officers in his younger days and he liked what he saw. Conveniently, there was a cadet college adjacent to his home and, after six months' training, he qualified as a radio officer. All he had to do was find a ship and he could realise his ambition to go to sea. One week before she was due to depart he was sent to the *Idomeneus* to be tested by the chief radio operator. He passed with flying colours and was excited at the prospect of his first journey at sea. As he left the ship he watched the shore crew preparing her for the long voyage to Australia.⁹

The *Idomeneus* was named after the illustrious warrior and King of Crete who had led the Cretan armies to the Trojan War.¹⁰ Homer's *Iliad* describes him as among the first rank of the Greek generals, leading his troops and engaging the enemy head-on, often narrowly escaping death. The Blue Funnel ship that carried the warrior name was to be less fortunate — she was carrying a mysterious cargo that would not only inflict serious injury on members of her crew, she was effectively to become a death ship.

Leaving the Holt offices and venturing into the gathering gloom of the late afternoon, Dark boarded the tram for the half-hour journey to the centre of Liverpool and then set out for the Birkenhead docks which were across the river. One of the busiest ports in the United Kingdom, Birkenhead handled on average four convoys a week carrying every imaginable material for the war effort including fuel, munitions, troops and food. Dark found his way to where the *Idomeneus* was berthed and stood gazing at his new command. She had clearly seen better days and there were rust patches showing through her paintwork in various places on her hull. But this was war and the *Idomeneus* was now a

Idomeneus
New South Wales State Library

workhorse carrying whatever was needed to where it was needed, this time to Australia.

A steel twin-screw motor vessel, the *Idomeneus* weighed in at 7792 gross tons and had a service speed of 14.5 knots. She was built in 1926 by Workman Clark & Co. in Belfast for the Blue Funnel Line and was officially registered in the names of China Mutual S.N. Co. and China Mutual Steam Navigation Co, two Alfred Holt companies.[11] This was the second *Idomeneus* that had been built for the line; the first had been transferred out of the fleet in 1922. It was to be Dark's first voyage on this ship.

The mysterious Y3 was stored in sturdy steel drums in the No. 1 lower hold. No. 1 hold was divided into three floors: the upper 'tween deck at the top, the lower 'tween deck in the middle and the lower hold at the bottom. The drums were tightly sealed, the contents assuming the harmless appearance of dirty dark car oil. This appearance was deceptive and disguised a 'mean character'. Its smell was hard to pin down. No two people could quite agree on what it resembled and it was

Y3 (Mustard Gas) Drums
Diana Nelson

variously described as smelling like garlic, onions or rotting vegetables. All agreed, however, that it was 'different'. The drums had two big metal bands, not unlike a modern-day beer keg, which protected them when they were tossed and rolled around. Some 628 drums were crammed into the hold at a total weight of 184 tons.

No. 1 wasn't an ideal shape to stow the drum cargo but, given the stringent regulations for the stowage of such cargo, there was only one other choice, No. 3 hold. No. 3 was ruled out as it was located immediately underneath the officers' quarters and, should a torpedo found its mark there, it could have deadly consequences. Although No. 1 was adjacent, it at least provided the slight buffer of a little distance. To fashion the hold to accommodate its cargo more snugly, drums of caustic soda were placed vertically in the bottom of the hold with a solid floor of wood placed on top. To prevent movement and possible damage, the drums had to be locked tight, but there weren't sufficient drums to fill the hold. The Y3 cargo was thus placed in the middle of the wooden floor where it occupied two-thirds of the hold space. Other cargo was jammed or 'chocked' in at the front and rear of the hold. To complete the loading, crated tractors were placed in the square of the hatch (the central hole). Every compartment in the ship had four ventilators and, as an extra precaution, No. 1 hold was hermetically sealed. The ventilators were plugged with wood, caulked with oakum (tarred fibre) and made tight. One of the drums was placed against a wooden rib projecting in the hold. It proved awkward to place and was knocked against the spur as it was loaded.

The *Idomeneus* had long been used to carry chilled beef to Australia. The carriage of beef on long voyages was problematic for ship owners who preferred to transport it in its frozen state. But frozen beef was considered inferior to its chilled counterpart, leaving ship owners with a problem: there was no method to chill beef for a lengthy voyage, particularly to destinations as far off as Australia.[12] A rival shipping company, the Blue Star Line, had deployed its fastest ships to carry chilled beef and gained an edge over its rivals. Alfred Holt's response was predictably innovative: he would gas-chill the meat. The *Idomeneus* was uniquely equipped with an insulated chamber in No. 4 hold in which the beef was chilled with a mixture of carbon dioxide and air — an innovation that was to revolutionise the transport of this cargo. The new technology proved a great success and was applied to other Holt

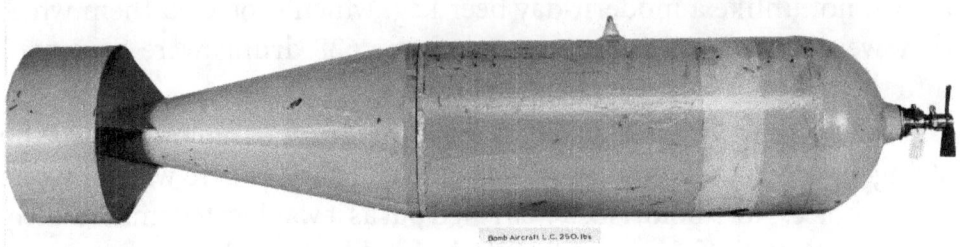

G1 (Phosgene) 250 lb Bomb
National Archives of Australia

ships on the Australia run. It now further proved its worth, providing the perfect storage environment for the G1 cargo.

The G1 weapons were obviously bombs — just under a metre in length with a rounded end. At least 3694 filled and 200 empty bombs, amounting to 393 tons, were loaded into the refrigerated No. 4 hold and sealed with the refrigerator hatches. The bombs contained a gas which was safest at low temperatures, so the chilled beef hold was ideal.

Convoy ON145 departed Liverpool on 9 November 1942 with four escorts. Stuart Glover described the ship's complement as she set sail for Australia:

> *The Idomeneus, when I joined her, had a crew of just over 100 and the deck officers were all British as were the radio officers. The engineers were British or Scottish and we had some Bren gunners and we had some British deck crew, the stewards were Chinese as were the cooks and those sorts of people. And surprisingly, by the time you totalled them all out, there were just over 100 people aboard. She was a very typical merchant ship of the time — typically Blue Funnel, with a single, very tall stack which housed the silencers and those things from the engines. Accommodation was good for the deck officers and the senior engineers — it was all in the centre castle. The rest of us were squeezed into terrible cabins in the engine room alleyway, which were very, very noisy and very, very hot. But you know, as ships went, she was just an average kind of a ship, about 8000 tons.[13]*

A week later, the *Polydorus* and 15 other ships from the convoy parted company and set course for Freetown in Sierra Leone. The remainder, including the *Idomeneus*, continued across the Atlantic in convoy, bound for New York. With its commercial and military cargo the *Idomeneus* was bound for Melbourne and Sydney via New York and Panama. Radio officer Glover remembers the journey well:

The North Atlantic in November was a wild, wild ocean. The ship climbed up to the top of a huge ocean swell and then plunged down the other side, burying the bows in the trough and emerging from all that with shakings and rumblings and things, and it was a pretty rough voyage. People were not really upset to have bad weather in the North Atlantic because heavy weather really was preferable to U-boat packs and the U-boats didn't operate well in heavy weather.[14]

Due to the curved shape of No. 1 hold it had been impossible to completely lock all the drums in. As the boat plunged into the troughs of the ocean swell, the drum that had been placed next to the wooden rib shifted and rubbed against the projection. A hair-line crack developed just below the rim at the bottom and a few drops of the oily liquid leaked as the ship ploughed on.

The convoy made steady progress and eventually reached Cape Race, Newfoundland, with only 190 miles of the Atlantic Ocean left to travel. They had survived the worst the seas could offer and the safety of the American coastline was now tantalisingly close. The weather settled and the first hour of 21 November brought a moonlit night with a gentle swell. It was a perfect night for U boat operations. Suddenly all hell broke loose. The ship in front of the *Idomeneus*, the *British Promise*, was torpedoed by U Boat U-518. Captain Dark had to take immediate evasive action to avoid the stricken *British Promise* and only narrowly averted a collision.

As he manoeuvred his ship away from the burning vessel, Dark thought he saw the submarine's conning tower break the surface close on his port beam and he opened fire with his port

U Boat U-518 Under Attack

Empire Sailor (formerly Cellina)
City of Vancouver Archives

Oerlikon cannon and swung his ship to starboard.[15] His response was justified: in the same action the *British Renown* in the adjacent column and the *Empire Sailor* in the outermost column were also torpedoed.

Merchantman Barry Ainsworth had just come off midnight watch on the tanker *Comanche* when he heard a series of explosions which sent him racing back to the bridge. A ship close by — the *Empire Sailor* — had been hit, but Ainsworth was puzzled by the sight of steam gushing out of her fractured hull. While the vessel appeared to have been hit in the boilers, Ainsworth understood the *Empire Sailor* to be a motor vessel in which case she would have no boilers.[16] Steam arising from a motor vessel was surely an aberration; but Ainsworth wasn't mistaken, although he could never have imagined that he was watching a lethal cloud of toxic gas drift from the ship.

Henderson, the Chief Officer on the *Empire Sailor*, saw a large column of water thrown up and noticed that the hatches and beams had been blown off No. 4 and 5 holds.[17] No. 4 hold was about half full with 300 tons of poison gas bombs. The hold had been specially sealed and fitted with ventilating pipes which stretched to a height some 20 feet above the deck. A total of six bombs were blown from the hold, falling onto the deck. Gas immediately started to escape and the men in the vicinity began to cough. Given the danger from the escaping fumes, the Captain immediately gave the order to abandon ship, and all four lifeboats were quickly lowered. Every man was clear of the ship within eight minutes of her being torpedoed although it was too late for those of the crew who had inhaled the poison gas. These men were already dying.

Henderson returned to the ship to check on the possibility of salvaging her. Fully aware of the nature of the white mist, he wore a gas mask as he could see that fumes were still present. He attempted to make a thorough search of the ship but everywhere was blacked out, making it difficult to see. In an effort to see more clearly he briefly took off his mask, but pulled it back on hastily and fled the ship. The choking effect had frightened him. The U boat fired another torpedo and the *Empire Sailor* sank to her watery grave.

The mysterious gas was a lethal choking agent. In his report Henderson noted that the toxic mist killed 20 men: four from one lifeboat and 14 from the other three. Another man subsequently died in hospital and naval gunner Bell perished on the way to the hospital. Two other naval gunners, Carter and Miller, died at sea.

A Phosgene Gas Trial in Queensland
Diana Nelson

Henderson made his way to a hotel and, some 26 hours after inhaling the gas, he collapsed without warning. Jones, the mess room steward, who had returned to the ship with Henderson, also became ill, but recovered. Henderson noted the delayed effect of the gas which caused his collapse up to a day after he had inhaled it.

The effects of the gas were puzzling to the crew. After recovering from the initial exposure they did not appear to suffer, but would subsequently start coughing, froth at the mouth, choke and die. At the hospital Henderson was given oxygen which he was told, along with complete rest, was the only treatment possible for this type of gas poisoning. Henderson was fortunate that he hadn't exerted himself after his exposure. Had he done so, his collapse might well have spelt his demise. It is still a poorly understood quirk of this poison that, once exposed to this gas, exertion can accelerate death.

'By way of assisting to square up our side of the convoy', Dark now increased speed to take up the station vacated by the *British Promise*. The *Idomeneus* continued her course, ploughing on towards New York, down through the Panama Canal and on to the Tasman Sea, to the east of Australia. The worst of the weather wasn't over. Dark recalled the 'exceptionally heavy weather in the Tasman Sea where it was necessary to heave the ship to.'[18] In heaving to, the ship changed its course and reduced its speed so it could ride into the sea more easily. However this was a dangerous manoeuvre as the ship was now more vulnerable to the prowling U boats. Dark knew this from grim experience.

Meanwhile, in the hold of the *Idomeneus*, the toxic sludge was oozing from the drum in a steady trickle. The oily liquid slid down the side of the hold to the bottom of the boat. It also penetrated the black tar pitch along the seam which proved an ideal absorbent.

After its long and eventful journey, the *Idomeneus* finally arrived in Melbourne and tied up at Victoria Dock 19 as instructed in Dark's military directive. It was 2.49 pm on Friday 8 January 1943. The toxic war cargo had reached its destination.

Chapter 2

Worse Than the Somme

Captain Dark's Ministry of War order had stated that:

When chemical explosives have been stowed in insulated spaces, a careful examination of the explosives and the stowage space must be carried out on arrival by a fully qualified person.[1]

At Victoria Dock in Melbourne, Wing Commander Raymond Le Fèvre was introduced to Dark as the local officer who would oversee the dangerous cargo in Nos. 1 and 4 holds and give permission to open the holds. Dark was reassured that his instructions had reached Australia. The war materials were in safe hands.

Wing Commander Raymond Le Fèvre
Australian War Memorial

For his part, Le Fèvre considered that his brief was 'to advise on the safety of the holds during the unloading of certain general cargo which was stowed over the chemical warfare items' and 'to give every possible assistance I could to the intaking people with the minimum of publicity of these stores to the storage depots.'²

At their meeting, Le Fèvre revealed for the first time the true nature of the cargo to the ship's Master. The *Idomeneus* had carried mustard gas in No. 1 hold and phosgene in No. 4 hold, the same layout as the *Empire Sailor* on which many sailors had perished. The *Empire Sailor* crewmen had drowned, not at sea, but in their own fluids as the misty white phosgene gas had destroyed their lung lining and allowed blood plasma to flood into their lungs in a process often referred to as 'dry land drowning'.

On 19 August 1943, some nine months after the sinking of the *Empire Sailor*, a confidential memo was sent to the Commonwealth of Australia from the Dominions Office, United Kingdom. While it does not name the *Empire Sailor*, the memo clearly refers to the fate of that ship:

> *I have the honour to state that the Minister of War Transport has had under consideration the need for special anti-gas precautions on ships carrying chemical warfare weapons and material. The question arose out of the case of a vessel which was torpedoed with the considerable loss of life caused mainly by leakage from phosgene bombs in the cargo which were damaged by explosion. Arrangements were subsequently made in February of this year for the crews of vessels carrying chemical warfare weapons or material or a substantial quantity of liquid chlorine as part cargo to be provided with service respirators and to be instructed and drilled in the care of wearing them.*³

These arrangements would come too late for the *Idomeneus*.

No. 4 hold in the *Empire Sailor* had held 270 tons of phosgene bombs while the *Idomeneus* held a far larger quantity, some 393 tons. The *Idomeneus* had been very fortunate. The *Empire Sailor* had also been carrying 60 tons of mustard gas and 100 tons of commercial cyanide in No. 1 hold while the *Idomeneus* had 184 tons of mustard in the 628 drums stowed in her hold. In the aftermath of the sinking of the *Empire Sailor*, the ship's Chief Officer, Henderson, had issued a cogent warning which may have inspired the Minister of War Transport to arrange training in

Phosgene Bombs from the Idomeneus

the use of respirators on ships carrying toxic cargoes. Henderson stated categorically: 'I consider that, when merchant ships are carrying poison gas amongst their cargoes, the crews should be especially warned of the necessity of carrying their gas masks, in addition to their lifejackets, at all times.'[4] The crew of the *Idomeneus* had been blessed with a lucky escape as none of them, including the Captain, had been prepared for such an incident and the ship had carried only a small number of gas masks, provided as a precaution in case of air raid.

Le Fèvre's revelation concerning the nature of his cargo prompted Captain Dark to send for the stevedore supervisor, Captain Grose. He then informed his Chief Officer,

> *No. 1 [lower] hold is battened down with three tarpaulins. That is the affair of the Royal Australian Air Force. Wing Commander Le Fèvre is the man who will tell you when you can open that hatch, because there is something in there that he knows more about than I do, so make sure you don't go down there until the ship's officers have been consulted.*[5]

Raymond James Wood Le Fèvre was born in North London in 1905.[6] At eight years of age, he became an altar boy and remained closely associated with his church, eventually becoming the Master of Ceremonies in his twenties. Le Fèvre developed an interest in chemistry and in 1928 was appointed lecturer in organic chemistry at University College, London. In September 1939 the college granted Le Fèvre temporary release and, for a short time, he was attached to the Ministry of Home Security training Gas Identification Officers.

In the early days of January 1940, Le Fèvre joined the Directorate of Scientific Research, Air Ministry, and acted as an adviser to the RAF Commands on certain chemical aspects of armaments. He also familiarised himself with the techniques of the manufacture, handling, storage and charging of toxic liquids and other materials.

Early in 1941, a supply of chemical weapons was earmarked for despatch to the RAF Command in Singapore. Le Fèvre, now granted the honorary rank of wing commander, set out for Singapore where he would act as adviser for the handling of the chemical weapons contained in the shipment. He travelled to Singapore through West Africa, Egypt, India, Burma and Malaya. In Cairo he inspected the reception and storage of chemical stocks in the Middle East.

Le Fèvre's first duties in Singapore concerned plans for the anti-gas defence of all RAF areas and arrangements for the receipt, storage and handling of the chemical weapons that were expected to arrive in a few weeks' time. The Batu caves just outside Kuala Lumpur were examined and found suitable for mustard gas storage. The successful use of caves in Malaya would influence the site selection for mustard gas storage in Australia.

Batu Caves
Imperial War Museum

With the Japanese invasion forces advancing rapidly down the Malay Peninsula in early 1942, Le Fèvre fled Singapore on a Yangtze River boat bound for Palembang in Sumatra. He hoped eventually to secure passage on the *Silver Larch*, a chemical weapons carrier due to dock in Batavia. From Palembang he set out for Batavia on a 500-ton RAF auxiliary vessel, the

Tung Song, travelling via Tjilatjap in south Java. Having missed the *Silver Larch*, he was forced to remain on board the *Tung Song* as it made its perilous journey to Australia. The *Tung Song* had left Singapore carrying a group of some 240 mostly RAF personnel and their wives, one of the last five Allied ships to leave the British colony before the Japanese occupation. The hazardous journey to the Exmouth Gulf in north-west Western Australia took around ten days to complete. On 14 March 1942 they reached Fremantle. Thus, by complete chance, Le Fèvre made his first contact with Australia.

There are some parallels between Captain Walter Dark and Wing Commander Raymond Le Fèvre. The importance of a strong religious upbringing is an obvious one.[7] They were also both highly respected. In the aftermath of the war, Le Fèvre moved to Australia and lectured at Sydney University where he was Head of the School of Chemistry from 1946 to 1970. A university colleague, describes Le Fèvre as 'an extremely modest man ... almost oblivious of honours or esteem accorded him. To generations of Sydney science graduates, Raymond Le Fèvre was an inspiration.'[8] Like Dark he had a sense of humour, described as wicked. However, both men made starkly contrasting decisions when faced with a contaminated hold. One man's decision led to a needless death by mustard gas.

In terms of technical knowledge, Raymond Le Fèvre was exactly the type of man the RAAF needed. Australia had just made the decision to import chemical weapons. Only a handful knew the dark secret the Japanese brought with them as they swept through South-East Asia in late 1941 — they carried a range of chemical weapons and had exhibited a willingness to use them. Samples were brought back to Australia for analysis and intelligence reports confirmed that the 'yellow peril' had previously used these weapons in Manchuria on an unsuspecting Chinese population. When Singapore fell, Australia sent an urgent request to the United Kingdom — the logical source of such stocks — for a retaliatory cache to use in case the Japanese launched a chemical attack. There was only one way the 1,000,000 weapons could be landed in Australia and that was by ship.

Le Fèvre was immediately given the Chemical Warfare Adviser role in the Directorate of Armament, Arm 6, at RAAF Headquarters in Melbourne. His deputy was Arthur Trewin. Flying Officer Trewin had spent some time on the RAAF reserve list while finishing university and was

Arthur Trewin
June Trewin

appointed to Armament 6 Division at Point Cook, Victoria, in 1941. He followed this with a posting to the Armament School in Hamilton, Victoria, as an instructor. It was in early 1943 that he was transferred to the Chemical Warfare Section at RAAF Headquarters to work under Le Fèvre.[9] Trewin would play a leading role in the decontamination of the *Idomeneus* and the storage of the unloaded weapons at Marrangaroo, west of Sydney.

As soon as the *Idomeneus* arrived in Melbourne, Le Fèvre, Trewin and a representative from the Munitions Department visited and inspected the arrangement of the cargo. They made their way through the sacks of soda ash in the upper decks and entered the lower No. 1 hold. Unable to detect a smell of mustard, they declared the hold free of 'obnoxious gases' and deemed it a safe place in which to work.

The operation to import chemical warfare stocks was classified Top Secret and Le Fèvre was unsurprisingly very perturbed when he thought he overheard a government official openly discussing the nature of the cargo. He later commented that the culprit 'did not restrain himself from mentioning mustard and phosgene by name quite freely in the hearing of labourers and stevedores standing around. Therefore these people were quite prepared to attribute any untoward effects to mustard gas.'[10]

On the morning of 9 January 1943, Le Fèvre entered the refrigerated alley through which the air of No. 4 hold was circulating. He could not detect any phosgene so gave the Chief Officer of the *Idomeneus* written approval to continue unloading the ship. Trewin and stevedore supervisor Grose also opened the lower hold in No. 1 sufficiently wide to gain access and provide a safety check and approval for the holds above to be unloaded. Supervisor Grose asked Wing Commander Le Fèvre to be present when the lowest hatch was opened early on Sunday as the wharfies would be directly entering the danger zone.

Percy Alexander had been a wharf labourer for 30 years. He had seen it all: the 1928 strike and the depression years when he had stood for hours waiting for a pick-up, finally leaving without securing a job. He'd done this week after week. But now times were better. With all the younger blokes at war there was plenty of work to be had and there were also plenty of lucrative night shifts. Many Blue Funnel ships had passed through the port, so it was with much familiarity that he started work at 8.00 am on Sunday morning in No.1 hold. He was instructed to go to the 'tween decks where he was tasked with unloading the bagged soda ash. It was back-breaking work manhandling the sacks into a sling before they were winched up by the hatch cranes.[11]

After three hours Alexander and his colleagues were ready to work the lower hold and remove the tractor cases that had been accidently loaded where the Sydney cargo should have been. Had the cargo been correctly loaded, they wouldn't have needed to access this area at all. Before they could enter the lower hold, however, they needed to secure clearance from Le Fèvre. Le Fèvre performed a nasal and visual inspection of the drums and gave the men approval to proceed. Percy Alexander and the gang were ready to move in to finish their work.

Alexander had spent half a lifetime on the waterfront unloading hundreds of ships. However, this time something immediately caught his experienced eye: 'There was something very conspicuous to me in the lower hold — three tarpaulins we had to remove, and that was very unusual.' He was unaware that the hold had been hermetically sealed due to its toxic cargo. Alexander and the other men removed the tarpaulins covering the lower hatch and then entered. They noted the tractor cases in the square of the hatch and were immediately assaulted by an acrid and unusual odour.

Ships' holds are characterised by unusual and varied smells, but this was different. To Alexander the odour resembled rotten onions and was strangely redolent. He couldn't place it at the time but, years later, he recalled serving in France in the Australian Imperial Force where he had been caught up in a mustard gas attack. On reflection the smell on the ship appeared similar, although the odour in the hold was 'much stronger than in the case of the Somme in 1916'. At the time of unloading he noticed that his eyes were tearing and were 'blood red'. He noted the same effects in his colleagues. Alexander felt exhausted and complained to the hatchman, William Duck, who was to be the recipient of many stevedore complaints about 'that smell'. As one of the stevedores in the lower hold had become too ill to continue work, Duck had relieved him after lunch, a little after one o'clock. The smell reminded him of vegetables.[12] It is a peculiar characteristic of mustard gas that, among a group of men exposed to its effects, none will agree on what the smell resembles. Each will interpret it differently.

Hatchman Duck was so concerned that he asked for the ship's Chief Officer to be sent down. Without discussion gas masks were produced. There was no context to their arrival and none of the stevedores associated it with the odour. Stevedore supervisor Grose was told that they were 'to be used in an emergency', although what sort of emergency he was unsure. He later recalled that 'they were not used as it was not deemed necessary by the authorities present.'[13] When one of the stevedores tried one on out of curiosity, he was told by a supervisor to 'stop playing around with it' and take it off.

Although none of the wharfies made a connection between the gas masks and the odour, hatchman Duck was more than a little curious. He knew gas masks were never used by the wharfies and that they had no training in their use. He noted that the officers were tight-lipped and guessed that there was something special about this cargo. He suspected that it was an obnoxious payload associated with the military. Duck was the only stevedore who had heard the rumours, most likely from the indiscreet government official of whose 'loose lips' Le Fèvre had complained. When the Chief Officer arrived Duck asked a direct question, 'Is this mustard gas?' The Chief Officer's response was to leave and return with the two Air Force officers, Le Fèvre and his deputy, Trewin. Duck observed them inspecting the tops of the drums, but was none the wiser. As a precaution, Trewin, Le Fèvre and the RAF advisers who had travelled with the toxic cargo on the *Idomeneus* remained in the hold while the cases were removed.[14]

As the afternoon progressed the situation deteriorated with some of the stevedores exiting the hatch, vomiting over the side, but feeling obliged to return to work. Finally, at 6.00 pm, Percy Alexander had reached his limit; he was too exhausted to continue and simply commented, 'I have had it.' At this late stage he heard that the Port Inspector had been called.

The Port Inspector, employed by the Stevedoring Industry Commission, was called to the ship at around 6.00 pm. He was shocked by the scene that greeted him. 'When I got to No. 1 hatch I observed men around in the vicinity of that hatch. I observed probably four or five or six men. The condition of those men, they were in such a state that they were unable to continue work on the hatch.'[15] He saw men draped over the edge of the hatches and others retching over the side of

Gas Masks such as these were Dumped on the Deck of the Idomeneus without Explanation
Australian War Memorial

the ship. He was shocked by their state but more shocked by the odour permeating the air.

The Port Inspector detected the acrid and pungent odour some three metres from the hatch opening. He had served during the First World War and had been at sea on HMAS *Australia* where he had received anti-gas training as part of his naval training. He noticed in particular the men's inflamed eyes and the tears streaming down their faces. Their appearance, the smell and vomiting led him to a quick but definitive conclusion — it was mustard gas. He reached this conclusion based solely on the evidence that confronted him rather than anything he had been told. At this stage he had spoken to neither Le Fèvre nor Trewin, nor to any of the RAF advisers who had travelled with the cargo.

Stevedore supervisor Grose was summoned and the Port Inspector told him that, as the men's health was his primary concern, he was sealing the hatch pending future investigation by the higher port authorities. The Inspector approached a senior RAAF officer, most likely Le Fèvre, and pressed him as to the nature of the cargo. 'Under security regulations I am unable to tell you,' was the unhelpful reply.[16] The Port Inspector was irritated by the officiousness of this response. He was bound by a secrecy oath himself and felt he had the authority to be told. Instead he was being kept in the dark when the health of his men was at stake.

HMAS Australia
Australian War Memorial

Captain Dark had no inkling of the evolving drama. He had been ashore taking a walk and, on his return, was met by his Chief Officer who reported that a number of men had been taken ill and the unloading had been halted. RAAF Chemical Warfare deputy Trewin visited the ship and 'advised first aid precautions as for mustard'.[17] By this stage one of the RAF advisers was also showing obvious signs of conjunctivitis and was removed to the RAAF hospital at Ascot Vale. Le Fèvre was recalled to the ship. He was accompanied by the RAAF medical officer from Ascot Vale.

Le Fèvre gave the Chief Officer 'a written and signed statement to the effect I was certain no mustard vapour had been present that morning to cause these effects.' But, if this was not the result of mustard gas, what could have caused such dramatic effects? While investigating the cause, Le Fèvre visited the deck storehouse and found an extremely strong sweetish tear gas smell. His opinion 'was that the wind direction may have been such that eddies of smell from the deck store' had caused the irritation.[18] As the stevedores were no longer available to chock the hole left by the now removed tractor cases, volunteers were asked to go down into the hold. Trewin and a team of stevedores answered the call and finished the job.

Hatchman Duck had, by now, struggled home. The condition of his eyes had deteriorated significantly. He dressed to go and seek medical help but, on the way into the city, 'went blind in the tram and had to be led to the hospital by my wife.' Duck was in hospital for some three weeks and, during that time, he saw all but two of the other men who had been working in the hold of the *Idomeneus*. 'After a week and a half I could just about see but it took nine weeks or so to be normal' was his recollection.[19]

Stevedore Percy Alexander later recalled, 'I don't know how I got home.'[20] Alexander's wife, as instructed, smothered his eyes with castor oil and took him to the doctor the next day. For a fortnight his wife took him back and forth to the doctor as he had temporarily lost his sight. Another wharfie colleague was in hospital for ten days with symptoms including vomiting, conjunctivitis and burns to the throat, skin and larynx. His treatment included the administration of atropine eye drops and sulphonamides by mouth. An extract from the deadly nightshade plant, atropine dilates the pupils and counteracts the closure caused by the mustard gas.

On Monday 11 January, Le Fèvre and several more RAAF officers revisited the ship. By this time another of the British RAF advisers had developed eye trouble and was sent to the RAAF hospital at Ascot Vale to join his colleague. The Third Mate from the *Idomeneus*, Hugh 'Gerry' Forsgate, informed the RAAF officers that 'he had been rung by a nurse from the Melbourne hospital at 2 pm and warned to boil all his clothes ...

as he was in danger from mustard gas contamination.'[21] On leaving the ship, Le Fèvre was interviewed by two representatives of the Victoria Dock Police who 'were particularly anxious to obtain a statement whether or not the injuries of the men were due to mustard.' His reply was unequivocal: 'They were not.'[22]

That afternoon there was a frantic round of phone calls for Le Fèvre who, at one point, conversed with a RAAF air vice marshal. By now, Le Fèvre's deputy, Trewin, had developed conjunctivitis and had been sent home. Le Fèvre later wrote that 'a rumour centring around mustard was fairly widespread.' With rumours escalating, the air vice marshal had recommended that Le Fèvre and RAAF medical services representatives visit the hospital that evening and talk to the men. The visit was duly completed.

'Gerry' Forsgate & Wife Betty
Brian Forsgate

Le Fèvre noted that,

> *For my part, nothing I saw caused me to alter my opinion ... namely that mustard vapours in concentrations below the threshold of detectability by smell could not have caused the injuries. They must have been due to soda ash dust in conjunction with traces of dichlorobenzene and possibly carbon tetrachloride and formaldehyde. The smallest amount of mustard vapour detectable by smell is 0.19 mgm/cu m and I have frequently noted I have a sensitivity to this at least.*[23]

Before the ship left Melbourne to continue its voyage to Sydney, Captain Dark asked Wing Commander Le Fèvre to provide him a written opinion that the wharfies' problems had not been caused by 'the stuff in No. 1 lower hold'.[24] Le Fèvre agreed. His opinion was included in a Sydney certificate written on 14 January which read: 'I have inspected the lowest section of No. 1 hold and as in Melbourne have been unable to detect the presence of mustard gas by smell.'[25]

By 11 January, the rumours had reached the press, with an article in *The Argus* entitled 'Seven Waterside Workers Injured'. It named six of those admitted to Royal Melbourne Hospital who were 'suffering from burns to face and eyes caused by a corrosive substance.'

The RAAF was taking no chances with the Sydney unloading. A 66 National Security (General) Regulation was signed by the Deputy Director of Ordnance Services which stated that:

> *A Senior Officer of the Movements and Shipping Section RAAF shall be present and perform duty at the said wharf and shall have control of the whole of the unshipping, handling, storage and conveyance of the said ammunition, explosives and inflammable substances.*[26]

It directed the *Idomeneus* to Walsh Bay in Sydney.

As the *Idomeneus* sailed to Sydney, the man with ultimate responsibility for the chemical weapons, Director of Armaments Wing Commander Lightfoot, was nervous. He recorded a missive which stated, 'Our preparations in this country for offensive chemical warfare as a retaliatory measure are highly secret and should be known by as few people as possible, even within the service.' He referred to the errant government official who

> *showed flagrant disregard for this requirement and it is suggested that suitable action be taken against him. I understand that while walking up and down the wharf, he shouted out such questions as, Where is the mustard gas? and Is that the hold with the phosgene in?*[27]

Lightfoot further noted that, while this action was a flagrant breach of security regulations, it was aggravated in this case by the casualties among the stevedores and their resultant attitude. The gentleman in question was later to deny the accusation.

Just before Le Fèvre left for Sydney he received further information from the medical officers at Ascot Vale RAAF Hospital. He was concerned by their findings, but continued to 'stake his reputation' on the fact that mustard gas was not responsible.[28] His reputation would be further tested in Sydney.

Mustard Gas Burns

Chapter 3

The Devil's Hour

On 13 January 1943 the *Idomeneus* approached Sydney Harbour. Radio officer Stuart Glover came out on deck just as the ship entered the harbour. He was taken with its magnificence. The harbour was at its best on what was a typical summer's day with a gentle breeze, a slight sea swell and that tropical warmth for which summertime Sydney is renowned. Seventy years on he could still remember that day vividly.[1] It left such an impression that he later immigrated and settled in Sydney permanently.

Stuart Glover
Stuart Glover

Idomeneus reduced speed, the pilots boarded and the ship slid under the harbour bridge with Glover nervously eyeing the mast clearance. By 6.20 pm the vessel was securely moored at No. 8 Pier, Walsh Bay, as ordered. It rode the gentle swell at its berth just a few hundred metres from the city's central business district.

Minutes later Captain Dark received a knock on the door. Having been used to greeting a shipping agent on his arrival in port, Dark was surprised to see three men lined up at his door. Le Fèvre had also arrived, having flown to Sydney to be *in situ* ahead of the ship. His job remained uncompleted as all the chemical weapons were yet to be unloaded. There was also a much larger group of senior RAAF representatives and wharf officials interested in the arrival of the ship.

The Blue Funnel's shipping agent had been so concerned by the events in Melbourne that the line had recruited its own specialist chemical expert. He was Harold McKenzie, an analytical chemist who was an Associate of the Australian Chemical Institute and an analyst under the Pure Foods Act. He was also the acting proprietor of the firm of Dickson & Byrne and his résumé extended to some 20 years' experience.

An impromptu meeting was soon in progress. Preliminary discussion regarding the stay in port and repairs was quickly out of the way and they proceeded to the crux of the matter which concerned the chemical warfare holds. While the precise identity of the RAAF officers who provided the various responses has never been clearly established, what followed was an extraordinary case of military obscuration and deception that is a matter of court record.

Recalling the casualties during the Melbourne unloading, Dark opened the proceedings with the obvious question, 'In view of what happened in Melbourne, what are we going to do to prevent a reoccurrence?' The military response was one of surprise: 'What do you mean?' Captain Dark then suggested that the wearing of gas masks was the only safe way to unload No. 1 hold. Hell bent on maintaining secrecy, the RAAF officers told Dark, 'What do you want gas masks for? It is not gas — it is soda ash.'[2] This response contradicted Trewin's advice following his visit to the *Idomeneus* in Melbourne when he had stated categorically that first aid precautions for mustard gas should be adopted. Trewin himself was not at this meeting — he was still recovering from being gassed.

Dark was an experienced captain. He told his audience that he had carried many thousands of tons of soda ash on previous journeys and had never seen such 'distressing symptoms' caused by soda ash. Perhaps he could accept that soda ash could cause eye trouble in a hot climate, but the vomiting was a different story altogether. He pressed the RAAF officers on the matter and was given the implausible response that the chemicals stowed in the fore cabin had become somehow mixed with the soda ash.

Dark naturally wondered how this had occurred and was told that the chemicals had been carried on the feet of the men who worked in the fore cabin and subsequently went down into the soda ash decks. Despite this explanation Captain Dark made one more attempt to enforce gas mask use in the hold, suggesting the display of 'a notice on number one and number four hatches saying that no one is allowed down here without a gas mask.'³ This suggestion finally produced a definitive response from the RAAF officers and one that revealed the crux of the affair:

*No, we shall reveal what is in the ship. We cannot do that for security reasons, we do not want everybody to know what is in the ship. No. 4 is phosgene and No. 1 is mustard gas. We cannot enforce gas masks, but when we get to the lower hold we will try to persuade the men to wear them.*⁴

Soda Ash Bags
Australian War Memorial

It could not have been spelled out more clearly. The wharf labourers were not permitted to know what they were handling as the importation of chemical weapons was classified Top Secret. Furthermore, despite the fact that they were handling a lethal agent, the adoption of gas protection could only be vaguely suggested to the workers as a precaution, it would not be mandatory.

In the face of solid opposition Dark, with the safety of the stevedores and his own crew at the forefront, insisted that, as a minimum, both Le Fèvre and the civilian chemist McKenzie would need to prove there was no chemical danger when the workers entered the weapons holds. McKenzie was also to test the commercial holds above the mustard gas before every shift. Dark gave explicit instruction to his officers that the tarpaulin on lower No. 1 hold should not be touched until Le Fèvre gave the word to open the hatch. During the meeting McKenzie glanced across to Le Fèvre and could see clearly that his eyes had been affected by the contamination in Melbourne. He was quite obviously suffering from conjunctivitis himself.⁵

The ship carried gas masks as required for air raid precautions but they had not been used for some time and were dirty. However they were Dark's only option as the RAAF refused to supply gas masks. Dark then asked the RAAF officers to assist him in cleaning them, but was told they had no means to do so. The ever-resourceful Dark found his own means of cleaning the masks and, despite their unhelpfulness, promised to make them available.

Dark now had official orders to work around the clock to clear the military cargo. The meeting over, Le Fèvre inspected No. 1 hold with McKenzie and two of the ship's officers. They used their sense of smell as a barometer. The drums of mustard were noted to be in good condition and they detected no odour. McKenzie issued a first provisional certificate for the labour in the two 'tween decks where work was to commence on the commercial cargo. He decided to return to the lab to perform a chemical test despite having heard, almost certainly from Le Fèvre, that a sense of smell could be as accurate as a chemical test for mustard gas levels. McKenzie promised to ring through the analytical result to the assistant wharf manager.[6] Some days later, again after a request from Dark, Le Fèvre provided a certificate of clearance for the unloading on this first night.

As instructed in the letter from the Ministry of War, preparations had been made for the raising of a decontamination squad. At lunchtime on 13 January, RAAF Flying Officer Harold Freeman was commanded to take charge of a party of 12 airmen and proceed to Sydney to form the squad. As a teenager, Freeman had served in the senior cadets and

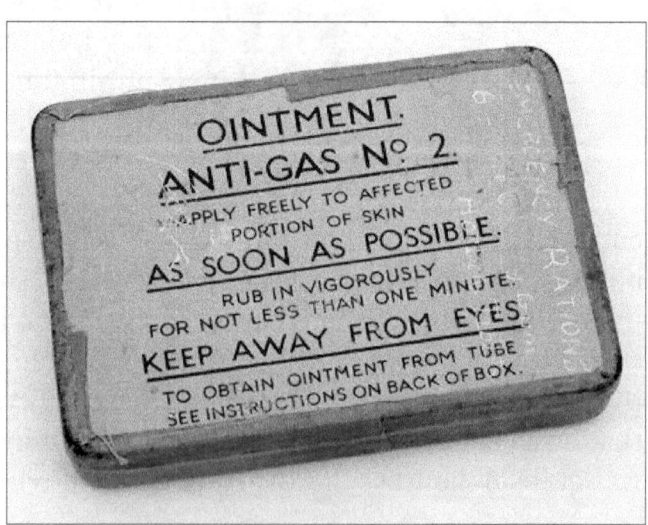

Anti-Gas Ointment
Australian War Memorial

had worked as a warehouse manager at Dunlop Rubber Company in Sydney since 1936. When applying for a commission in the Equipment Branch of the RAAF he declared his expertise to lie in 'all activities in warehousing from receipt of orders to dispatch' and was assigned as an equipment officer at the combined RAAF/Army establishment at Marrangaroo (west of Sydney).

Freeman gathered decontamination suits, respirators, rubber gloves, mittens, oilskin gloves, three drums of bleaching powder, two jars of No. 2 anti-gas ointment, gas detector paper (litmus), eye shields and a complete set of decontamination equipment. He reported to RAAF No. 1 Movements and Shipping Office where Le Fèvre gave instructions on the decontamination procedures, should they be required. The men were to be accommodated on the wharf for the duration of the unloading.

Freeman had little experience in chemical weapons. His training amounted to a one-week RAAF officers No. 3 gas course which he had undertaken only weeks earlier. Freeman arranged a roster so that two of his men were on board at any one time, one supervising the stevedores in No. 1 and one supervising those in No. 4. With the experts having granted their approval, it was time for the stevedores to move in. The night gang went aboard and unloading commenced at 7.00 pm. Arthur English was given charge of No. 1 hold.

Harold Freeman
National Archives of Australia

Central Wharf Stevedoring Company
City of Sydney Archives

English was a foreman stevedore employed by the Central Wharf Stevedoring Company and had been with them for one year. As per his routine, he first spoke to the timekeeper, who assigned him to a ship for the night. He was told he was looking after the *Idomeneus* and that Sammy Smithers would be the overall ship supervisor.[7] English took charge of his assigned 'gang' of wharfies: Williams, Muggivan, Roach, Swinton, Whitton, Quentin, Pearce the watchman, Kearney the hatchman, and two winchmen on the top deck.

This was not a long-established work gang in the usual sense, but rather one assembled for the task of unloading this particular ship. In total, English had seven men working below decks, including the six stevedores, while three worked above — the hatchman and two winchmen. Events in the hold were to reunite the team seven years later — at least those who were still alive.

As the night progressed the steering gear was oiled and examined. A continuous watch was maintained on the ship's defensive weapons and three ships' gunners were employed on sabotage watch. The crew also mustered at the boat stations wearing lifejackets and the lifeboats were swung inboard. Blue Funnel had a proud safety record to maintain and Dark had firsthand experience of its importance. The gang worked five and a half hours on the Wednesday night shift and it passed without incident.

On Thursday morning just before 8.00 am, McKenzie the chemist returned to the ship and handed the formal clearance certificates to Captain Dark. McKenzie had remained in his laboratory until after midnight performing tests in which he had used three test reagents. The chemical test result was negative.

The stevedore day gang consisted of wharfies Flanagan, Jones, Spiteri, Gillanders the foreman, Smith, Horton, Minor and Wilson. On Thursday morning they continued the work of the night gang and, in

No. 1 'tween decks, moved soda ash bags onto the slings and out of the hold. Le Fèvre made his only chemical test, later describing the process that he had used:

> *You have a pump and at the end of the pump a small vessel in which you can lay a piece of paper impregnated with a testary agent and you draw up, making a definite number of pump strokes, you draw a certain number of air pump strokes — 100 as I look back was the figure I had to use. Then you tested the paper ... a blue colour indicated the presence of mustard gas. I got no blue colour.[8]*

Le Fèvre issued a certificate on Thursday evening which stated:

> *I have inspected the lowest section of number one hold and — as in Melbourne — have been unable to detect the presence of mustard gas vapour by smell. A chemical test has also been made and has shown a similar negative result. I am therefore certain that number one hold does not contain a concentration of mustard gas vapour sufficient to endanger men working there. However, in view of the events occurring in Melbourne under the same circumstances, I recommend that the men should wear respirators. I have instructed Flying Officer Fleming [sic Freeman] that he is to place two airmen in respirators at the bottom of the hold to keep a watch in case any of the drums are accidentally damaged.[9]*

As they progressed down the hold the men started to notice an unusual smell. They later described it variously as 'peculiar', 'like decaying stuff' and employed a range of other descriptors.[10] It affected their throats and made life uncomfortable. The stevedores called a Board of Reference. If there was a dispute between the employers and employees an independent arbiter could be called in.

Mr Welbourn, the Conciliation Officer, Federal Arbitration Court, arrived to make an assessment of the uncomfortable work environment in which the men had found themselves. He could assign the men extra pay for working with 'damaged, difficult and obnoxious cargoes'. The stevedores believed the conditions in which they were working warranted some extra pay, but Welbourn deferred the decision. Although he had been told there was a gas on board Welbourn did not pass this information on to the labourers.[11]

McKenzie saw some gas masks during the day and, remembering the directive to encourage the stevedores to wear them, he asked, 'Why don't you wear the masks?'[12] He received no reply. The gas masks were in a pile on the top deck, some still in their haversacks and some sitting out. A few of the stevedores saw them on the top deck in a heaped pile, others failed to notice them as their attention was never drawn to them. Although the environment was uncomfortable, they had been reassured that there was no danger and so continued to work.

The situation at this point is best summarised by the Assistant Wharf Manager who recalled hearing complaints about the smell and noted,

> *There were masks available for the workmen, [but] no instructions were given to them to use them and ... I depended on the reports given me by McKenzie and the RAAF officers that the hold was gas free. If the report had been that there was any trace of gas we would have pulled the men out of the hatch immediately until some arrangements were made.*[13]

By this time the night shift had returned. Before entering the hold, however, the men needed McKenzie's approval. At 6.00 pm he inspected all three levels. There was now an expectation that the men would enter the very lowest hold and work in the area that had caused the problems in Melbourne. The night gang boarded and proceeded to No. 1 hatch and opened the uppermost hatches. The hatches were covered with big timber hatch covers, wedged on the outside to hold them tight. The bottom one was covered in tarpaulins as an extra precaution.

Once the hatch covers were removed the stevedores clambered down through the various levels of hold. About an hour or so after they had started work, Supervisor English began to receive complaints from all his men about an unusual smell. English was completely unaware that this was a replay of incidents both in Melbourne and during the previous shift when identical complaints had been made to the supervisors.

The men continued to work and took some cargo out of the fo'c'sle head, including drums of oil and cylinders of chemicals (in liquid form), and continued to unload the soda ash bags using the on ship's 'hawk' crane. The smell increased as they burrowed deeper into the hold and the problem soon became more than simply the smell. Stevedore Swinton now noticed that the odour was 'irritating my nose and throat'.[14]

THE DEVIL'S HOUR

There were too many complaints to ignore. Foreman English approached the *Idomeneus* officer in charge of the night shift, William James Stewart Eynon, the Fourth Officer, soon after the start of the shift. Eynon was the son of another Blue Funnel master and Stuart Glover remembers him as a 'nice guy and very efficient'.[16] Eynon replied that the odour had been 'left there by the cargo that was discharged in Melbourne'. He told English there were some gas masks on the main deck but English received no instructions as to their use and had no idea why they were there. He didn't inform his gang they were there as he saw no need. English also reported the musty smell to his boss, Smithers the ship supervisor.[17] Based on the information Smithers had received from the RAAF and ships' officers, he assured English that all was in order. However Smithers was puzzled when he saw the masks and asked English, 'Who put them there?'[18]

Later in the night an emergency saw chemist McKenzie recalled to the ship by Freeman. There was some concern over a number of the phosgene bombs in No. 4 hold. But it was a false alarm; condensation had formed on the outside of the bombs causing the workmen to believe that they were leaking. It was now past midnight, the early morning of 15 January, and chemist McKenzie decided to remain on the ship. The men were closing in on the mustard drums.

At midnight a meal break provided the men some relief from the summer heat and the strange exhaustion they were feeling. After the meal break they went

A Winchman
Imperial War Museum

to No. 3 hatch and, at 2.00 am, returned to No. 1. There were only a few more soda bags left on the floor above the lowest hold. The job was almost done. But something caught the experienced eye of these men who had worked the docks for years. Stevedore Whitton's attention was drawn to the lower hatch covering: 'It was a thing I had very very seldom seen on a ship, battened down, the lower hold.'[19] Having tarpaulins on the top hatch to keep the weather and sea out made sense, but at three levels down, it certainly didn't. Others noticed the same incongruity.

They also noticed that, when a sling of soda ash dragged across and pulled the tarpaulins back, the smell grew worse and their discomfort increased. When they replaced the displaced cover, the situation improved. Finally, the two 'tween decks were cleared and it was time to unload the mustard gas hold. It was 3.00 am, the start of the devil's hour.

Chapter 4

Green Vomit

As agreed at the first conference in Dark's cabin, an inspection was to be conducted before the men moved into the danger zone. Between 3.30 and 4.00 am, prior to Friday's early morning shift, chemist McKenzie inspected the lower No. 1 hold, clambering over all the drums. He was accompanied by Freeman, the decontamination supervisor, who brought with him a leading aircraftsman from his squad, and Eynon, the *Idomeneus*' officer in charge. Inexplicably, there was no Le Fèvre, despite the fact that his presence had been part of the agreement. He was quite clearly the chemical cargo expert but was absent when his expertise was most needed, despite the issues that had arisen in Melbourne. No explanation was ever provided for his absence. Most of the inspections were then based on an assessment made by smell as McKenzie had only performed one chemical test which had been conducted on the first day.

Puzzled by the substantial military presence, stevedore Whitton asked one of the Air Force personnel, 'Is there anything down here crook?' The reply came back immediately: 'If there is, we will detect it before you will, and will let you know and give you time to get out.'[1] Wharfie Pearce lent one of the airmen a torch as he clambered down to make his inspection. He noticed that one of the uniformed RAAF officials was carrying a yellow tin of ointment with a handle on it and his curiosity got the better of him. 'What's that you have there?' he asked. 'Oh that is some ointment to put on anyone who comes into contact with this stuff that is in the drums,' came the reply.[2] It was anti-gas ointment, although the stevedores were not permitted to know this. The RAAF inspectors finally gave their approval to Eynon who in turn nodded to ship supervisor Smithers. The final clearance had been given and the fate of the stevedores was now sealed. They had been given permission to enter a highly toxic environment.

The night gang moved into the lower hold. They began to clear the boxes of crockery and general cargo in the square of the hatch which had been loaded in Melbourne so as to chock the drums and replace the tractor cases. The steel drums beneath the boxes were now visible.

By this time stevedore George Whitton had 'a dry sort of feeling in the nostrils, and the mouth, and the eyes burning'. His eyes felt 'as if they were full of sand under the lids'.[3] The labour crew could not have known that the free gas in the superheated hold was water soluble; it attacked the eyes first as they were constantly moist.

Wharfie Whitton was partnered with wharfie Andrew Williams. 'I noticed especially the chap I was working with …Williams. His eyes, well, you could not tell any whites from the pupils of the eyes. They were just like — clods of practically raw steak it appeared to me under the light of the [ship's hold] lamp lights. We passed a remark about one another's eyes.'[4]

Andrew Williams lived in Millers Point, a stone's throw from his worksite, Walsh Bay, and had worked there most of his life, having been a coal lumper in his early twenties. Coal lumping was an essential service as the lumpers moved coal from colliers onto steam-driven vessels, and was an incredibly tough occupation requiring great stamina. Williams was born in Dunedin, New Zealand, and, at age 63, had very few assets to his name. But he did boast 'perfect health' and a happy family life and was content in his senior years. His life was insured by the Metropolitan Life Insurance Co. for £70 pounds and he had the same amount in a Commonwealth Bank account. He was by no means a rich man.[5]

Andrew Williams' Residence

Like the Melbourne stevedores before them, the Sydney labour gang could only surmise that it was the soda ash dust leaking from the sacks that was causing their eyes to inflame. But soda

GREEN VOMIT

Clontarf Coal Lumpers Union Picnic, 30 October 1907.
Andrew Williams (Back Row, Leftmost); Elsie Williams (Font Row, Middle)

Beryl Miller

ash dust usually only caused irritation and sneezing and was generally regarded as 'not detrimental to anyone ... because it is handled so often'.[6] It made no sense that it should now cause this reaction, although the men could not pinpoint another cause. Nevertheless the complaints persisted. By now everyone was 'hostile about the smell and the taste there', the men had begun to feel considerably worse and most had begun to cough.[7] But these were tough men and they persevered until their shift was over, emerging just before 7.00 am to make their way home.

Stevedore supervisor English later recalled that he 'got home about 8 o'clock that morning, and I had a wash and went and had my breakfast, and I laid down to have a rest for the day, and as near as I could say it would be about 11 o'clock there was this tremendous burning and pain in the eyes.'[8] Swinton was in a similar state: 'When I got home I could hardly see and I was retching. I went straight down to my own doctor in Manly.'[9] The doctor was puzzled; he noticed the acutely inflamed eyes and sore throat and also detected some bronchitis, but was at a loss to surmise a cause.

Elsie Williams
Beryl Miller

Stevedore Pearce was the last to leave the hatch. He boarded the tram and, feeling sick in the stomach, made his way to the back platform where he vomited 'green stuff' over the side. His eyes were excruciatingly painful. By the time he arrived home at Woollahra in North Sydney, 'it was very bad'. He stumbled through the gate, went upstairs and asked someone to ring the doctor as he felt terribly ill. He was unable to make the call himself, his eyes so badly affected that he could not see the telephone. He was ordered straight to hospital.[10]

Andrew Williams also stumbled home. What was habitually only a few minutes' walk was now agonisingly difficult. Fortunately, he had walked this path so many times that he could do it blindfolded as, like the others, he could barely see by now. He crossed Hickson Road and staggered up the 50 steps to Windmill Street, turned right at the Nelson Hotel and then onto High Street. He finally reached his house, number 16A, at 7.30 am. It was a walk that took him less than five minutes to complete, but it was the toughest he had ever endured.

At first his wife, Elsie, noticed nothing out of the ordinary, although she thought her husband was very quiet. He had a cup of tea and made himself toast, but didn't eat it, instead taking it out to feed the pet cockatoo. He had a wash and then wandered about the yard. It was then she saw him sitting with his hands to his face. She asked him if there was something wrong and he replied, 'I got something at work on the ship. I think I swallowed some alkali [soda ash]. I have dreadful pains in my chest and my eyes are watering that bad that I can't see out of them.' She suggested that he should go to bed, but he replied, 'Go away and leave me for a little while until I get alright.'[11]

Mrs Williams resumed her household duties. At around 9.00 am she heard her husband making noises as if he were vomiting. He lost control of his bowels and was by now suffering acute diarrhoea. He then became very restless, getting up and down all the time. At about 12.30 pm Mrs Williams called for her son Gilbert, also a waterside worker, who conveniently lived next door at 14 High Street. Gilbert rushed in and noticed his father in the back bedroom where he looked 'very bad'.[12] He raced to the Central Wharf for advice and was told to order a taxicab to take his father to Dr Colin Ross of Macquarie Street, a ten-minute drive away. By the time he returned home his father was too ill to be taken by taxi, so Gilbert retraced his steps and sent for an ambulance. Williams was taken the short distance to Dr Ross' rooms. Ross, an eye specialist, hurried out of his office to the ambulance, examined Williams and immediately despatched him to hospital. Ross described him as 'so sick … he was rather comatose and sleepy'. In fact Williams had been so badly gassed that Ross himself received a 'slight attack' from his clothes which had readily absorbed the toxin.[13] As a result, Williams continued to suffer the effects of the gas now absorbed in his clothes. The ambulance sped to Royal Prince Alfred Hospital at Camperdown. Andrew Williams was not the first wharfie Ross had seen that day.

As these events were unfolding, it was business as usual at the wharf. Once the night gang had departed, McKenzie tested again prior to the start of the day shift. Inexplicably, he had not been informed of the night's dramas and thus gave approval for the day shift to begin. The stevedores on this shift developed the same symptoms as those on the night shift.

Les Parsons was a rookie RAAF recruit with no gas training. Decontamination head Freeman had assigned him the task of supervising the wharfies in No. 1 hold. He remembers being addressed by a wing

Gilbert Williams
Beryl Miller

commander with a 'pommy accent'. Le Fèvre had gone down into the hold wearing a gas mask and came out still wearing it. Parsons is adamant that the wing commander directly addressed members of the decontamination squad and told them, 'You do not need to wear a gas mask, it is clear.'[14]

But something was clearly astir. It came to a head just minutes before wharfie Flanagan had made up a sling of soda. As he and his partner bent down, they caught each other's eye and hesitated. They knew something was terribly wrong. Their eyes felt as if they were on fire and were so badly affected that the whites were indistinguishable. Flanagan had seen nothing like it and knew they were in trouble. Confirmation came soon after when a stevedore delegate yelled down the hatch for all workers to get out of the hold immediately as the cargo had now been blacklisted. 'We all could not get up the ladder quick enough,' Flanagan related.[15]

Dr Colin Ross
Royal Prince Alfred Museum & Archives

The stevedoring supervisors had shut up shop, realising belatedly that they were working in a toxic environment. One of the dangers of mustard gas is that, at non-acute levels, its effects are delayed; but by then the damage is done. The penetrative power of the vapour was one of its outstanding features. It became fixed in the skin in a few minutes; by then its effects were irreversible

Les Parsons

as it reacted with enzymes, proteins, Deoxyribonucleic acid (DNA) and other biological molecules, causing irreparable damage. The workers had been affected for life.

Meanwhile some members of the stevedore night gang were drifting back. Swinton's wife took her husband to the gate of the Stevedoring Office. By then Swinton could only recognise the timekeeper by his voice and was told to go straight to Royal Prince Alfred Hospital. An emergency conference was held and 'it was decided that, if possible RAAF men should work No. 1 and 4 holds to the exclusion of wharf labourers and that No. 1 and 4 should be closed forthwith until such time as the Air Force could commence operations.'[16] A decision that should have occurred before the unloading had started was now forced on the military.

When RAAF recruit Parsons emerged from supervising the hold he knew he was in trouble. He was vomiting and fell to the ground where he rolled around in agony. In 'a big panic' he was taken off to the RAAF sick quarters in Ultimo.[17] In time many RAAF casualties would be admitted. Wing Commander George Blakemore, a consultant eye specialist, examined eight of the 11 RAAF patients and found them to be exhibiting classic mustard gas symptoms: allergy to light, watering eyes and, in the worst cases, shedding of the cornea epithelium. The RAAF now had a crisis on its hands — contaminated labourers and RAAF personnel, and a blacklisted ship right next to Sydney's central business district.

By now there were also casualties among the ship's crew. Fourth Officer Eynon came off with the night gang at 7.00 am and, after breakfast, reported to his boss, Captain Dark, that he had eye trouble. He was transferred to St Vincent's Hospital with bilateral conjunctivitis, his eyes 'pale pink all over'. With the crew now affected, others on the ship discovered that something was amiss. Unaware that they were carrying chemical weapons, radioman Glover was stunned:

And somebody even said poison gas — mustard gas. And I think we were all duly shocked. Particularly when the stories became a little bit more fleshed out and we understood that there'd been some sort of a spillage and I think some wharf labourers had been affected and I think also that from that moment on, the wharfies decided that they wouldn't work the cargo on Idomeneus any more.[18]

At least 15 crew members of the *Idomeneus* became casualties.[19]

The arbiter, Mr Welbourn, went back to the ship at 3.30 pm, this time with Dr Gordon Smith, Assistant Medical Officer of Industrial Hygiene and a representative of the Department of Health. On being pressed by the employees' representative to fix an extra rate for work already performed and for discharging the drums of gas and other cargo in the hold, Welbourn informed him that there were indications that the men's health might be affected and that he would not consider fixing a rate until he had received Smith's report.[20] That same afternoon Smith wrote in his report, 'An odour resembling that of mustard gas was discernable. In my opinion, mustard gas should only be handled by trained personnel.'

The day shift now also began to suffer. Flanagan went to Dr Ross at Macquarie Street but was quickly sent to Royal Prince Alfred Hospital. He was discharged and sent home to Kensington: 'Well, I had to be helped off the tram ... as my eyesight was leaving ... and the eyes were starting to close up.' Dorothy, his wife of 31 years, opened the door and was shocked to see the state he was in. 'He was staggering in. He was blind. He was very distressed.'[21] Flanagan was treated with bicarbonate of soda and water which the eye specialist Dr Ross had recommended. At the time, irrigation with bicarbonate of soda and water was thought to neutralise the mustard, although it has since been proven to be ineffective.

Crewman Glover recalled:

There was a story that I've always believed that I can't actually confirm that one of our crew people went down there and got a bit of liquid mustard on his dungarees which he promptly spread onto a toilet seat in the crew's quarters and there were lurid stories of injuries of various people who had subsequently shared the same toilet seat. There were injuries, there were hospitalisations, there was a story current, that I've always believed that somebody — and I think it was supposed to be a wharf labourer — was affected by mustard gas and actually suicided out of the window of the Balmain Hospital. That was the story anyway.[22]

Chapter 5

A Fall

Richard Harris, a medical practitioner from Camperdown and a respected resident and registrar at Royal Prince Alfred Hospital, was on duty when a wharf labourer was admitted at 3.15 pm on the afternoon of Friday 15 January. He recorded the man's name as Andrew William Williams. Harris noted that Williams was complaining of sore eyes, vomiting, diarrhoea and a cough.[1]

Later that evening Gilbert Williams visited his father. He looked 'very bad' and was strangely uncommunicative. Gilbert resorted to talking to the nurse, who reported that his father was bronchial and his eyes were in a very bad state. In fact Williams' eyesight had now completely failed and he recognised his son only by his voice. Gilbert turned his attention to the wharfie in the next bed. He asked this man how his father had been since his admission. The wharfie's eyes were closed and he simply replied that he could not see. This was the last time Gilbert saw his father alive.[2]

Richard Harris
Royal Prince Alfred Museum & Archives

Wharfie Flanagan arrived at the hospital on Saturday morning having been referred by his local doctor. He had presented at the Royal Prince Alfred the day before and had been sent home. But his condition had since deteriorated considerably. 'I had lost my sight. I was led there, and led out of the car,' he recounted.[3] He was seen by a young nurse, Margaret Miller.[4]

With the outbreak of the Second World War, Margaret Miller had decided that she should make a contribution to the war effort. A resident of the tiny country town of Temora, some 300 miles from Sydney, she travelled to the Royal Prince Alfred Hospital and was interviewed there by the hospital's matron. She was duly called up for nursing duty in May 1940 and joined the nursing staff at the Royal Prince Alfred. She recalled 'a very strange incident' while temporarily in charge of the men's section of Ward D2 on Saturday 16 January 1943:

I was working in D2 which was a general surgical ward for both men and women. Even though I was a junior nurse I remember — for this day — being in charge of the men's section and I can recall it was a weekend as we were short of staff. Although we had 24 beds, on the weekends we always kept two of them spare — made up and ready — to receive any emergency patients we might receive from casualty. In the late morning or afternoon two ambulance officers rushed in with two patients on stretchers. We understood they were burns victims although they had no obvious signs of such. One of the most basic things we were instructed to always do was to put their ailment on their record but as I was preparing to find out the problem I was told by the senior residents and doctors that I was 'not to ask anything at all of the illness they were suffering or its cause and not to put anything on their admission sheet' and 'not to speak to anyone about them'. This was highly unusual to say the least. All we were told was that they were labourers who had had an accident while unloading a ship, nothing else. After much discussion by the residents and doctors the patients were transferred to another part of the hospital and that was the last I saw or heard of them. With such an unusual event it's impossible to stop the nursing staff from talking and the gossip around the hospital at that time was that the patients had been involved in moving mustard gas on the wharves and had become contaminated.[5]

Stevedore Flanagan was then moved to Vic 1 ward on the third floor where Williams and his other fellow colleagues were housed. Nurse Phyllis Heydon recalls:

It was a classic RPA ward where you had women down one end and men down the other with the nurses in the middle with a basin for washing and scrubbing. The ward had a very high ceiling and windows down the side looking onto Missendon Rd. There was no air conditioning although the big windows could be left open. At the end of the ward there were lavatories and a sluice room for washing.[6]

Flanagan's stay proved nightmarish: 'Well the voice went, and then the throat was absolutely raw. You could not see. That was 20 hours or thereabouts afterwards. The throat was bad for months afterwards, months and months afterwards, but I got my voice back.'[7] He took to wearing green glasses to protect his eyes from the light.

Flanagan was suffering from a classic case of mustard gas poisoning which included photophobia. Photophobia is hypersensivity to light with pain resulting from light exposure. The characteristic pink/red colour is due to inflammation of the eye. It is partly an immune response, with more blood carrying antibodies, and partly a protective mechanism. With overstimulation of the photoreceptors, the damaged eye is closed as a risk avoidance measure. Many of the stevedores wore dark glasses for several months afterwards to protect their eyes from the light. As with the Melbourne stevedores, one of the eye treatments administered was atropine. It is still used today to dilate the eye given the same symptoms.

Having first attacked the eyes, the mustard gas then targets the other moist areas of the body, particularly the respiratory system and groin area with resulting rashes and blisters. The blisters are formed by the separation of two skin layers, the mechanics of which are still not fully understood. Flanagan described them thus: 'I started to get sores and blisters around my testicles and between the legs, and the blisters then all

Margaret Miller
Royal Prince Alfred Museum & Archives

D2 Block, Royal Prince Alfred Hospital
Royal Prince Alfred Museum & Archives

Royal Prince Alfred Hospital Ambulance
Royal Prince Alfred Museum & Archives

ran together, and it just became one whole sore. We had to dress [our testicles] ourselves in hospital and I had sore testicles anything up to four or five months afterwards.'[8]

Flanagan's hospital records reflect his verbal testimony: '18th slight cough, 19th throat sore and cough, 20th throat ulcerated, much coughing and itchy rash and 25th very hoarse.'[9] Most of the stevedores were in hospital for three weeks with the same symptoms: ulcerated throat, cough, respiratory distress, blisters and allergy to light.

Nurse Phyllis Heydon was also on duty at the Royal Prince Alfred when the wharf labourers were admitted. During her years at boarding school, Phyllis Heydon had given much thought to the career she might eventually pursue. There were few options for women: 'I could be a teacher, I could be a secretary or I could be a nurse.' As it was very difficult to get into university, 'I thought about it carefully and decided I would go nursing.' One of her inspirations was Dr Flynn's Flying Doctor Service. 'Well I looked at all the hospitals and RPA was the pre-eminent hospital in Sydney at the time so I decided that was the one I would go to and I started there on 20th September 1940.' Heydon remembers that there were few specifics for disease, no antibiotics and no penicillin: 'People had to get better with good nursing and by eating good meals. That was what good nursing was about.'[10]

While Phyllis Heydon was working in Vic 1 ward:

> *I think there were about four or five patients were brought in and we were told they were wharf labourers and they had been unloading gas and some of them had been burnt. They were in one part of the ward and only the more senior sisters attended to them. We were told they were 'gas' burns, that they were unloading gas and came into contact with it in some way. We were told that on no account were we to tell anybody about it. We were very surprised as we didn't know there was gas in Australia. It was kept very quiet.*[11]

By a strange coincidence she was soon to meet and marry another *Idomeneus* gas victim, but this was a little way into the future.

Mrs Williams came in on Saturday to see her husband. His condition appeared to have deteriorated. 'He was dreadfully sick' and was coughing and could not see.[12] He was given a cough mixture (linctus) and throat gargles to relieve his ulcerated throat. Andrew Williams' daughter Jean saw her father for the first time on Saturday between 2.30 pm and

4.00 am. 'He could not see any of us on account of his eyes and was coughing a great deal. He said his eyes were very painful and, "I can't distinguish any of you."'[13] He was also visited by Dr Ross who noted that he could see dimly and that there was 'a remnant of haze on the eye cornea'. Ross' primary treatment was continuous irrigation of the eyes with an unnamed lotion. Ross considered Andrew Williams the worst of the 12 afflicted stevedores, although he remarked to a nurse that 'he was a bit of a Briton to be so cheerful about it'.[14]

On Sunday 17 January, Joy Rablah, a senior night duty nurse at the Royal Prince Alfred, noted that Williams' mind seemed to be wandering a little. She had seen him sitting on the side of his bed pulling at his bedclothes. She asked him what he was doing and he said, 'It is time to make my bed.' She told him not to get out of bed as she would attend to him if required. He had also been mumbling 'a good deal to himself' and was constantly worried about his eyes and asking if they would recover. He had asked

Jean Williams
Beryl Miller

Nurse Rablah this question repeatedly since his arrival. She had been told that he was suffering the effects of some chemical irritant and knew that others on the ward were suffering from the same affliction. Despite all this she noted that he eventually slept quite well.[15]

Joy Rablah
Elizabeth Russ

Olive Tampe, a fellow Royal Prince Alfred nurse, remembered Joy as being 5' 6" tall, of medium build with brown hair, and in her third year of training. She was a dedicated and compassionate nurse 'as you would expect all nurses to be but exceptionally so'.[16] Joy Rablah's colleagues portrayed her as very dedicated and thorough, pleasant and unassuming, as well as someone who liked to have fun. Andrew Williams was in good hands.

On Sunday, Mrs Williams was told by her husband that 'the Air Force have been here, and asked the men not to divulge anything about themselves.' She asked him, 'Why is that?' He said, 'Well Mum the enemy listens.' Williams then instructed his wife not to talk to anyone about his illness.[17] While Mrs Williams never saw her husband again, she kept her promise to maintain the secrecy of his condition. Dr Ross also visited Andrew Williams on Sunday, recording that he was experiencing a great deal of irritation on the scrotum which had spread up his chest. He did not prescribe painkillers to relieve the pain and discomfort although he did acknowledge that Williams must have been suffering a great deal.[18]

Jean Williams visited her father again on Monday 18 January between 7.20 pm and 8.00 pm with her sister and a girlfriend. She noted that he was still coughing a great deal and remained very sick although he was more cheerful than on her previous visit. He was still blind: 'I can't distinguish any of you,' he told them. His chest was problematic and he didn't say much. He had an eyewash while she was there and another just as she left. Strangely, he said, 'These hospitals. You know what they are like. Now when I am able to give myself the eyewash they might put me out.' She helped with the eyewash as he couldn't manage it unaided: 'He was fumbling about a great deal to find the water.' He had some cotton wool which he had to dip in a basin and sponge his eyes. He gave the impression he might be sent home the following day. Jean asked him, 'Do you fancy anything to eat?' He replied, 'I haven't been eating. You can bring up a jam tart and bring me 2 shillings for a shave.' She observed that he was not despondent, and was 'even a little bit more cheerful than on Saturday.' He added, 'I'm tough, I suppose I will get over it.' Jean noted that 'he was still in great pain but seemed quite rational'.[19] She said goodbye for the last time.

Nurse Rablah recalled that Williams seemed to worry more than the other stevedores although they were all complaining about their eyes: 'He was one of the worst in there.'[20] His sight had been very bad throughout the four nights he was a patient. He was given an eyewash every hour and had three eyewashes before midnight. After midnight his eyes were not washed to allow him to sleep. He was not given a sleeping draught (medicine) on his last night. After lights out, Joy Rablah carried a lamp on her rounds.

When Nurse Rablah completed her rounds at 12.15 am on 19 January Andrew appeared to be asleep. His eyes were closed and he lay very quietly in his bed. At 12.35 am:

> *I was attending to a child patient in the ward when I noticed a patient get out of bed and go out towards the bathroom. At the*

time I could not leave the child I was attending to. My junior had just returned from supper and was not actually in the ward at the time. About two minutes later, I first of all heard a door bang. Then I heard a sound like lattice breaking. I went out and looked for him first. I then could hear someone calling out as if in pain, it was a loud groan. As I was going out of the door I had looked to see who was out of bed and realised that it was Williams. When I heard the loud groaning I looked in the bathrooms and lavatories and I then noticed a broken lavatory window. I looked out the window and saw a man on the pavement below. I told another nurse to go down to the deceased. I rang Sister Williams [night matron in charge of whole hospital] and informed her.[21]

At 12.45 am Richard Harris was called. He saw Andrew Williams' broken body lying on the concrete at the bottom of Victoria Pavilion. A little later Williams was brought back to the ward on a stretcher by two wardsmen. Joy Rablah 'did not see him until after, because I had received a bad shock myself. When I went to him he was conscious but could not tell us anything.'[22] Doctors and nurses crowded around

Typical Ward Layout, Royal Prince Alfred Hospital
Royal Prince Alfred Museum & Archives

Williams, including Sisters Williamson and Harris. He died 45 minutes after the fall.

Joy Rablah never mentioned the event until her final nursing reunion prior to her death. Talking to the other nurses at this gathering, she mentioned that she had gone to court after someone had fallen out of a window. She added that she had been told not to talk about it.[23] Rablah's daughter, Elizabeth Russ, remembered her mother describing the incident as a 'top secret matter' and that she had warned the hospital staff that Andrew Williams was an at-risk patient. Joy Rablah had been annoyed by the hospital's inaction over this matter.[24]

Sergeant Hilton Kelly received a call at Police Station No. 2 at 6.30 am and went to the Royal Prince Alfred Hospital. The body was identified to him by Andrew Williams' son Gilbert and removed to the City Morgue. On inspection it was surmised that Williams had made his way to the lavatory which had one window 1'8" wide and 4'6" high which was situated directly over the toilet seat. Williams had apparently climbed onto the seat and broken a one-inch slat across the centre of the window which was found hanging down on each side of the window. On the outside he had grabbed the horizontal water pipes. He then slid down

A Williams' Picnic. Andrew & Wife Elsie to the far Left.
Beryl Miller

A FALL

a vertical pipe for 16 feet leaving marks on and next to the pipe. He put a foot through a window on his descent and seemed to be trying to put his foot on the sill of a lower window. At the junction of the pipes at the second floor there were three small marks as if made by fingers and then blurred marks further down where Andrew Williams had apparently been falling.[25]

Wing Commander Le Fèvre was interviewed by Sergeant Kelly on 22 January: 'I described the general cargo as I saw it at Melbourne and Sydney, but I said that the nature of the RAAF consignment was secret and that I could not discuss such facts without permission. I therefore suggested that the Police should approach the Air Force officially.'[26]

Andrew Williams' granddaughter, Beryl Miller, remembers the death vividly, although she was only five years old when her grandfather died. Beryl clearly recalls going to the Williams house in High Street: 'The scene still sticks in my mind's eye.' The entire family was gathered around the dining-room table — the room was literally packed with people

Williams Family Members Present on the Day Andrew Died. Elsie (Wife, Back Left). Front Left to Right, Gwen (Granddaughter), Bill Russell, Elsie (Daughter) & Gilbert (Son)
Beryl Miller

as Mrs Williams had a number of sisters and they were all assembled as were their children. Three of Andrew Williams' children and five grandchildren were also present. Beryl can still see Mrs Williams crying and repeating over and over 'My Bill!' — the name by which the family knew Andrew. 'It was extremely traumatic and something you can never forget,' adds Beryl.

Beryl Miller 'never found out what truly happened until I was married and in my thirties and it wasn't until my father, John William Williams, was dying.' John was the eldest of Andrew Williams' four children. In the last year of John's life, he was cared for by Joyce Elsie, his eldest daughter. Beryl recalls:

… they were close and it was at this time he mentioned the story to her. He knew he was dying. He had never ever talked about it to any of us up to this moment. He told her Andrew had been exposed to leaking mustard gas while unloading a ship and had then thrown himself out of the hospital window.

The explanation John Williams gave was: 'He had been driven crazy by the effects of it.' Adds Beryl Miller, 'Joyce Elsie then told me but that was all we ever learnt about it. We were all duly shocked. Why he left it till his death bed we will never know.'

Beryl's father was away fighting in the war at the time Andrew Williams died and came home on compassionate leave. He then had to return directly to his unit. He never talked much about his father and Beryl never thought to ask:

As we never knew him [Andrew] we didn't pay much attention to his death. Another comment Dad passed to my sister was that mustard gas had been banned after World War I and it was 'never to be used again'. It must have been a surprise to everyone that it was being brought to Australia on ships at the time. Although it was never to be used again, they did have it and it was not to be talked about — sadly my grandfather paid the price with his life and with no compensation.

More recently Beryl asked one of her aunts on her mother's side — now aged 82 — about the death of Andrew Williams. Her only comment was, 'Everybody knew about it, but you weren't to talk about it.' Beryl laments, 'It's awfully sad, they should have had gas masks. He wanted to get out of hospital, he wanted to go home.'

Beryl grew up in Millers Point, the same neighbourhood as Andrew Williams, where all the wharfies lived. She lived near 'Griff', one of the older wharfies who had a burnt face. 'He looked awful with "bubbles" all over his skin. How he got them we never found out officially but I came to the conclusion they were mustard gas burns,' she remembers.[27]

On 20 January 1943, a funeral notice appeared in *The Sydney Morning Herald*:

> *Williams – The Relatives and Friends of Mrs. Elsie May Williams and Family of 16a High Street, Millers Point are invited to attend the funeral of her beloved Husband and their dear Father, Andrew Williams; to leave the Private Chapel of Motor Funerals Limited.*

The day after Andrew Williams died, Wing Commander Le Fèvre asked the Principal RAAF Medical Officer 'if he and Wing Commander Blakemore could again contact the cases in hospital to prevent guesses concerning the causes of the injuries being presented by the hospital staff.' He further stated that an accurate diagnosis could only be based on full consideration of all the available medical facts based on toxicological tests.[28] He must have known that this would not end speculation as to the true nature of the cause of Andrew Williams' death.

Chapter 6

Hell Hold

The next question concerned the fate of the black-banned cargo. The first decision was to move the ship. Radioman Stuart Glover remembers that the mass contamination

> … *seemed to be the signal to batten the hatches and take the ship around to Balmain, or Rozelle Bay, to a dedicated wharf around there and then we seemed to be inundated with nice Air Force people who took charge of the unloading and the decontamination of number one hold.*[1]

The ship was moved to a reserved RAAF berth, No. 9 wharf, at Glebe Island (Balmain), where the unloading recommenced. As had been agreed at the impromptu meeting on the *Idomeneus* two days previously, only RAAF personnel were to be employed for this task. There were three groups of RAAF men comprising two officers and some 15 men from No. 1 Movements & Shipping Office, a party from Bradfield Park No. 2 consisting of 40 men, and a party of 15 men from Richmond led by an officer.

Geoff Burn, a RAAF chemical warfare armourer, recalled:

> *And we used to go down into the hold; the wharf labourers had woken up to it and they wouldn't touch it. I don't know whether it was ten minutes down in the hold and twenty minutes out, or twenty minutes down and ten minutes out. Well, it was stifling — the heat down there was absolutely stifling because you were all rugged up in this impervious clothing and you couldn't breathe, you couldn't. It was just like trying to work in an oven — it was a stifling situation, absolutely shocking. A lot of the blokes were carried out; they collapsed down there and had to be carried out and sort of revived and then like going into a bloody football game, go in and get your head knocked off and then we'll revive you and we'll send you back down again, you know, to get the stuff out.*[2]

Geoff Burn with 250 lb Bombs at Marrangaroo Tunnel
National Archives of Australia

Kevin Garr, a fellow armourer, concurred: 'It was so damn hot. By the time we got down in the hold, within three or four minutes, you were covered in perspiration and we were working in Wellington boots.'[3] It was the height of summer. While the first two days had been trouble-free, the men were now closing in on the leaking drum and the Air Force personnel suffered very serious injuries as a result. Ken Heydon started the war in the cavalry and the light horse and finished his career as a RAAF flying officer:

> *They sent me to Richmond air base for six weeks to get my maths up to scratch. They asked for volunteers for an unpleasant job and anything was better than mathematics and I went into this large hall where they put a guard on the door, they shut the windows and put an armed guard outside. The officer told us if we said 'yes', under no circumstances were we ever to divulge what we were doing; we were sworn to secrecy ad infinitum.*

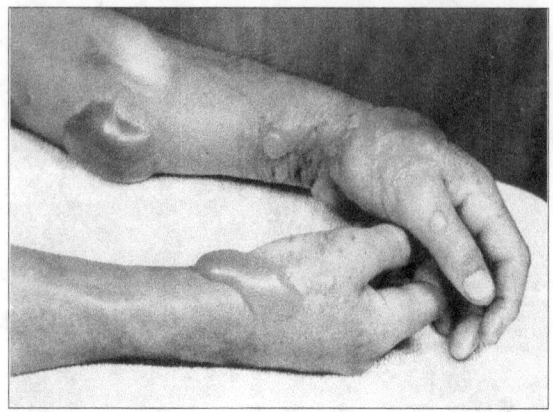
Wrist Blisters from Mustard Gas

Interestingly, the officer told them that the ship had suffered a machine-gun attack and that the drums were now leaking as a consequence. 'He told us the wharf labourers had refused to unload it, the Army had refused to unload it, the Navy volunteered to unload at wharf labourers' danger pay, that was refused so the Air Force was being asked to do it and we would fairly certainly get the wharf labourers' danger money.' Heydon had not received any gas training. Curiously, he couldn't see any damage to the ship. He was given the job of hosing each layer of drums with a huge two-inch hose pumping seawater to wash the mustard off the drums. Then another crew would move in and spend a maximum of 20 minutes down in the hold. 'It was extremely hot, we were in full gear, no flesh exposed at all, gumboots, gas mask, hat, heavy coat and trousers and huge gloves that came up to your elbow, everything in heavy plastic. It was hot work, bloody hot. We were given no instructions whatsoever in case of an accident, there wasn't meant to be one.' The combination of water spray and summer heat resulted in a superheated fog laden with mustard vapour. The conditions were intolerable, with sweat filling the gas mask. For Heydon,

> ... it was a case of swallow it and vomit or take my glove off and blow the sweat out which I did. The air was full of hot steam and I didn't know it but I got burnt on the wrist and burnt on the right hand side of my throat. The resulting blister was enormous, it was about three inches across and all I can remember is the nursing sister saying we must not puncture it.[4] The blister was there for nearly three weeks. We were really ignorant of the effects of mustard.

Unfortunately his assistant holding the hose, desperate to relieve himself, 'lowered his pants and urinated, no more than 10 seconds, and did his pants up again. I saw him later in the air base hospital in

Richmond and he was a sight you just didn't want to see twice — he was a hell of a mess around the nether region, it was one big blister. We told him he'd had it for life.' There were many more injuries. One RAAF member was splashed in the eye by a drop of mustard-contaminated water from a drum being lifted out of the hold. Heydon stared in amazement as

> ... the guy went berserk and tried to knock himself out on the wharf by bashing his head on the wooden decking. A sailor from the boat who was standing there jumped into a lighter moored alongside, shoved his head into the harbour, got a mouth full of water, gouged the bloke's eye open and spat into the guy's eye. He probably saved his eyesight. I'd thought I'd hosed the drums down enough but there was still enough mustard remaining to burn like hell.

While on deck having a spell from the mustard hold, Heydon watched the phosgene bombs brought up. He recalls the supervising officer (Third Officer Forsgate), 'a most amazing striking good looking man — tall, flowing beard and moustache, deep voice, he used to stand leaning over the hold directing the winchman and you used to hear him bellow "under below" as the huge steel mesh sling feet came down.'5 A gas sergeant who was standing nearby instructed Heydon and several others to 'come over here and get a sniff of the phosgene'. They were asked if they knew how it smelled and were told that the smell resembled musty

Ken Heydon
Ken Heydon

Cranes Used to Hoist the Mustard Gas Drums from No. 1 Hold
State Library of New South Wales

hay. 'There was a bloke in front of me and a bomb lying on the deck with the nose cap twisted half off. The bloke took a good sniff, enough to get some phosgene in his lungs. He hit the rail of the boat and coughed and spluttered. I walked forward and instead of sniffing in, I blew out of my nose and I pretended to cough and I said "yes sergeant, musty hay" and that was it.' The phosgene bombs that had lost their nose caps had L-E-A-K-Y written on the side in large letters. The drums and bombs were loaded onto a train that was close to the wharf. The entire operation was meant to be top secret but there were civilians watching through the fence. In Heydon's opinion, 'they could put two and two together and get the right answer'. There were half a dozen young girls watching the operation and talking to the RAAF personnel:

> *What they said I don't know but there was no secret, the whole of Sydney would have known. Secrecy, oh it was a joke, with the Glebe population around the outside of the fence and young girls talking to us through the mesh wire. It was obvious they weren't a conventional weapon. Whether they were told or guessed I don't know but I would say it was horribly obvious with people in this heavy gear going into and out of the hold, ripping it off as soon as you got out of the hold. It was obvious something nasty was happening.*

Heydon was told to go to Mount Victoria in the Blue Mountains to recover from the burns he received while decontaminating the *Idomeneus*. He recalled,

On the way back I got on the train at Mount Victoria and this good looking chick got on the train with an extra large bag. There was only one vacant seat and that was beside me, thank god. I helped put the bag up on the rack and got talking to her and she said she was a nurse at RPA and she later became my wife. When we got back to Sydney I put her in a taxi back to RPA.[6]

Phyllis Heydon (nee Suttor), the nurse in question, who had seen the gassed stevedores at RPA, unsurprisingly remembers the meeting well:

I'd gone up to see a friend and we came back on the same train. A few days later he rang me and said he couldn't wait as he'd booked every theatre in Sydney on the Saturday. He asked, 'Which one do you want to go to?' But he hadn't booked anything! I didn't know what I was going to do so finally we went out and we spent our time going backwards and forwards on the ferry as you could do that for sixpence and that was very interesting. He must have shown his burn to me.[7]

Ken Heydon knew he had broken the code of secrecy. He had told Phyllis that he had been burnt with gas but hadn't told her where. Heydon also told her that some of the labourers had gone to the RPA and had heard that one had committed suicide. Phyllis then replied that she already knew as she had looked after some of them and had heard of the death. Heydon reflected,

It's a long time ago and all I can say is volunteering for that job is the best thing I ever did — I found a wife. I don't know where I'd be. Had I not been burnt I'd be in an earlier course at Bradfield Park, a different squadron, I'd have got to England, probably shot down in England. Volunteering for that job really changed my entire life.[8]

By Tuesday 19 January 1943 all the drums of mustard had been removed and were 'in good condition' with the exception of three. They were among the last 18 mustard drums removed. Two of these showed signs of dampness around the bung in the centre of the end of the drum. The third had a hairline crack just below the rim at the bottom. In the first two cases no liquid was visible nor was there any sign of the drum having leaked. In the third case the men told their supervisors that the drum had been stowed against a shelf-like projection above the floor and that, in removing the drum, and before they had noticed any damage, they had knocked it with some violence and either caused or increased the damage.[9] Only one or two cubic centimetres of leakage were detectable. RAAF chemical officer Le Fevre stated that:

> *No signs were visible to me of any mustard having reached the floor upon which these drums had been standing or moved over. Nevertheless as a precaution these areas were treated with bleach etc and the damaged drum (after decontamination) plus the undamaged drums standing close to it were taken to the slings by personnel in fully protective clothing.*[10]

This precaution was certainly necessary as the initial assessment had been erroneous. This was the drum that had been leaking since the journey began and it was now lashed to the side of a rail truck for the final leg to its destination. At Glenbrook station the drum was weighed on government scales where it was calculated to have leaked 80 to 100 lbs of mustard, a substantial amount. The knock had not contributed to the spill as most of the liquid had already escaped.

The Mustard Gas Drums at Glenbrook Tunnel
National Archives of Australia

Chapter 7

The Tunnels

On the day Andrew Williams died, the unloading of all bulk mustard from No. 1 hold had been completed with the last 18 drums removed. The bulk mustard had been placed on rail trucks which ran along a track that wound its way conveniently alongside Glebe Island. On their arrival at Rozelle, however, it was discovered that there were only six rail trucks instead of the 18 that should have been present for escort to the Glenbrook rail siding. By the time the trucks and their escort arrived at Penrith on 20 January the 12 missing trucks had been located. Two trucks had arrived at Glenbrook the previous night and ten earlier that morning. All were now accounted for.[1]

Tim Miers was a sharp-eyed youngster who had grown up in a house next to the Glenbrook siding where he was to spend his entire life. He watched with interest one day as hundreds of drums arrived by rail and were loaded onto semi-trailers. What caught his eye about this load, as distinct from the many other loads he had watched previously, was the secrecy surrounding it. If they were simply petrol drums as he had initially assumed, why was each load taken by a different road route to the nearby abandoned tunnel? There were four roads from the siding and each was used in turn. This was clearly a precious cargo. 'They obviously wanted

Tim Miers
Tim Miers

to avoid any attempts at sabotage,' Miers surmised. But what could those drums contain? Miers pondered the mystery for some time before he stumbled on the answer. He later recalled the incident that provided the solution:

> *One afternoon at about 4.30 pm a RAAF trucker was transporting drums from the Glenbrook railway siding to the tunnel. While he was driving up Raymond St, which in the war years was all dirt and potholes, and when he was just behind the home and butcher's shop of George and Jessie Bunyan, two of the drums fell off and busted open. Next we had a high ranking Air Force officer visiting all the nearby homes advising mothers to 'shut all the doors and windows and keep your children inside until we are able to clean up the mess.' There was a strange smell around which I recall was like a rotting egg smell.*
>
> *Two guys in full anti-gas gear then turned up and rolled the drums into a gully where they dealt with them. As kids we were too scared to go down and investigate the drums although they may have removed them. Although the mustard gas stored in the commandeered mushroom tunnel was supposed to be a secret, all the locals knew it existed. My late mother told us as children, as did all the other mothers, not to talk about the mustard gas as it would sabotage the war effort. It was a matter of 'We knew but pretended not to.'*[2]

While locals were fully aware of what had happened at the time, many others moved to Glenbrook in the post-war years and some residents, to this day, have no idea that mustard gas was ever stored at Glenbrook.

One of the chemical warfare drivers was Harry Evans whose task it was to drive the mustard drums from the Glenbrook rail siding to the nearby tunnel. He was not permitted to wear a gas mask: 'It'd look a bit queer, wouldn't it? The world would know about what was going on. So I couldn't have a gas mask, I carried one but I couldn't wear it.' Evans had to tie down his loads with rope and he did so with great care as it was a court-martial offence to lose any of the drums from his load. But he was unable to wear protective gloves as his gloved hands simply did not have the dexterity to tie the knots. As the mustard impregnated the

THE TUNNELS

Siding at Glenbrook Station used to Offload Mustard Gas
Tim Miers

Above: Truck Used by Harry Evans to Deliver Mustard Gas from the Siding to the Tunnel
Chemical Warfare Armourers

Left: Glenbrook Tunnel Being Used as a Mushroom Farm by the Rowes
Penrith City Library Photographic Collection

rope Evans was inevitably burned on his hands and arms which soon erupted with huge blisters 'just like bunches of grapes'. The frequency of his burns eventually forced Harry Evans to change jobs and it was with little regret that he parted company with the deadly drums of mustard gas.[3]

Fanny and Herbert Rowe were long-time residents of Glenbrook. In the early 1930s they developed an interest in growing mushrooms close to their property. They felt sure they could build a thriving business supplying the Sydney markets and looked long and hard for a suitable site, aware that mushrooms require high humidity as well as complete darkness. Fanny soon heard of an abandoned 660-metre railway tunnel at Glenbrook and completed a lengthy inspection of the site. It was perfect. It met all the requisite growing conditions and also boasted a significant additional benefit — it was close to the existing railway station where the morning train could take the mushrooms to Sydney for delivery to the markets. The Rowes approached the Commissioner of Railways and petitioned successfully for use of the tunnel. In June 1934 they secured a lease for a period of 12 months at £13 per annum.[4] Fanny, Herbert and daughter Gwen soon embarked on a mushrooming career, although it was not until 1939 that the farm showed any return for their efforts.

In the early days the Rowe family endured primitive living conditions. Bats and rats were constant companions. It was Gwen's job to deliver the mushrooms to Glenbrook station each night and she later recalled the hard years spent living a spartan existence as the family built the business:

> *For years we lived in an old Wirth's Circus tent with a small rock cave as a kitchen and our water supply was gathered in a pool my father dug to catch whatever came through the culvert under the main western highway. The culvert was also our refrigerator. Very shortly after dad collected corrugated iron to roof over the tent of four rooms, and put up outer walls of Wunderlich steel panels with the aim of removing the many ropes and pegs from the tent.*[5]

The family worked hard, scraping and saving to make their venture a success. Just as the farm was coming into profit, the Rowes' world was rudely disrupted.

THE TUNNELS

Mustard Gas in a Cutting at Glenbrook Tunnel
Ernie Moore

Around April 1941, Air Force officers from the Richmond RAAF base made an initial inspection of the Rowes' mushroom-growing tunnel. What they told the Rowes at the time is unclear. Records indicate, however, that on 2 January 1942 the RAAF was searching for an explosive depot in NSW and, according to notes from the time, 'It has been found that an eminently suitable site for one such, is in the old railway tunnel at Glenbrook on the line to Katoomba.' At that time they were considering options for the safe storage of conventional explosives, as the decision to import chemical weapons had yet to be taken. The Railways Department agreed to hand the tunnel to the RAAF to use for its own purposes. By January 1942 the Rowes had been leasing the tunnel for over seven years, with the lease at three months' notice. Their notice was soon to be rapidly and summarily invoked. By 27 January 1942 the Rowes and their mushrooms had been moved and the RAAF had occupied the tunnel in pursuance of an order under Regulation 54 of the National Security (General) Regulations.[6] The tunnel was ostensibly destined for use as an ammunition store.

Railway tunnels were not only ideal for growing mushrooms but also for storing mustard gas which required a low temperature and high security. With the entry of chemical weapons into Australia, Glenbrook tunnel, with its easy proximity to the major shipping terminals in Sydney, was a logical storage choice. It replicated the environmental conditions in the Batu caves in Malaya. Storage of the *Idomeneus'* mustard gas drums at Glenbrook tunnel began with the arrival of the first consignment on 20 January 1943 and, after a day's careful unloading and movement, was completed on 21 January 1943. All drums were in good condition apart from the leaker in No. 1 hold.

With the tunnel now in military hands, Herbert Rowe moved to Cowra where he was employed as a carpenter and joiner from January 1942. A year later, in January 1943, he returned to Glenbrook where he remained until October 1946. He was a master builder and completed carpentry and maintenance tasks at the Glenbrook chemical weapon storage depot, where he was placed on the maximum scale for labourers at £250. He became a much-loved member of the chemical warfare depot and was affectionately known as 'Pop'. Fanny Rowe was also placed on the civilian establishment of the unit as compensation for the loss of her livelihood and, in 1947, received £400 compensation for the loss of her mushroom business.[7]

Ron Hughes lived in Glenbrook from 1943 to 1947 when his parents were proprietors of Kelgoola Guest House, an old sandstone building in the centre of the village. He clearly remembers the secrecy of the time:

The wives of the Air Force personnel used to stay in our guest house and Mrs Makin who ran the Lapstone hotel [just above the tunnel] used to call up if she had no more room. We invariably took them in. One day one of the Air Force men came in to see his wife, as they often did, and I could see his arm was covered in huge blisters which I was told were caused by mustard gas. It was all hush hush and my parents told me to be quiet about it and I did so. I was 11 or 12 at the time.

Another incident I remember at the guest house concerned a chap, perhaps in his 50s. He stayed at the guest house on three occasions. On the first occasion he wore a full beard, on the second he wore a moustache and on the third occasion he was clean shaven. He was apparently asking too many questions about operations at the camp so the Air Force guys had him followed as they were concerned he may have been a spy. From memory, I do not think it amounted to anything. He was just interested but it showed how paranoid people were at the time.[8]

Once the drums of mustard gas had been stored it was time to deal with the phosgene bombs from No. 4 hold. One phosgene bomb with a slight leak was found on 19 January and two further leakers were discovered the next day. By 23 January all the phosgene weapons had been unloaded from No. 4 hold. While Glenbrook was used to store the bulk stocks, another abandoned tunnel cutting at Marrangaroo, on the same railway line, was used for the phosgene bombs.

Rail trucks from Rozelle carrying the phosgene bombs began arriving at Marrangaroo on Friday 22 January 1943, pulling into a siding built at the combined Army-Air Force Marrangaroo depot. The siding was opened in May 1942 and had been purpose-designed for the receipt of explosives to the base. The phosgene bombs were then loaded onto road trucks and taken to the nearby abandoned rail tunnel a few kilometres away. The bombs were inspected at all points: as the rail trucks were uncovered; as the lorries were loaded; as the lorries were unloaded; and as the drums were stacked.

The tunnel at Marrangaroo was initially inspected on 6 May 1942 by Wing Commander Le Fèvre and the Commanding Officer of the base.[9] Although it was deemed too small to hold all the chemical stocks, the tunnel cutting's excellent condition, its natural ventilation, level

Ron Hughes
Ron Hughes

flooring and access road, were all noted approvingly by Le Fèvre: 'I strongly recommend that an attempt should be made to acquire it. Very little work would be required to bring it into usable condition.' His recommendation was accepted and, in May 1942, the RAAF Chief of Air Staff approved the expenditure of £1,544 to convert the tunnel for explosive storage. By late 1942 it was deemed necessary also to acquire the house that stood next to the tunnel for security reasons.[10] Originally owned by the Hansen family, the house was converted into a guard house and still stands.

As the building of open-sided sheds to house the phosgene bombs and the roads that would provide access to the site had not yet commenced, the phosgene bombs were temporarily stored in a cutting at the northern end of the tunnel. Phosgene cannot be stored in an enclosed tunnel due the lethal nature of the gas. In any case the tunnel was already filled with 250 lb mustard gas bombs which had arrived on another ship, the *Nigerstrrom*, in August 1942.

From 22 to 25 January 1943 the rail trucks continued to arrive and the 250 lb phosgene bombs were unloaded and stored, shipment after shipment. By 25 January, 3183 filled and 200 empty bombs had been moved in 23 trucks accompanied by 12 trucks of tail units, with two more trucks due to arrive. The bomb bodies were exposed to the sun, although an attempt was made to provide cover using branches from trees overlaid on the surface of the bombs. Trewin noted that, 'As a consequence of the bombs being heated (exposed to summer sun), I anticipate an increase in the number of leakers as many are in a very bad condition.'[11] This did not augur well.

As the first days passed, numerous leaking bombs were separated with some stored in an unidentified isolated area known as 'the graveyard' and buried nose-up to a depth of 12 inches. Some bombs developed leaks after storage and, in many cases, could not be located precisely in the stack due to the intermittent behaviour of the leaking. Eddying winds that played around the dump and the elusive nature of the phosgene odour also added to the difficulties in identifying leakers. According to the records, 'Guards were especially warned to patrol upwind of the storage.' After the third day of storage the men handling the bombs, questioned on their physical health, complained of physical weariness and exhibited an increased tendency to contract colds in the head and chest.[12]

THE TUNNELS

Phosgene Bombs from the Idomeneus at Marrangaroo Tunnel
National Archives of Australia

Phosgene Shed Foundations Today

Due to both the constant handling processes and the sudden movement from a refrigerated state to semi-tropical temperatures, approximately 25 phosgene bombs leaked intermittently, 23 through the nose cap of the ejection charge container. 'Leakage is occurring in dozens of bombs through the nose cap, owing to corrosion of the ejection charge container, and I have found many of the bombs leak as soon as the nose caps are removed. The leakage was intermittent due to the action of the escaping gas on the luting around the nose cap.'[13] Later inspections showed 15 bombs to be completely unserviceable and, alarmingly, almost empty.

In mid-1943 sheds were finally erected to store the phosgene bombs. While very few physical remnants survive from Australia's chemical warfare past, the foundations of these sheds remain, a testament to the solidity of the structures that contained the phosgene. Now overgrown with wild blackberry and eucalypts, they lie forgotten.[14] The burial of these bombs at the nearby Marrangaroo Army depot was to attract international attention in 2008 and 2009 in events that will be described later in this narrative.

The leaking phosgene bombs caused many casualties. All personnel who operated close to the defective stores were told to wear face masks. One RAAF airman vomited and was ordered to rest. Three other RAAF personnel were sent to Lithgow hospital. Trewin, who was in charge, noted:

> *I made the error of allowing the remaining men go on evening stand down if they wished after the compulsory rest taken during the afternoon. Practically every man went into the township. I saw the men before they left and they were all fit, fit enough anyhow to go to a local dance they had been looking forward to attending. Five additional casualties were admitted to the hospital for observation between 2200 hours and 2359 hours that night, three of these entering hospital from the township after feeling ill at the dance and two from the unit, one of these having returned from an evening in Lithgow. I have been to the hospital this morning and all nine patients to my mind are looking quite fit.*[15]

The Alsatian guard dogs were also poisoned and had to be taken off duty.

However, one staff member was deliberately exposed to phosgene. Trewin took a civilian medical officer out to the storage area one evening to give him some idea of the conditions under which the men worked. He showed him a leaker 'to experience a concentration of phosgene, which he had never smelt before.'[16] This was to be an experience the medical officer would never forget.

Chapter 8

The Clean-Up

Back at the wharf, the *Idomeneus'* No. 1 hold was now empty and ready to be reused. This required a massive clean-up and decontamination, particularly as the hold was to be used for food transportation. With up to 100 lbs (45 kg) of mustard gas loose in the hold, there was much debate over how precisely the decontamination would be achieved. Captain Dark's letter of instruction had stipulated:

> *Such insulated spaces which have been used for the storage of chemical weapons, must not be used for the storage of food until they have been certified clear of contamination and suitable for food stowage by a fully qualified person.*[1]

Idomeneus crewman Stuart Glover remembers the protracted and complex clean-up process that eventuated:

> *Now this went on for a long time — it seemed to be weeks. And every time the Air Force people confessed that they had decontaminated as well as they could, somebody would go down and again be affected by the mustard gas. Apparently the stuff was stowed in drums and a drum had developed a split.*
>
> *I remember that when we were relocated to Balmain for the actual unloading and decontamination of the mustard, we were aware of the Air Force personnel doing these things. And there was a young chap who was a young officer, a young RAAF officer, and I've always thought that he was a flight lieutenant but I may be wrong. And I remember talking to him one day, about chemical weaponry and mustard gas in particular. And he showed me a large circular scar that he had on the back of his wrist and told me that was the result of one drop of mustard gas. So we knew a little, but not very much. And over and over again, it seemed that these poor RAAF blokes were sent down to number one to re-decontaminate but the stuff must have been very, very persistent because they went down there*

over and over again and I don't know how they decontaminated, I never saw it myself, but I always had an idea that it was a dilution and soap and water job or something like that.[2]

Le Fèvre's chemical warfare deputy Trewin oversaw the decontamination with two RAAF personnel in support as supervisors.

On 25 January 1943 the RAAF declared the clean-up completed. As per his instructions, Captain Dark sought 'a certificate to say my ship was free of mustard gas, and taint, and was suitable for the carriage of food stuffs.'[3] But he was told by Le Fèvre,

I am not able to give you the certificate you want, while I can give you a gas free certificate, I cannot give you a taint free certificate. I am not a shipping man, but I have brought with me Squadron Leader [Buttfield]. I can identify him by saying that he is shipping manager for the Orient Line. He knows about these things and does not feel I should give you [a] taint free [clearance].

No. 8/9 Pier at Glebe Island
State Records of New South Wales

THE CLEAN-UP

Dark was not convinced and suggested they have one last look at No. 1 hold.

As Le Fèvre, Dark and the squadron leader entered No. 1 for the final inspection, Le Fèvre recalled, 'The place looked extraordinarily clean. The treatment had been the most exacting treatment I had ever heard of in decontaminating.' The hold and the walls had been sluiced with seawater. The men had used a vast quantity of bleaching powder, scrubbed the place with yard brooms, hosed it down with salt water, drained it and repeated the bleaching procedure. Le Fèvre learned that the ship had a fire extinguishing system consisting of superheated steam which could be piped to the hull, battened down for that purpose. 'The chemistry of mustard gas is such that even at ordinary temperatures it should be destroyed if ordinary cold water gets in touch with it.' Le Fèvre argued that if one increased the velocity of the destructive reaction by raising the temperature and supplying superheated steam, it would easily destroy any remnants of the mustard gas.[4]

Bleaching Powder in a Bucket
Imperial War Museum

The ship's top hatch was closed and the fire extinguishing steam system turned on and pumped into the hold and the hold left battened with the steam system in full force for 24 hours. The following morning it was cooled, hosed with salt water and, when opened for inspection, it was 'found to be like new'.[5]

Le Fèvre could see nothing with the potential for contamination except at the sides of the bottom of the hold where the floor joined the walls of the ship. The join was sealed with a layer of pitch. The inspection party checked the site where the leak had been discovered, scrutinising the pitch at that point and discovering that it was soft. Le Fèvre could not believe that mustard could have survived the treatment to which the hold had been subjected.

Dark was less convinced. He scraped some of the pitch at this location and examined it closely. He thought he could detect a suspect smell. He told Le Fèvre to smell it, asking, 'In view of the fact we have a good chemist in the employ of the company could he take it to the laboratory and analyse it?' The Wing Commander responded, 'What are you afraid of — mustard gas?' to which Dark promptly replied, 'Yes.' Le Fèvre asserted that he could prove there was none with a two-minute experiment.

Le Fèvre scraped out some of the pitch with a stick that was standing nearby and told Dark that, if mustard was present, it would react with bleaching powder. He picked up a handful of bleaching powder and threw it on the pitch in question. Le Fèvre was utterly 'astonished' when it immediately reacted and caught fire. Dark recalled, 'It blew up into flames. We were all gassed.' Le Fèvre was justifiably flummoxed. 'The chemistry of mustard is such that it could not have remained in its active form under all that treatment, unless of course it was protected by something or dissolved in something, which subsequently proved to be the case where the pitch was concerned.'

The casualties, including chemist McKenzie and the assistant wharf manager, retired to Dark's cabin and washed their eyes with saline and distilled castor oil. The squadron leader and Le Fèvre made plans to return under cover of darkness to treat the pitch 'so that the darkness would in some measure screen our operations from the observation of the wharf labourers, who were now working in the other holds of the ship'. The decontamination equipment and truck (returning to Glenbrook) were recalled by radio. The squadron leader and Le Fèvre

THE CLEAN-UP

were exhausted, ill and vomiting. Le Fèvre described the after-effects of his gassing:

> *I also registered a marked smarting of the eyes, and fearing the later development during the night, obtained a morphine tablet from the [RAAF] Medical Officer. I arrived home about midnight and immediately took a hot bath. I woke about 2 am with pain in the eyes, observing blepharospasm and photophobia. Even the light of the moon through the window was painful. Vision was quite indistinct. I therefore took the morphine and slept until 6 am by which time the symptoms were very painful and sleep was impossible.[6]*

Le Fèvre was treated in hospital with drops of atropine and castor oil. On 27 January he was transferred to Concord, by which time cod liver oil was being administered instead of castor oil. He was finally discharged on 6 February but had been allowed out three days previously for the historic Chemical Warfare Plan conference at US Colonel Copthorne's office where a plan for the use of chemical weapons in the South West Pacific was drafted. Captain Dark remained in hospital until 30 January.

Crewman Stuart Glover recalls the incident well:

> *Captain Dark, I do remember, like a good skipper, did things that he asked his other people to do and he went down number one hold himself at one stage and the chief problem then, was people having their eyes affected. And this happened to Captain Dark and I think he went ashore for a couple of days probably, to hospital and then came back again and resumed playing deck golf.[7]*

The clean-up had to resume. On 26 January the pitch was removed to a depth of one inch from the seam around the hold. The next day the contaminated pitch was swept to the square of hatch to be removed and placed in a steel tip-truck for dumping. Some 1300 lbs of chloride of lime were used to neutralise the impregnated mustard. Thick bleach paste was applied to the floor to a height of eight feet, the paste scrubbed into the steel structure and the wooden spar ceiling. Two days later, on 28 January, the material in the tip-truck was taken away and buried — in Botany Bay rubbish tip! Further scrubbing and bleach was applied and the hold closed and made airtight. Steam at 80 lbs per square inch from three fire extinguishers was injected into the hold for eight hours non-stop. The next day the hold was reopened, inspected, steamed for another three hours and hosed for three and a half hours with cold water. Remarkably, positive results from the pitch were still obtained.

Trewin conducted a further clearance test — a seemingly bizarre experiment which ultimately compromised his health. This 'physiological test' was performed on 29 January with Trewin binding contaminated pitch to his forearm for four hours. The result was a faint erythema (redness) one hour after removal and the emergence of a shallow blister several days later.[8] On 30 January all the pitch on the starboard side was removed. Again the No. 1 hold was thoroughly scrubbed with bleach paste and the hold washed out.

Ron Patfield was yet another RAAF 'rookie' tasked with removing the pitch. He was waiting at Bradfield Park to move north when an officer told him, 'You are tasked for a job at Rozelle wharf.' He and the other men with him were not volunteers. They were led into the hold of the *Idomeneus* and told to remove the tarry pitch. It was hot; they were given gas masks but were told they didn't need them. In any case they could not see with the masks on. They had no idea of the nature of the operation and were given only a pickaxe to complete the task. Patfield subsequently developed a large burn on the left thumb and on his right leg and in the groin area.

Ron Patfield

Later, when ill from the effects of mustard (and possibly malaria) he went to see a doctor. He was told that there was no mustard gas in

Australia in World War II and that his problem was that he 'was obsessed with Jesus'! Ron Patfield later became Rector of Annandale, although a persistent cough prevented him delivering sermons. He also developed a hypersensitivity to light. A surgeon friend, having watched a documentary on mustard gas, was the first to suggest that Patfield may have been exposed to the gas, as his symptoms closely resembled those described in the documentary.[9] Chronic bronchitis, an itchy scrotum and a chronic heel problem (like another mustard gas veteran, Frank Burkin) were just some of the lingering health problems.

Iris Warn was engaged to Frank Bourke, another RAAF rookie recruited to clean up the *Idomeneus*. Bourke had always loved aircraft and, realising that he would be conscripted, joined the Air Force at 18. Iris had seen World War I gas victims in oil baths but never believed that this could happen to her future husband.

Iris was working in the Technico electronics factory with Frank's sister Kathleen. She received a call one day and was told that Frank was very

Iris Bourke
Iris Bourke

Frank Bourke
Frank Bourke

badly burned and was going to die and that she should go to Concord Repatriation Hospital (Yaralla Military Hospital) immediately. By the time she and Kathleen arrived Frank 'was very sick and yellow. He looked horrible and smelt horrible'. Frank Bourke had been decontaminating the *Idomeneus* wearing his overalls. He had no protective gear whatsoever.

Iris watched as 'the nurses used to come every day and with a needle, burst the blisters which were from his neck to bum'. They were told he wasn't going to live. As his family was Irish Catholic, Kathleen sent for a priest to give the last rites. The priest duly came.

On her next visit, Iris discovered that Frank had been removed from the critical list and was now in a wheelchair. Like the wharfies, he was morose and uncommunicative and wanted to be left alone. He was allowed home for two weeks and given dispensation to wear civilian clothes as he couldn't bear the rough Air Force uniform against his skin. Iris recalls, 'Frank was a beast for a while, very moody, very angry after the event.'[10] We now recognise this as Post Traumatic Stress Disorder (PTSD) which is well documented in mustard gas victims. Frank Bourke later joined the Returned and Services League at Granville. The welfare officer there suggested, 'Why don't you go down to repatriation for some assistance regarding the exposure?' Frank agreed. However, the doctors who made the assessment told him that there was no mustard gas in Australia and dismissed his claim out of hand. He was told that he had an allergy to tomatoes, was a nervous person and was then referred to a psychiatrist.[11] The medical establishment had no idea that these weapons had been present in Australia.

Frank Bourke and his mates drank to forget. Although he survived, the health legacy included pains in the chest and exhaustion after completing certain tasks. Iris Bourke laments, 'It affected him greatly all his life.'[12] Frank had lifetime problems with rashes, pigmentation and wart-like growths in the genital area (possibly what is referred to as mustard-induced angioma). In fact, because of the scarring and growths on his genitals, the doctors told him that he wouldn't be able to have children. Iris and Frank were shocked when they had four daughters whom Frank proudly told had been conceived against the odds.

The only treatment Frank Bourke received from Concord Hospital was a series of creams to relieve the skin rashes and irritations. One of the few ways he could relieve his itchy skin was to take frequent showers. Seventy years later Iris remains very upset over his treatment. 'He was always told there was no such thing as mustard gas. He was a very very honest man, he could never accept being called a liar and told that he was mad. He simply gave up trying to persuade the powers that be that it really happened and said "I'm not going to deal with these idiots any more."[13] After the rejections Frank never again sought treatment for the effects of his exposure to mustard gas. This is a theme common in the lives of many of Australia's chemical warfare veterans. No-one believed they had been exposed and the government remained firmly in denial. The men's war records provided no assistance. Almost universally there are no references to the chemical sites where they worked. Instead they are referred to as 'attached to a headquarters' and then on 'secondment' while, in fact, they were working with gas.

Frank & Iris Bourke
Iris Bourke

On the last day of January the hold was scrubbed repeatedly, given a final sluicing and yet another 'physiological test' was conducted. Seven pieces of pitch from different places on the port side were placed on Trewin's left arm and seven small fragments of pitch remaining in the trough on the starboard side were attached to his right arm. The fragments were placed under cellophane paper, strapped on tightly and left for two hours, the arms then exposed to the sun to obtain maximum vaporisation of any remaining mustard gas. Half an hour after removal faint erythema appeared in six places on the left and two on right. Trewin

DEATH BY MUSTARD GAS

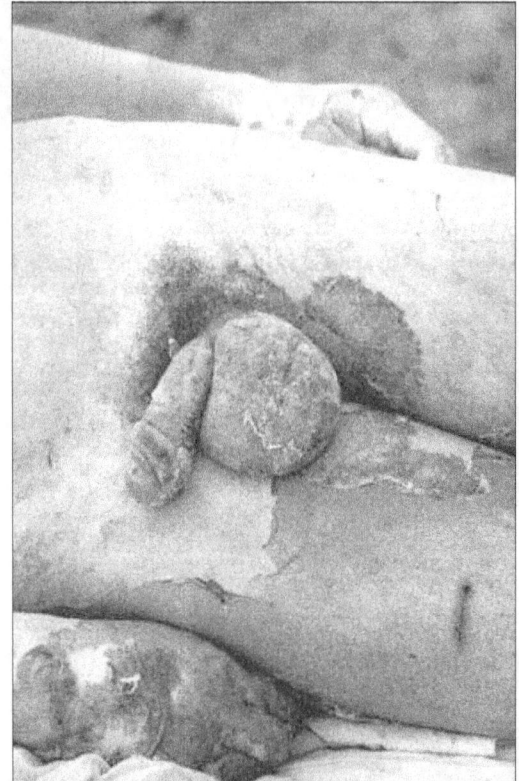

The Devastating Effects of Mustard Gas on the Penis & Scrotum

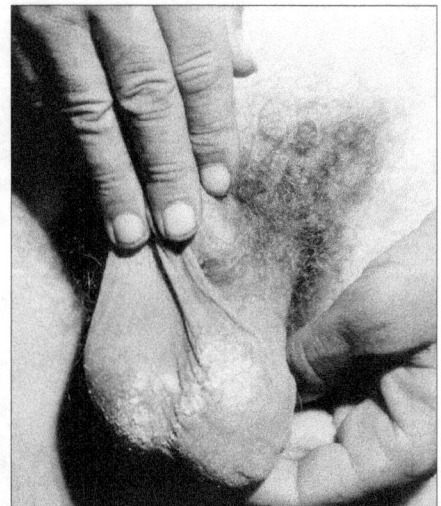

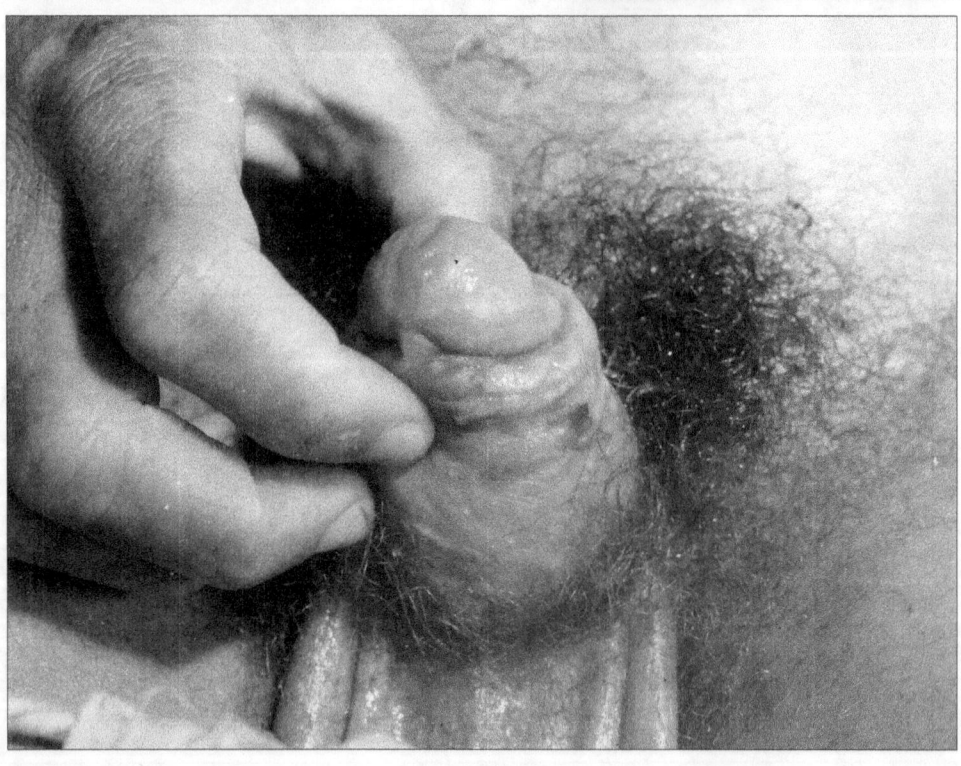

was to pay a price for this brave experiment. He had placed his health on the line to ensure the safety of food movement.

One small area of starboard pitch still gave a positive mustard result. This area was treated with hydrolysing agent (caustic soda and methylated spirits). Then, on 31 January at 9.30 pm, a certificate was written and issued to Dark, with another inspection promised in Melbourne as the *Idomeneus* was stopping there on its way home.

Two weeks after the gassing, Flight Lieutenant Hamilton submitted a report describing the Air Force casualties. He counted 76 afflicted men, the majority with vapour burns. There were six 'fairly' severe scrotal burns due to vapour and one had a 'serious' liquid burn on the whole leg, scrotum and penis. He concluded, 'In my opinion no case will suffer any significant after-effects.'[14] The Medical Officer at RAAF sick quarters in Ultimo noted one patient, 'the worst', had marked erythema of the scrotum. 'I do not consider that there will be any material permanent disability occurring in these cases.'[15] He was wrong. He was referring to Les Parsons who was to suffer from the effects of mustard gas for the rest of his life.

The *Idomeneus* crew also became casualties during the cleansing process with at least 15 men gassed. The affected parts were listed as the eyes, larynx, hips, chest, arms and neck.[16]

The unloading and decontamination process also produced unsung heroes such as Mrs McKillock, a voluntary worker,

> *... who with different women friends prepared excellently cooked meals for the men on the wharf and maintained a constant supply of tea, bringing it on board personally and ensuring that men all received their personal share. This service in view of the exhaustion of the men after working in complete oilskin suitings, was not a luxury but a physiological necessity.*[17]

The total volume of material removed or destroyed included 375 running feet of timber, 15 rope slings, 20,000 running feet dunnage of wood (taken to sea in a ship and sunk), two dozen brooms, 100 tons of fresh water and 480 feet of spar ceiling.

The worst possible outcome had occurred. Someone had died during the top secret process of importing mustard gas into Australia. No-one was meant to know and now too many people did. The Air Force scrambled into damage control. There were to be two quick inquiries, one external and one internal. Someone was responsible, but whom?

Chapter 9

Fall Guy

While the decontamination was proceeding an internal RAAF inquiry was convened with a Court of Inquiry commencing on 21 January 1943. Squadron Leader Martin was appointed President of the Court with Flight Lieutenants Harding and Read its members. Their brief was to enquire 'into the circumstances giving rise to injuries alleged to have been suffered by service personnel'.[1] The plight of the stevedores was simply ignored.

Le Fèvre was called as the first witness. He was a busy man and gave evidence to the Court in between supervising the decontamination of the *Idomeneus* and inspecting new tunnels for chemical weapons storage. He explained that he had been tasked to advise on the safety of the holds during the unloading of general cargo. He had noted that the cargo comprised soda ash in jute bags and that a fine powder had filtered through the bags onto the ladders and walls. Explanations of complex chemistry dominated the answers he provided to the court. Le Fèvre explained that a drum of paradichlorobenzene had burst in the deckhouse and the contents had spattered the floor and were consequently spread by the wharfies who had trampled it on their shoes. Formaldehyde solution had also leaked throughout the voyage and a strong odour of carbon tetrachloride was present. Le Fèvre described the inspections, adding that no smell of mustard gas had been detected but 'as the situation was the same as Melbourne he advised the wearing of respirators.' Le Fèvre had Dark to thank for insisting that this caveat was placed on the certificate and was available in writing.

As the testimony proceeded Le Fèvre appeared happy to lay the blame at the feet of one the RAAF supervisors. He asserted that he had instructed Flying Officer Harold Freeman to place two airmen in respirators at the bottom of the hold to keep watch in case any of the drums were accidentally damaged. In evidence he said, 'My certificate was shown to Flying Officer Freeman before it was handed to the Captain and Mr Freeman appeared to understand the instructions which it implied ... I asked Flying Officer Freeman why his men had not worn respirators.

His reply was to the effect that it would not have looked good for his men to wear respirators when the wharf labourers were not wearing them.' During a later court case he was to comment that Freeman 'was in no way really under my orders' and 'could not have been [under his control].'[2] In other words, he could not have been under Le Fèvre's command.

Le Fèvre concluded his evidence by asserting his opinion that mustard vapour in concentrations below the threshold of detection by smell could not have caused the injuries and that these must have been due to soda ash dust in conjunction with traces of dichlorobenzene and possibly carbon tetrachloride and formaldehyde.[3]

Harold Freeman
National Archives of Australia

Four days later Le Fèvre was recalled for further evidence. Flight Lieutenant Trewin had informed him by phone that he had weighed the drum with the hairline crack on government-tested scales in use at Glenbrook railway station and found it to be 666 pounds. By way of comparison, 11 undamaged drums were found to have weights between 748 and 779 pounds. It was possible, therefore, that the damaged drum may have lost upwards of 80 lbs of mustard gas. There were now definite signs of mustard contamination of the wood floor above where the drums had been.

Le Fèvre revised his hypothesis. The negative test was obtained when the hold was first opened as his sampling always occurred *on top* of the cargo. As the leaking drum was in the very front of the hold and the air was still, the heavy vapour never diffused at a level high enough to be detected near the square of the hatch. A positive test was obtained in the region of the damaged drum when there were only 17 mustard drums still to be unloaded and all corners of the hold were completely accessible.

Since the symptoms of the earlier Sydney cases had resembled those in Melbourne — severe eye symptoms 'without parallel effects on their bodies', Le Fèvre reiterated his view

> ... *that the soda ash etc was the chief responsible agent at first. However, as the hold became clear and the airmen were working in the neighbourhood of the detected leakage, the casualties began to present a typical mustard picture, reddening of the skin, of the crotch and armpits as well as eye trouble. I am convinced that the chief responsible agent with these later casualties was mustard gas vapour.*

Thus, he concluded that, while the health problems suffered by the men in Melbourne troubles were not due to mustard, the injuries that occurred *later* during the Sydney unloading were.[4]

Next to give evidence was the decontamination supervisor Flying Officer Freeman. Freeman was still a patient in the RAAF sick quarters at Ultimo and had been unable to attend the court while the previous evidence was taken. As a consequence the evidence had to be relayed to him at the sick quarters. Freeman disputed Le Fèvre's evidence. 'I have been shown the evidence of Wing Commander Le Fèvre in which he states he asked me why men had not worn respirators and I had replied that it would not have looked good for the men to wear respirators when the wharf labourers were not wearing them.'[5] Freeman was adamant that this conversation never occurred.

However Chemist McKenzie corroborated Le Fèvre's evidence, commenting that he had heard Le Fèvre telling Freeman to tell his men to wear respirators so as to impress on the wharfies the need for protective clothing. Despite his World War I experience, ARP training and chemical background, McKenzie could never account for the fact that none of his tests and examination had detected the presence of mustard gas. He told the court that there was 'some unusual condition there which I am unaware of.'[6] McKenzie was correct, but it would take seven years to discover this as the full facts of the situation were withheld not only from McKenzie but also from the Court of Inquiry.

Captain Dark's evidence was very brief. He was clearly of little interest to the court as he was dismissed in less than ten minutes.[7] Freeman's version of events was, however, supported by a member of the decontamination crew. While this RAAF member could not recall whether Le Fèvre had ordered respirators to be worn, he commented, 'I thought it was safe in view of the fact that all the tests I knew of had revealed no trace of gas.'

In its concluding comments the court recorded:

Concerning Flying Officer Freeman's responsibilities as Officer in Charge of the decontamination squad, the court is of the opinion the officer who has practically no experience in handling of mustard gas, relied more on the certificates issued by the competent authorities than on his own judgment in deciding what precautions were necessary.[8]

One statement in particular is worth examining: 'someone who had no experience relied on chemical warfare experts rather than his own intuition'. The irony of this statement must have been lost on the members of the court and their only defence can be that they signed the document without reading it as the conclusion is so ludicrous as to be risible.

The court found the RAAF responsible for the injuries that the men had suffered. The injuries were found not to have been due to any pre-existing physical pathological cause, but solely to mustard gas liquid from the leaking drum. The court further stated that 'the eye injuries were due to a lack of discretion on the part of Flying Officer Freeman in not ensuring that the decontamination party wore respirators at all times when on duty in the lower No. 1 hold.' The court recommended that Freeman be reprimanded as his oversight had led to the eye injuries suffered by the men.

The RAAF had found its 'fall guy'. Freeman alone was held responsible. Unsurprisingly, he left the Air Force soon after the war ended and returned to his former occupation at Dunlop Rubber Company.

The court also recommended that material such as mustard gas should, in future, be handled by specialists as 'the standard of anti-gas training in the RAAF is much below that needed for personnel who are required to handle chemical warfare gases.'⁹ Amateurs such as Freeman should not be involved.

While the RAAF accepted responsibility for the eye damage, this was never relayed to the victims. RAAF recruit Parsons never heard about the Court of Inquiry, never heard the result and its admission of responsibility, and he certainly

The Effect of Mustard Gas on Eyes
Australian War Memorial

never received any compensation despite the fact that he had to pay expensive eye-care bills for the next 65 years. But he continued to maintain that he had heard from Le Fèvre directly that he did not need to wear a gas mask.

With the conclusion of the Court of Inquiry a coroner's inquest was convened and the RAAF was quick to seek to exert an influence. Le Fèvre, in particular, sought to influence the coroner through RAAF Security Officer Shields:

> *I generally described the facts connected with the Idomeneus and particularly those connected with the wharf labourer who had died. I said I could not understand why the coroner was not satisfied that the verdict should be accidental death since the facts as stated by Sergeant Kelly seemed obviously to point to this side ... if the man had been desirous of committing suicide he would not have climbed part of the way down a drainpipe but would have jumped straight out of the window, while, if he were so blinded and in pain (as his relatives might be maintaining) he would not have found his way to the lavatory, through the window, and on to the pipe. Mr Shields said he would see the Coroner and endeavour to arrange that proceedings will either be in camera or will be fixed so*

that no mention is made of mustard gas in relation to the RAAF. He agreed to attempt to trace all civilian medical officers who were given certificates for various purposes in which the material is mentioned by name.[10]

It worked, as recorded in RAAF archival material:

The date for the Coroner's inquest on the death of Williams has not yet been fixed – the assistant coroner Mr Harris has been interviewed by the security officer in this headquarters and has been requested to conduct the inquiry in camera, and to impress upon all parties concerned, the necessity of maintaining secrecy as to any facts brought out at the inquiry. Mr Harris agreed willingly to this and proposes taking all necessary steps to have our request carried into effect.[11]

The Coroner's Court was at The Rocks, a stones throw to Walsh Bay. Joan Hunt, a fellow RPA nurse, provided an escort for Nurse Joy Rablah. Hunt recalls leaving early in the morning to go to the inquest. She had been assigned by the Matron of the hospital, Matron Heatherington, to accompany Nurse Rablah to the court for 'moral assistance'. They walked down Missenden Road and boarded a slow tram. They had to be there early and spent the entire morning sitting around waiting for proceedings to commence. No senior person from RPA went with them which came as a surprise to Hunt who felt that Rablah needed higher level support. At some stage Rablah mentioned to Hunt that the deceased had been terrified of going blind and, although Rablah was 'terribly upset' by Williams' death, she did not show it.[12] At about lunchtime Rablah was called in as a witness. As this was a closed court Hunt remained outside.

The coronial inquiry into the death of Andrew William Williams, aged 63, was held before the city Coroner, Mr Oram, on 22 February 1943. The first witness to be called was his wife Elsie. She described him leaving home to go to work, the events that followed his return home, his admission to hospital and his behaviour once there. 'He had always been a very happy man,' she told the inquest. Gilbert Williams agreed: 'My father was always a happy, carefree man.'[13]

Nurse Joy Rablah provided a long and detailed description of the days prior to Williams' death and the events of the early hours of

Coroner's Court
State Library of New South Wales

19 January. Medical Practitioner Stratford Sheldon described his internal examination of the body of a man at the Sydney morgue identified to him by Sergeant Kelly of No. 2 Police Station. Dr Collins and several doctors from the Microbiological Department had attended the autopsy. He described Andrew Williams' condition in some detail. The heel bone of the right foot was shattered. The left knee was dislocated and there was a fracture of the lower end of the thigh bone on the same side. The right side of the pelvis was widely broken and this fracture extended through the sacrum. There was free blood in the abdomen. The eighth left rib was broken in front. There was no gross change in any of the organs except the heart which was very large. Parts of the heart were sent to the Microbiological Department and some of the organs were sent to the government analyst. The report from the analyst, using the tests available at the time, found no evidence of the presence of di-chlordiethyl sulphide, the scientific name for mustard gas.

Dr Sheldon surmised, 'It seems quite feasible to me that the deceased would have a considerable amount of irritation but not only from his eyes but also from his mucous passages, his air passages and alimentary passages. I see nothing unreasonable in a man being mentally affected at night time from that alone.' He did not find any previous history of 'mental instability'. He continued:

> *If he was a healthy man and a happy, cheerful man, it would be reasonable to explain what had happened from the fact that he was confined in hospital in strange surroundings and he would have the irritation of his eyes, his chest and air passages and his alimentary tracts. Frequently you see people with less than that put off their head at night time. There is a constant irritation from his eyes. The nerve impulses from his scrotum and his eyes would be quite sufficient to upset his mind without knowing absolutely.*[14]

This was a commonsense and accurate conclusion.

The coroner concluded that 'the death of the deceased was due to injuries received by him through a fall whilst climbing down from the third floor of the hospital to the ground', that 'the deceased was suffering from the effects of mustard gas to which he was exposed' and that he 'did not commit suicide'.[15] While the coroner ruled that there was no criminal or culpable negligence, the question remains as to whether he had all the facts in front of him. Was Williams' death pure accident? Time would tell.

Soon after the conclusion of both enquiries Le Fèvre, believing that his reputation had been impugned, added a statement to the RAAF record in his own defence:

> *I would be grateful to make written comments on the following points which concern me personally. In point of fact – if the men upon whose cases the RAAF Court of Enquiry has sat had worn their respirators as ordered [they] would have escaped with only a few minor skin burns which in all probability would not have necessitated their [admission] into hospital or even stopping work. In my own interest I want to stress the point … [the] fact that later we definitely found that mustard <u>had</u> [leaked] and that there <u>was</u> detectable mustard at the bottom hold – <u>and</u> that I gave evidence to this effect at [an] appearance before the court – does not affect the [fact that they should have worn respirators]. In justice therefore, the technical advice which I [gave as] to the lower hold being opened should be judged <u>only</u> [on] the evidence*

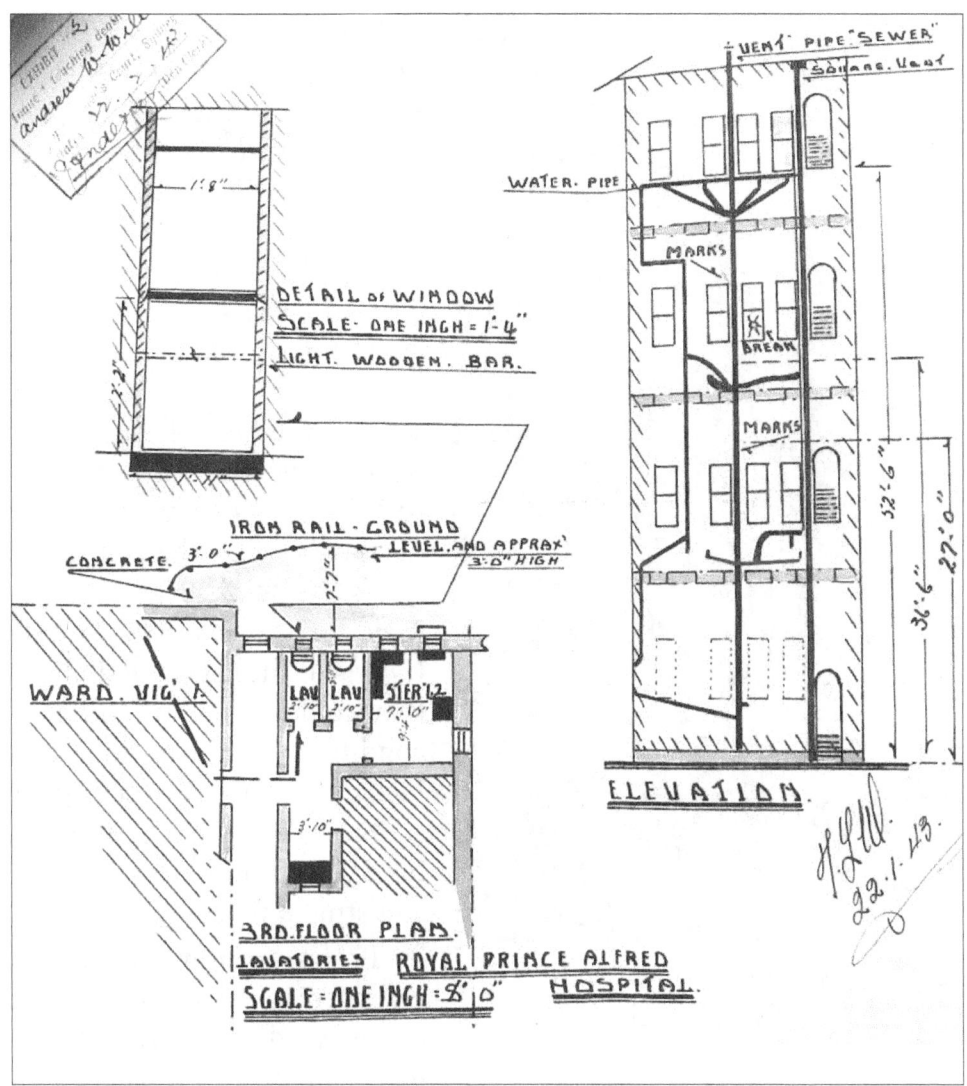

Diagrams from Coroner's Inquest
Coroner's Inquest

that was available to me when that advi[ce] was given. When I first learned of the limited terms of reference in the No. 5 Court of Enquiry, I feared that the recorded proceedings might be taken by readers as an authoritative account of the whole series of incidents presented during the unloading of instead of only part of the story concerning one ship.[16]

Since the Court of Inquiry had cleared Le Fèvre, and his actions were not examined during the proceedings, these musings appear symptomatic of a troubled mind. Was it possible that he was hiding something?

Is it possible to understand why Andrew Williams climbed out of the hospital window? Can a single label be applied to his psychological state or can it at least be narrowed to a restricted number of possibilities? There are a number of specialists who believe that this is possible based on reference to their diagnostic bible, the *Diagnostic and Statistical Manual of Mental Disorders, Fifth Edition* (DSM-5). The list of possibilities that could describe Williams' condition is lengthy and includes confusion (delirium), acute depressive episode, brief psychotic reaction, or adjustment reaction.

Professor Sandy McFarlane, an expert in trauma and PTSD, having read the records related to Williams' physical and mental state, made the following observations:

The Wall from which Andrew Williams Fell

Concerning Andrew's mental state, I think PTSD is not likely. I would believe that almost definitely he had delirium. Serious physical illness, associated with pain not uncommonly leads to delirium. This condition is essentially brain failure. It often is worse or only evident at night and is more severe due to the effects of relative sensory deprivation. In this way Andrew's blindness from the mustard gas would have interacted with the severity of his lung injury. Hence he may have been hypoxic [low oxygen], may have had an infection [as mustard gas notoriously leads to lung infections] and been in severe pain. He had acute brain failure.

The symptoms of delirium are confusion, problems with concentration and hallucinations and delusions. The treatment is to treat the primary condition and give adequate analgesia [painkiller, which he did not receive]. Increasing sensory stimulation by light, music and the presence of another is also part of the treatment.

His escape from the hospital and fall could have been due to either confusion or paranoid beliefs or a combination of both. He could have been in the bathroom and been confused about where he was. He may have believed he was trapped and had to escape. This would not be surprising given the fear he may have had being in confined spaces after being in the ship's hold. Given the secrecy and rumour about the ship, it is not hard to see that he may have become paranoid and had some conspiracy belief about what had happened to him. He had no certainty his ordeal had ended when he was in hospital [noting that RAAF officials had visited him in hospital and told him to remain silent].

You can see how these factors all added up to determine his actions that night which arose from his fear and confusion. He was not mentally ill other than in response to the impact of the mustard gas on his physical health. This is the opinion I would offer to the courts if this matter became an issue of compensation, in my role as an expert witness.[17]

What is clear is that there was absolutely no evidence of any previous mental illness. There is also no question that exposure to mustard gas caused his death. He would not have died on 19 January 1943 if he had not been gassed four days previously — this was, and never can be, disputed. He died as a result of mustard gas exposure which led to a state of mind in which he was compelled to climb out of the window of a three-storey building, something that, in his normal state of mind he would have considered completely irrational. As the coroner concluded, he may not have consciously set out to end his life, but the exposure to this poison led him to place his life in extreme jeopardy by climbing down a drainpipe some 52' 6" (16 metres) above a concrete pavement.

Chapter 10

Aftermath

The motor vessel *Idomeneus* sailed for Melbourne en route to the United Kingdom on 1 February 1943. It was to return at least once more, in September 1943, bringing another 265 tons of mustard gas drums. Fortune at last smiled on the ship, albeit during what was its homeward journey from the disastrous unloading on the Australian docks.

At dawn on 7 May 1943, while the *Idomeneus* was travelling to Liverpool as a member of convoy SL 128, Captain Dark saw one of the port wing escorts attack an unidentified object. Later that morning a Liberator dropped depth charges on the same side of the convoy. Then, at 11.25 am, while Dark and radio specialist Stuart Glover were out playing deck golf, Able Seaman Jones, who was on watch as masthead lookout, sighted splashes around a mile away on the port bow, and at once hailed the bridge with a warning shout of 'Torpedoes!'

There were, in fact, two torpedoes making for the *Idomeneus*, their underwater track hitherto unnoticed. It was only when they briefly broke the surface in the choppy sea that the alert lookout sighted them. Third Mate Forsgate at once applied full port wheel, and the torpedoes passed so close under the ship's stern that the gun's crew could clearly see their tubular shapes as they flashed under the log line. However the *Idomeneus*' good luck spelled doom for a fellow ship. Having missed the *Idomeneus*, which was in station No. 41 (the leading ship of the fourth column from the left), both torpedoes hit the second ship in column No. 5 (*Lakonikos*) which exploded almost immediately in a violent flash and sank in less than a minute. The vigilance of the lookout and the quick response of the third mate had once again saved a Holt ship.[1]

Radioman Stuart Glover thought there had been three torpedoes, commenting that they

> ... were obviously intended for us because we were one of the larger ships of the convoy and they streaked across the intervening lane and encountered a Greek ship called the Lakonikos. The first torpedo struck Lakonikos a little forward of the engine room, the

second one I think hit her in the engine room and I can't remember what happened with the third one. There were colossal explosions of course and fire and flame and the Lakonikos started to sink instantly and very rapidly and there was a general thought she went down in seconds rather than minutes. I saw a number of ships torpedoed and sunk, the very adjacency of the Lakonikos and the speed in which she went down has never left me as an active image in my mind.[2]

While the *Idomeneus* was evading torpedoes off East Africa, those who had been gassed by her deadly cargo of mustard continued to suffer ill effects.[3] Despite his gassing, Stevedore Flanagan initially remained on the waterfront on the 'disability book'. This was a scheme for older or disabled stevedores that allowed them to remain employed on the waterfront completing less strenuous work. Flanagan was unable to complete tasks involving flour or cement as contact with these items led to 'violent coughing and irritation'. Described as similar to whooping cough, Flanagan's coughing attacks were relieved only by vomiting. In 1948 he was finally forced to leave his employment at the wharf to work as a hire car driver employed by his son and earning £7 per week, a great deal less than the £10 paid to workers on the wharf. He could not work full time and his wages dropped by a third. 'I may work a full shift one week and be sick the next,' he explained. He never regained his strength

Lakonikos

or his former weight. Some 18 months later Flanagan developed a hernia which he attributed to his constant coughing and resorted to wearing a surgical truss to ensure that the hernia did not rupture. The cough eased a little after he left hospital, but it never completely left him, 'and periodically it comes on me five times a week – possibly during the day it will come on. I have always a continuous cough, but when I get the violent fits of coughing it is something cruel. It will last 10 minutes when I get a violent fit of coughing.'[4]

Flanagan's story was common among the stevedores. Wharf labourer Swinton was off work for three months after the gassing and remained on the disability book for five years. He could no longer perform heavy work and became a hatchman, giving signals to workers on the wharf and to the winchman. Again, this was lighter work which required no lifting but, like Flanagan, he could not work with dust, flour or cement, having developed an allergic reaction to these.[5]

The ill effects of the mustard were not confined to the wharf workers. Chemist McKenzie also suffered badly. He was advised by a doctor to transfer to a dry climate 'to clear up the trouble persistently arising from the mustard gas'. He closed his business (which had been established in 1872) in March 1944 and sold his chemical plant and equipment to meet debts accumulated through his inability to carry on his profession. He also developed allergies and could not work with irritant vapours in the laboratory. As a

Les Parsons Cross Eyed After being exposed to Mustard Gas on the Idomeneus

Les Parsons

professional chemist, this was a particularly devastating blow. He was unable to obtain employment either in the city or country and was compelled to draw social service benefits of £2.10 per week. Although registered with the Commonwealth Employment Service, no suitable work could be found for him due to his persistent health issues. By October 1948 he had become housebound, both his hands completely wrapped in bandages.

McKenzie sought £10,000 compensation from the RAAF citing its 'moral obligation'. However the Deputy Crown Solicitor in Sydney found that the Commonwealth was not legally liable to compensate him for his injuries and financial losses as he had been engaged by the shipping company and 'any injury caused to him was not caused by any act of this Department or its agents'.[6]

The RAAF officers also continued to suffer the effects of mustard gas. While Le Fèvre regained his sight after being gassed during the decontamination of the *Idomeneus*, he permanently lost his sense of taste and smell. Trewin's health problems in later life were numerous and included the appearance of wart-like growths on both arms. This is unsurprising considering that his physiological tests for mustard included binding mustard gas-contaminated pitch to his arms. He was later given blood transfusions to alleviate a low white blood cell count, an indication of a compromised immune system. In his later years he also suffered laboured breathing and bronchial pneumonia. When Le Fèvre left, Trewin took over as head of Australia's Chemical Warfare Section.

Les Parsons, the RAAF rookie, experienced chronic eye problems his entire life which included permanent photophobia and a pitted cornea. Mustard gas penetrates the cornea even more rapidly than the skin. Parsons recalled:

It seemed to me that I was in hospital about three months. I was in a dark room — had all the curtains blocked off, everything ... pitch dark ... couldn't stand the light at all. I never got out of the bed. For days, I couldn't see. I had been burnt under the crutch and they called me 'the nappy boy'. Changing my nappy a couple of times a day and under the arms and they were feeding me. I heard a doctor come in to look at me, and he talked to another doctor and the thing he said was a bit frightening, because I could hear

> *it. He said, 'I don't know if this bloke's going to see again.' That was a nice thing to hear. Well, [at the hospital] I don't think they knew what to do for a start. They were putting in a drop [in my eyes] to try and cut the blisters off and then putting another one to soothe it, because it was giving me hell, these drops, trying to get the blisters out. That went on day after day.*

The blister covered Parsons' eyes so effectively that the nurses were unable to distinguish his eye colour. He also developed double vision. In 2005 Parsons reflected, 'I can't do anything about it. Can't even fix it up with glasses. Well, according to the specialists, the skin of my eye is like hard rubber sort of thing, it's made it hard, the cover of the eye, over the eye.' Clinical Associate Professor Dr Philip House, who saw Parsons from 1998, observed that he had significant corneal scarring. 'A lot of it was in the peripheral part of the cornea, but there was a small component centrally which reduced his vision a lot in the right eye and a little in the left.'[7]

Soon after being gassed Les developed double pneumonia. Bronchopneumonia can lead to death in mustard gas victims, particularly given the limited health care available in the 1940s, but Parsons maintains that one of the nurses saved his life.

> *If it wasn't for a sister, I think I would have kicked the bucket. She stayed up with me all night. She was on duty all day and every half hour — I was delirious — she was pouring some sort of drink into me. Orange drink or something. She reckons I told her all my history of my life. God knows what I told her. I've never had so many eggflips in my life either — they were for my lungs or something.*

When he was released from hospital Parsons was unable to keep food down. 'For no reason at all, I'd sit up and shoot it clean over the table — whole dinner, very embarrassing.' He was eventually to succumb to oesophageal/stomach cancer which has been linked to mustard gas exposure. Doctors always remarked on his chest rattle and he wheezed his entire life. 'Different doctors have said to me over the years, "Gee you've got a rattle in your chest, in your lungs." I cough every now and again, for no reason. I cough and if I walk too fast, I get a wispy breath.' Like Pearce his voice changed, becoming noticeably hoarse and deteriorating to a croak as the day wore on.[8]

AFTERMATH

Idomeneus Veterans Les Parsons (Right) & Geoff Burn being Filmed at Glenbrook Tunnel for an Upcoming Documentary

Those known to have been affected by mustard and phosgene numbered some 140 individuals, although there are certainly more whose plight remained undocumented.[9] Interviews with the survivors clearly indicate that the official description of their injuries was woefully inadequate. As has been described in this chapter, the effects were chronic and debilitating. Further, the long-term effects on the majority of victims remain unrecorded. As mustard gas is a Group I carcinogen on a par with asbestos, one can only speculate as to its ultimate influence in this respect.

On 19 February 1943, a few days after the gassing, Le Fèvre recommended that the unloading of future shipments of chemical weapons be restricted to service personnel. 'I realise that such a proposal implies additional work for the services', he acknowledged, 'on the other hand our recent experiences show that it would contribute towards secrecy and security. We have formed and are now training a specialist CW [chemical warfare] Section for the purpose, inter alia, of handling, transport etc of dangerous chemical stock … This Section will replace waterside workers on such duties.'[10] At the same time the Assistant Director-General of Munitions wrote to the Defence Committee informing its members that accidents had occurred during the unloading of chemical munitions by inexperienced civilian personnel. He recommended that, in future, all chemical weapons should be handled by experienced service personnel only. The Defence Committee (which advised the Minister for Defence on all matters affecting Defence policy) met on 29 April 1943 and agreed to the Director-General's recommendation.[11] It was to come too late for the affected stevedores in both Sydney and Melbourne.

Chapter 11

Security Reasons

In September 1948 the stevedores poisoned in Sydney took legal action in a quest for some form of compensation and writs were issued in the New South Wales Supreme Court.[1] The first case heard was that of Stevedore Flanagan who had been on the Friday day shift. He sued the *Idomeneus* shipowners China Mutual Steam Navigation Company Ltd and the Ocean Steam Ship Company Ltd for damages for negligence. Those companies, in effect, sued the Commonwealth of Australia for an indemnity or contribution, believing that the Commonwealth had indeed played a part in the gassing. The two shipping companies traded under the name of Alfred Holt & Co.

New South Wales Supreme Court

In law, stevedore Flanagan was known as an 'invitee' (onto the ship) of the defendant companies. Flanagan's legal representatives argued that a duty to exercise 'reasonable care' existed to prevent damage from an unusual danger of which the occupier knew or ought to have known and of which the plaintiff was ignorant.

Mr Clemens, representing the plaintiff Flanagan, submitted a threefold argument: 1. the failure to warn the plaintiff of the danger; 2. failure to prevent escape of gas in the hold; and 3. failure to provide protection (gas masks) with suitable instruction as to their use.

The Commonwealth (termed the 3rd party) pursued a strategy designed to show that the damage was the result of a storm that had hit the *Idomeneus* during her voyage to Australia. The Commonwealth legal team also set out to verify that all the known tests had been conducted. In addition, the Commonwealth sought to show contributory negligence by the plaintiff as Flanagan had not worn a gas mask when he should have done so.

The first day of the trial was 26 June 1950 and stevedore Flanagan was called to testify. He made a poor start and his testimony was confused. He described the smell in the hold and the subsequent attention drawn to the bloodshot appearance of the stevedores' eyes. He recalled that the men had a lunch break at 12.00, came back at 1.00 pm and then worked in No. 3 hold. He described the struggle to reach home and the period he had spent in hospital. During cross-examination Flanagan was told that the hold had in fact been closed at 10.30 am on Friday. Flanagan was actually relating the events of the night shift in which he had played no part. He had worked on Friday morning. Flanagan's testimony had been clouded by discussions with his colleagues and he had become confused over the intervening seven years. Three members of the Melbourne contingent were the next to testify, wharfies Cook, Alexander and Duck. They described the gassing in Melbourne and their resultant pain and suffering.

Le Fèvre spent only a matter of minutes in the stand. Under cross-examination by Mr Ferguson (who was acting for the defendants) as to why he had recommended the use of masks he replied, 'Because of the occurrences in Melbourne, of which I take it you have information, which had occurred and in which in no way proved indubitably to me that mustard gas may have caused it, but it may have been due to mustard gas.'

Professor Raymond Le Fèvre
National Archives of Australia

This was the first time in seven years that Le Fèvre had admitted the possibility that the Melbourne incident may have been in any way related to mustard gas. Ferguson was clearly taken aback, for he then asked, 'What was the last part?' whereby Le Fèvre repeated the admission: '… **it may have been due to mustard gas** …' Ferguson pressed, 'Did you at that time have any opinion as to the cause of the sickness in Melbourne?' '**Not a definite opinion, I was inclined to the belief that mustard was the cause**,' was Le Fèvre's answer.

The door was ajar, a significant development from the evidence previously garnered under oath. At the RAAF Court of Inquiry Le Fèvre had strongly argued that mustard was <u>never</u> a possibility in Melbourne. After denying it under any circumstances he later admitted that it was a possibility in Sydney but only after the leaking drum had been discovered at the end of the unloading process. Now he had stated that it was a possibility in Melbourne.

The critical question then arose: could Le Fèvre have been certain that mustard gas had contaminated the stevedores in Melbourne prior to the commencement of unloading in Sydney? The implications were seismic, both morally and legally. If the RAAF had known or strongly suspected this to be the case, then they were responsible for both the tragic death and the catastrophic health effects on the wharfies in Sydney. Had military secrecy led to the death of Williams? If so, an innocent man had suffered and died needlessly. There could be no excuse, despite the fact that this was a wartime situation and the importation was a highly secret business. And there was also an obvious solution to the situation, one that was implemented after the wharfies had refused to unload the cargo. A RAAF crew in full protective gear acting under military orders should have been brought in to unload No. 1 hold, as had eventually happened at Glebe.

Ferguson let the matter drop temporarily but returned to it later in cross-examination. This occurred while he was again exploring the question of who was in control of the cargo, which was central to the case. He asked Le Fèvre, 'After the Melbourne incident, where the people went down. You were inclined to the view, weren't you, that it was not mustard gas at all that caused it?' And again he received an unexpected reply, '**Officially, but in my own heart** …' Ferguson cut him off and pursued the opening. 'Officially you expressed that view?' and was answered, '**The whole matter was graded as secret, at that time, so for the purposes** of public discussion I spoke about the possibilities of soda ash and these other chemicals having been responsible, **but in my own mind I thought mustard was at the bottom of the whole thing.**' (author's emphasis)

Under oath Le Fèvre stated that he had always believed mustard to be at the bottom 'of the whole thing'. After seven years the truth had finally emerged.

By the time he reached Sydney Le Fèvre had become convinced that mustard gas was responsible for the Melbourne injuries, but he had been constrained by military secrecy. Concerning

Walter Francis Dark
Arthur Dark

the issue of the Allied use of mustard gas he admitted, 'Oh yes. Britain was a signatory to the Geneva Convention and so on. We were just not supposed to know anything about it.'

That there can be no doubt that secrecy was the central issue was confirmed in the following trial which featured stevedore Pearce as the plaintiff. Le Fèvre was asked: '**And, of course, your reason for making that public utterance [that it was not mustard that caused the Melbourne casualties] was the security reasons?**' Le Fèvre replied, '**It was.**' He was also asked, '**That is the way you desired to deal with it, to disguise the fact – I can quite appreciate why – for security reasons, that the men had been affected by mustard gas?**' Le Fèvre answered, '**Yes.**' These are among the numerous admissions in the series of three trials by Le Fèvre that he had believed mustard gas to be the cause but had been unable to reveal his conviction to anyone, including his chemist colleague, McKenzie, whom he had assisted in assessing the safety of the holds.

In the third and final trial, with wharfie Swinton now as the plaintiff, Le Fèvre admitted to telling an untruth at the Sydney conference when the ship had initially arrived. When asked, '**So far as you were concerned, at the conference you expressed the view that it was not mustard gas but these chemicals [soda ash]?**' Le Fèvre answered, '**That is so – that was the story that I was then generally adopting to practically everybody that was not entitled to know that the Australians were receiving a cargo of this noxious chemical.**' Ferguson again sought clarification: 'Of course the reason for that was, as you say, security reasons?' Le Fèvre replied, '**Two reasons: security was the predominant one, and the second one was that I could then proceed to make the right recommendation for mustard gas on the wrong reasons – even if they were the wrong reasons.**'

Le Fèvre believed that he could protect the stevedores from the mustard gas fumes by recommending they wear gas masks for protection from other chemicals. Although this would have protected the face and respiratory system, the men were given no reason to use them. In any case the mustard vapour would still penetrate all the other exposed areas of skin. As the stevedore supervisor Captain Grose had stated, he would have insisted that the men use the masks had he known of the existence of any dangerous free gas in the hold. However this had been categorically denied throughout the whole process.

Court Testimony from Professor Raymond Le Fèvre
National Archives of Australia

Ferguson, acting for Blue Funnel, immediately realised the legal implications and, during the summing up for Flanagan's case, urged Justice Herron to emphasise the point to the jury that

> ... so far as Wing Commander Le Fèvre is concerned, the evidence is that he always suspected that the Melbourne episode was due to gas and told us [the defendants] that it was not due to gas. Now that is important in that event – assume the jury finds we [the defendants] are in control. Then to that extent we were misled and had we known Le Fèvre suspected it was gas but told us definitely it was not ... the captain had owed a duty to me [each stevedore] in order to see that I [Flanagan] was not injured and the captain employed you [Le Fèvre] to advise him and you deliberately misled him so that he would not take the precautions.

He continued, reiterating Le Fèvre's previous testimony: 'Now the position is that he was there on behalf of the Commonwealth and he was there in order to see that people were not injured and he was there for the purpose of advising the captain so that the captain could take such steps to prevent injury as he thought fit, and assume that he deliberately goes to the captain and gives him wrong advice, well that is a breach of his duty towards the plaintiff.' This was the right question to ask. Although the Captain and the ship's officers were in charge of the ship, were they being misled concerning the true extent of the danger? Clearly they were.

There were more revelations during this series of trials. At one point Le Fèvre was asked: '**Then you found out at a very early stage, before you left Melbourne, that the men had marks on their bodies?**' He replied, '**That is so.**' When asked: '**And you got these reports about damage under the arms, on the body, the body marks and so on. That indicated pretty clearly that it was mustard gas?**' Le Fèvre responded: '**You mean the report from Melbourne hospital? Yes. Yes, it pointed that way.**' The medical reports had confirmed to Le Fèvre that mustard gas was the cause.

Le Fèvre also admitted that, by January 1943, he had known about the increased intensity of mustard gas in warmer climates. Ferguson seized on this point: '**Did you have any belief about the possibility of heat increasing the time within which mustard gas became effective, in January 1943?**' Le Fèvre replied, '**Yes.**' Major Gorrill had been in

Melbourne at that time, fresh from his mustard gas experiments in Townsville. These experiments had shown that mustard gas was four times more effective in warmer conditions — that is, a quarter of the dose had the same effect as a single dose in cooler climates. Gorrill was destined to head the Australian Field Experimental Station in Innisfail where tropical experiments on mustard gas were systematically conducted on Army personnel. These experiments are now infamous. Hundreds of Australian service personnel were exposed to a variety of chemical warfare agents in gas chambers and in trials with real chemical agents. They, too, were to suffer lifelong ailments. Le Fèvre had all the knowledge available to understand the amplifying effect of the summer heat in the *Idomeneus*' hold on the mustard gas, and that smaller quantities of mustard gas would be extremely dangerous to anyone exposed.

Le Fèvre made an even more stunning admission to the Commonwealth counsel while preparing the trial brief. The details of this admission can be found in the notes Le Fèvre made at the time, buried in Air Force records. He wrote:

I had advised Flight Lieutenant Trewin towards the latter stage of his decontamination operations, that the only conclusive test for complete decontamination would be a physiological one. This advice was given because of two factors (i) Y3 [mustard gas] contains an involatile constituent. Therefore quite apart from other considerations such as sensitivity, no test involving only the air in the hold could be a complete basis for a certificate of clearance. This point was not made publicly on the ship to the civilian chemist since the constitution of Y3 is highly secret (ii) it has been shown that [the] concentration of mustard vapour beneath the threshold of detectability by chemical test or smell can cause eye casualties to men working continuously in such atmospheres. Details of a procedure for suitable physiological tests were therefore given to Flight Lieutenant Trewin during a discussion in my room at the hospital at which, fortunately, Major Gorrill was also present. [2]

Le Fèvre had known all along that atmospheric tests using the sense of smell were inconclusive, that only by testing the surface of the ship's hold for the non-volatile component could he be sure that there was no mustard present. What is more, he had withheld the information from the Blue Funnel chemist. This now explains Trewin's strange physiological test using contaminated pitch bound to his arm. Unhappily for the stevedores, the third party counsel, although fully aware of the revelation, successfully kept this out of the court cases. The pre-trial Commonwealth counsel 'Advice on Evidence' states only: 'It is admitted by W/Cdr [Wing Commander]Le Fèvre that tests involving the air only are inconclusive due to the involatile constituent of Y3, but that he could not publicise that in making the earlier tests in conjunction with civilian experts for reasons of security.'[3] The stevedores never discovered this as it was not revealed in the trials or any other forum during their lifetimes.

The medical testimony at the trials was mixed, primarily because the constant coughing and other ailments were not apparent on X-rays and there was little other physical evidence. Soft tissue scarring caused by mustard gas cannot be seen on conventional X-rays. Had modern imaging technologies such as magnetic resonance imaging (MRI) or computed tomography (CT) been available it may well have revealed

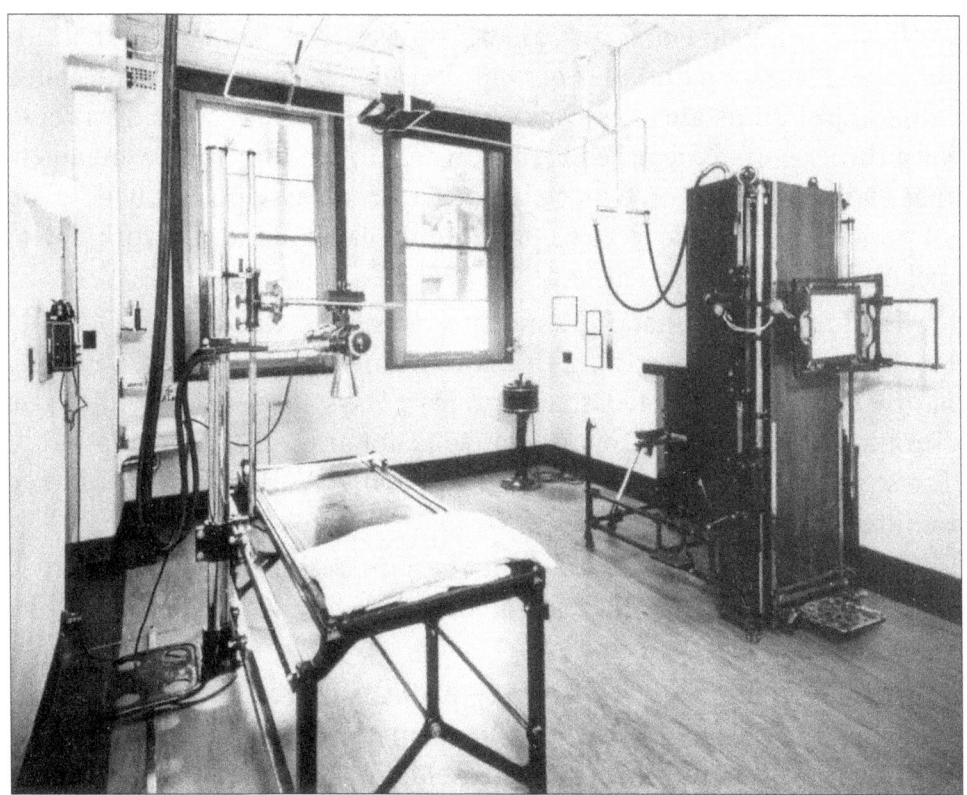

X-Ray at Royal Prince Alfred Hospital
Royal Prince Alfred Museum & Archives

these lesions. In any case recent studies have shown that mustard gas has its most damaging effect on the upper respiratory airways.

During the court cases Le Fèvre suggested that he told Captain Dark at the time that mustard gas had caused the casualties in Melbourne. When asked by Ferguson, 'The fact is you made it plain to the captain in private conversation that you inclined to the belief that mustard was the cause of the happening in Melbourne?' he replied, 'Yes.' Dark emphatically denied this, exasperatingly responding, 'Definitely not,' and 'I deny that wholeheartedly,' adding that the assertion was 'absolutely untrue'. All the evidence points to the fact that Dark was telling the truth. Any suggestion that Le Fèvre told Dark is completely untenable. Indeed Le Fèvre consistently denied mustard gas as a cause to all concerned, including to senior RAAF officers at an enquiry. Le Fèvre never told any of the RAAF workers or the Blue Funnel chemist that he believed this to be the case, so any suggestion that he would tell the captain simply beggars belief.

In summing up Flanagan's case, Justice Herron pointed out that this was a war situation and that perhaps reasonable care was not provided under the circumstances as a 'necessity for continuity of work in order to keep things going'. He noted Ferguson's argument that tests were taken, that Dark had relied on experts and even recruited one and had 'taken all possible reasonable steps to protect the plaintiff and his workmates', including supplying gas masks.

The Judge noted that, if Flanagan was entitled to damages, it would be a moderate award, adding that 'the plaintiff's pain was of a passing nature'. He further noted that Flanagan 'says that he has suffered a chronic bronchitis, now that of course is not anything of great gravity.' The stevedores and Australians gassed during World War I would beg to differ.

On 30 June 1950, at 12.12 pm, the jury retired. At 2.27 pm they returned a verdict for the defendant, the shipping companies. The stevedores had lost their first case.

In the second trial involving the plaintiff Pearce, the ship's Fourth Mate, Eynon, claimed that he had seven masks and handed one to each stevedore as he went down into the hold. 'As each man went below he took a gas mask with him.' He also claimed that a certificate had been read aloud to the men and agreed that one of the clearance certificates, read to him in court, was the one: 'Yes, this was what was read to the men,' he responded. This assertion was untenable as every stevedore and supervisor witness denied it and testified so. In any case there were eight men below deck on the night they were gassed, so the defendants' case was severely weakened. A key point in the plaintiff's case was demonstrated: the defendants failed to provide protection by way of gas masks. Indeed the ship did not carry sufficient gas masks for all the workers. Eynon was caught out by Ferguson in cross-examination: 'And the idea was to keep it away from all people other than the Air Force men and ship's agent and the ship's officers that it was mustard gas,

Sir Robert Gordon Menzies
National Archives of Australia

wasn't it?' Eynon replied, 'The idea was to maintain security.' Eynon was then asked why a certificate naming the secret cargo would be read to the stevedores. It didn't make sense and again was clearly a fabrication. In the second judgment the decision was reversed, this time finding for stevedore Pearce with £500 damages awarded to be borne equally by the defendants and third party.

On 9 October 1951 Pearce wrote to Prime Minister Menzies concerning the award of an MBE to his son. In the course of his letter he related the substance of his case:

> *During the war years I felt that I should be doing something for my country, and being too old for an active part therein, I became a watchman on the Sydney waterfront and was engaged throughout on war cargoes for the forces. In January 1923 [sic 1943] whilst engaged on that duty, I was gassed with mustard gas, together with wharf labourers on the SS Idomeneus.[4] A good many of these men have since died and we spent considerable time in hospital. I myself am still suffering from the effects and have never been the same. Owing to the War Precautions Act, a considerable time*

elapsed before anything could be done in the matter regarding compensation. Finally the matter was taken before the Courts and in August 1950 a verdict was returned for me, against the China Steam Navigation Coy and the Commonwealth Government, 'jointly', to the amount of £500.

When the verdict was given, Mr McLennan (McClemens), now Judge McLennan who appeared on my behalf, gave expression to his feeling in the matter, by saying to me, 'Well Pearce, I did my best for you, but I did think you should have got more. However that's better than a Kick in the Pants.'[5]

Pearce then commented that nothing had happened since the verdict was given. 'I am sorry to have bored you with this matter dear Mr Menzies,' he wrote, 'but I am 67 years of age and not endowed with much money these days and don't intend to live on a pension as long as I can be actively employed.'[6]

Menzies replied on 18 October:

I have received the letter you sent me on the 9th October and am glad you wrote. I am especially interested to learn that your son is Group Captain C W Pearce who is our Air Attaché at Washington. You may well be proud of your boy and of the distinctions he has earned for himself. I am making some enquiries in connection with the delay in paying you the amount of damages granted you by the court in August 1950, and as soon as I am in a position to do so I will write to you again. In the meantime I send you all good wishes.[7]

Whether the payment was finally made is unclear.

Stevedore Muggivan had also been listed as one of the plaintiffs but died just prior to his case coming to court. The RAAF was relieved, a feeling evident in the archives of the time: 'The immediate problem is this, there is another case starting tomorrow, the plaintiff being Muggivan. So far as I can see from the medical evidence he was the most seriously injured and he may go down rather

C W Pearce

well with jury.'[8] Fortunately for the RAAF, although not for Muggivan, he died the day before his case was to start and the Justice decided to take Swinton's case as next on the list.

The third trial ended at 12.32 pm on 14 August and the jury returned to the court with a verdict for Swinton for £1,050 of which 25% was to be paid by the Commonwealth. This was the second consecutive trial in which the stevedores had found success. Dissatisfied with the result the defendants lodged an appeal in the Supreme Court of New South Wales for the judgment to be set aside and a new trial granted on the grounds that the 'verdict was against evidence'.

The appeal was heard by the Supreme Court on 20 and 21 November 1950. In a reserved judgment delivered on 7 December 1950, the full court ordered a new trial. Swinton then appealed to the High Court, the highest court in Australia. This appeal was heard on 20 and 23 July 1951 before Sir Owen Dixon, Sir Dudley Williams, Sir William Webb, Sir Frank Kitto and Sir Wilfred Fullagar. The appellant Swinton argued that the evidence showed that the shipping company defendants knew

Top Left (Clockwise)
Sir Dudley Williams
Sir Wilfred Fullagar
Sir William Webb
Sir Owen Dixon
Sir Frank Kitto
High Court of Australia

that there was danger in the hold and failed to provide any warning. He also argued that the full Supreme Court gave undue weight to the chemical tests.

The High Court made the final decision as to culpability and it was squarely against the ship's owners. The Court concluded that the owners did not exercise reasonable care to prevent injury from an unusual danger. Examining the facts of the case the court accepted (because the Supreme Court jury so found) the plaintiff's evidence that there were no gas masks and the men were not, therefore, wearing masks. They rightfully rejected the evidence of the Fourth Officer, Eynon.[9]

The High Court found that the shipowners (represented by the master) may not have known that it was mustard gas until the ship reached Melbourne. From the outset, however, they realised that the contents were dangerous. Because of what occurred in Melbourne, they knew that, from then on, they had been carrying mustard gas and had reason to believe ('grounds for apprehending') that it might be escaping. The danger was the possibility only ('contingency') of escaping gas; the owners were not required to know that the gas was escaping. This was despite the explanation Le Fèvre had given.

The defendants argued that the order made under National Security Regulation 66 and the conduct of the RAAF officers passed the responsibility for unloading/managing the danger/duty of care from the master (defendants) to the Commonwealth. The Court rejected this assertion.

The regulation certainly concerned the handling of munitions (mustard gas drums) and their unloading; however the danger arose not from the presence of mustard gas in the drums, but from the presence of poison gas in the hold (the workplace). The injury was inflicted by escaped gas in the hold. Hence the workplace was unsafe and the defendants were responsible for the workplace. This may seem a fine distinction to a layman but it is 'legally and factually sound'. Legal readers of the court judgment assert that it is clear the court was sympathetic to the plaintiff and was determined to grant a remedy by upholding the jury's decision.

The High Court ultimately found that the defendants had breached the duty of care owed and were negligent. The decision was upheld for the plaintiff, the Supreme Court order was reversed and the original decision for Swinton stood. The jury's verdict in favour of the plaintiff and the 25% contribution of the Commonwealth was restored.

Years after the original gassing at the wharf, on 13 February 1953, the Deputy Crown Solicitor concluded, 'In the light of the previous actions arising out of the unloading of this cargo it cannot be disputed that the Commonwealth and the shipping companies concerned are liable for the damage caused by the gas.'[10] On 18 March 1952 the Prime Minister's Department was advised in writing that, following protracted negotiations, it was agreed that the Ministry of Transport (on behalf of the government of the United Kingdom) and the Commonwealth of Australia would respectively bear 66% and 33% of the expenses, 'arising out of the settlements to be negotiated in the remaining cases'.[11]

Consent verdicts (where the case did not come to trial) were entered for the last eight cases and there was a shifting of 'the burden of compensating these eight plaintiffs from the shipping company to the United Kingdom government which was to bear two thirds of the cost and the Commonwealth government which was to bear one third of the cost.'

Stevedores Spiteri, Roach, Gillanders, Wilson, Whitton, Minor, Horton and Smith received consent verdicts for amounts from £1,008 to £1,607.[12] Flanagan was given a £1000 ex gratis payment (where the government provided compensation but did not admit liability), even though he had lost his case.[13] He was the only surviving Sydney member who had not been given compensation.

On February 1955, 12 years after the stevedores and others had been poisoned with a chemical weapon, it was finally over: 'The Ministry of Transport and Civil Aviation have informed this office that all outstanding claims they have had under negotiation have now been settled.'[14] It had cost the governments of the United Kingdom and Australia £18,183 sterling. The cost in physical and mental suffering was far greater and its legacy has continued for over 70 years.

Since McDonald[15] and seven other Melbourne stevedores had received compensation under the Workers Compensation Act 1928 of Victoria, it was deemed that there was '... no right of action against the Shipping Company or the Commonwealth for damages by virtue of Section 62 of the Workers Compensation Act (Victoria) ... McDonald received his injury whilst working on the *Idomeneus* at Melbourne in January 1943, and there is probably not a case of negligence against the Shipping Company or the Commonwealth in so far as the happening at Melbourne is concerned.'[16] There was also a six-year limit for making the claim.[17] While the Melbourne men had been just as badly affected as the Sydney stevedores, their payments had been a pathetic £84 to McDonald, £33 to Mathews, to Prazenica £22, to Rowden £41, to Alexander £64, to Campbell £19, to Dahlstedt £21 and to Duck £22.[18]

Wharf labourer O'Brien, of whom little is known, is reported in the records to have 'died of tuberculosis aggravated by mustard gas.'[19] The reverse is just as likely — mustard gas aggravated by tuberculosis as the immune-suppressive effects of the mustard gas would allow the tuberculosis free reign. The South British Insurance Company paid £679 in compensation for his death. Williams' life was worth £913. The insurance company made a claim against Alfred Holt for reimbursement. The records do not state whether this succeeded, however this much is recorded: 'The Commonwealth is agreeable to the proposal that the solicitors for the South British Company Limited be informed that the Ministry of Transport is not prepared to accept liability in respect of the Company's payments to any persons who were not plaintiffs in the actions in the Supreme Court.'[20]

Chapter 12

Conclusion

In October 1947 Albert Einstein, in an open letter to the United Nations General Assembly, wrote that military secrecy was 'one of the worst scourges of our time and one of the greatest obstacles to cultural betterment.' This is clearly an overstatement as military secrecy certainly has its place. For instance, the ability to design and produce nuclear weapons should be protected from 'rogue' states with the potential to destabilise the globe. However military secrecy must never directly cause the death and maiming of innocent people, which is exactly what occurred in 1943 at Walsh Bay in Sydney. It was military secrecy that prevented chemical weapons expert Wing Commander Le Fèvre telling the stevedores, the ship's staff, the chemist recruited by the Blue Funnel Line, his own staff in the RAAF and senior officials at a RAAF court that, 'in his own heart' he knew that mustard gas had contaminated the men who had entered the *Idomeneus* No. 1 hold in Melbourne.

Indeed Le Fèvre denied that mustard gas was present and provided complicated chemical explanations to support his argument. To a lay audience his expertise was beyond question and his explanations sounded

No. 8 Pier, Walsh Bay

extremely plausible. But the injuries he saw in the stevedores who had worked on the *Idomeneus* bore the classic symptoms of mustard gas poisoning: severe conjunctivitis, coughing and the rashes and blistering described to him later. Crucially, only he knew of the involatile nature of mustard gas. He also knew that mustard gas was four to five times more dangerous in warmer conditions, precisely those found in the No. 1 hold of the *Idomeneus* at the peak of summer. Thus his assertion that chemicals other than mustard gas caused the injuries in Melbourne was a sham, plain and simple. That he believed another truth was put beyond doubt when he testified under oath in a court of law.

Even before the *Idomeneus* reached Sydney the evidence of mustard gas contamination was apparent. Hospital staff in Melbourne had notified the crew, as had chemical warfare deputy Trewin, that those taken ill in Melbourne were the victims of mustard gas poisoning. Le Fèvre himself had suffered from mustard exposure by the time he reached Sydney as McKenzie had recognised this during the Sydney conference. The Port Inspector in Melbourne smelt and immediately recognised mustard gas, despite not being informed of its presence. The Health Inspector, clearly not a specialist, identified it on 15 January and mentioned mustard gas contamination in a report on the same day. Yet Le Fèvre continued to pretend that there was no evidence of mustard gas. He maintained this pretence for seven years as the wharfies struggled with the health and psychological legacy of their poisoning.

What is apparent is Le Fèvre's conviction that he was unable to reveal the truth. He was asked in court, 'As a matter of fact, your job was to keep it well away from the wharf labourers that it was mustard gas,' to which he replied, 'It was part of my job to keep it away from the Press also — not only wharf labourers. Wharf labourers were not singled out for the secrecy.'

The irony was that the RAAF's top expert evidently did not understand the international law regarding chemical weapons. He believed that the stockpiling of chemical weapons was counter to the Geneva Protocol (1925) and that Australia 'shouldn't have anything to do with it.' While the Geneva Protocol certainly prohibited the initial use of chemical weapons, its terms did not prevent a nation either manufacturing or importing these weapons and thus reserving a capability for retaliatory strikes. And this is exactly the purpose for which Australia stockpiled

CONCLUSION

these weapons. It is nothing short of staggering that Australia's leading authority on chemical weapons was so poorly briefed.

The decision to employ untrained civilians to unload top secret toxic gas only hundreds of metres from the central business district is also hard to fathom — particularly as a reserved RAAF wharf was located close by. Perhaps the best guess is a combination of complacency and price. It was cheaper to rely on civilian labour although, ultimately, the resources were found when the need became urgent. RAAF personnel were sent to decontaminate the ship and to move the toxic cargo to tunnels west of Sydney. These men, who had some experience in the handling of toxic chemicals, should have been used during the initial unloading of the drums, not called in once disaster had occurred.

Ironically, permitting untrained and unprotected personnel to work these holds threatened the very secrecy that Le Fèvre worked so hard and sacrificed so much to protect. Even if there had not been a leak in one of the drums, workplaces are typically the home of gossip and speculation leading to the spreading of rumour. The wharfies in Melbourne naturally asked questions concerning the nature of the cargo — as they probably asked about every cargo they unloaded. The gassing

The Now Abandoned Marrangaroo Tunnel

prompted the publication of an article in a Melbourne newspaper and, ultimately, the convening of an inquest in the Coroner's Court. The RAAF presence was noted, its officers described as 'tight lipped' — the inescapable conclusion was that the cargo was obviously military. The stevedores, nurses and doctors in Sydney discovered the secret with little difficulty. Police appeared on the dock making inquiries and the locals at Balmain watched the men work in anti-gas gear.

There was, however, one positive result. Directly as a consequence of this tragedy, the RAAF formed a specialist unit to unload, transport and maintain these lethal toxins — the RAAF chemical warfare armourers or 'mustard gas men'. Later ships which carried chemical weapons were unloaded without major incident.

The term 'chemical weapon' was mentioned once in Dark's brief: 'Such insulated spaces which have been used for the stowage of chemical weapons, must not be used for the storage of food'.[1] Interestingly, the use of the term 'chemical weapon' aroused no suspicion. Mustard gas and phosgene were referred to as 'poison gas' at the time, at least by lay persons. The term 'chemical weapon' did not indicate mustard gas to Dark. He could not have known that mustard gas and phosgene were being imported into Australia. Rather, he most likely linked the reference to chemical explosives which included torpedo warheads, mines and other war weapons.

In any case, the fact that Dark did not know that his hold contained mustard gas was confirmed by the Office of the High Commissioner for Australia in London: 'In accordance with the usual wartime practice, the Captain of the vessel was merely notified that he had on board certain dangerous and hazardous cargo, but was not told exactly what it was.'[2] In addition, the gas was loaded by a shore crew, the sea crew joining the ship some days later. The crew had no involvement in the loading whatsoever.

For his part, Le Fèvre asserted that he had a 'moral responsibility, a watching brief for the cargo and therefore people working around it.'[3] He specifically mentioned the safe unloading of the commercial cargo. He clearly did not discharge this responsibility.

Dark's response (and effectively that of the Blue Funnel Line) was text book: an attempt to enforce gas masks, the recruitment of a chemist — all

CONCLUSION

without the knowledge that mustard gas was the cause of the Melbourne incident, albeit in the understanding that a toxic environment existed. Dark took these measures despite being told by the experts — Le Fèvre in particular — that the hold was safe. It was Dark who insisted that the use of gas masks should be written as a recommendation as he was told that their wearing could not be enforced. It was Dark who provided the gas masks as the RAAF was unwilling or unable to provide these, despite the fact that a large number was produced when they were needed at Rozelle and despite the fact that the RAAF had its own decontamination squad. Dark was told by the RAAF officers that they would try to persuade the labourers to use the gas masks — although there is absolutely no evidence that this occurred. Only chemist McKenzie is known to have made an attempt. In fact there is contrary evidence that Le Fèvre told his own men not to wear them, as stated by RAAF recruit Parsons: 'I was wearing just overalls and underpants underneath, that's all — and a beret. Because he [Le Fèvre] said I didn't have to take my gas mask. We had them with us, but didn't wear them. But he said that because if those wharfies had seen us wearing gas masks, they wouldn't have gone near that ship.'[4] Le Fèvre, on the other hand, attributes this statement to Freeman.

If Le Fèvre considered the masks so important, it was clearly his responsibility to supply them. Instead he allowed unused, dirty and unserviced gas masks from the ship to be made available to the stevedores who were untrained in their use. He also wrote a false clearance certificate for Dark stating that mustard gas poisoning had not occurred in Melbourne. McKenzie recalled that Dark 'was very insistent, and he really wanted the men to wear them [masks] the whole time they were down there — that was his idea of it.'[5] While the fact that gas masks had been written into the certificate provided an escape route for Le Fèvre, it was Dark who had insisted on the certificates in the first place and on the inclusion of the entry on gas masks. Le Fèvre admitted this much in the third trial: 'I only gave certificates to the Captain at his own request,' with Dark having told Le Fèvre, 'If you make a remark on your certificate about wearing gas masks I will put them there.'[6]

For his part, McKenzie was always under the impression that the RAAF would unload the lower hold. He was also convinced that the recommendation to wear gas masks in case of accidental damage to a drum, not because one of the drums was suspected of leaking.[7]

Only Le Fèvre knew that the masks would not provide protection against the involatile constituent, as they only protected the face and lungs. The stevedores wore no protective clothing whatsoever. Had they touched any leaked mustard they would have been burnt just as the RAAF recruits were during the decontamination. Masks would only have protected the face and respiratory system. The vapour is just as dangerous and would have penetrated the skin of the labourers even if they had been wearing gas masks.

Arthur Dark, the Dark family historian, knew Captain Dark's son, Victor, very well. Victor told Arthur that the events surrounding the gassing of the men on the *Idomeneus* had an enormous impact on his father's life. Captain Dark believed that it reflected badly on him personally and reiterated that he had been entirely ignorant of the mustard gas and phosgene in the ship's hold. In fact, Victor was convinced that the incident had clouded his later years with the company, as he believed that the Blue Funnel Line had let him down. Arthur Dark observed that 'Walter was certainly a man of principle, like Victor, and whereas other men might have shrugged it off on the grounds that their own conscience was clear, Walter would

Glenbrook Tunnel Today

CONCLUSION

have wanted unambiguous and public acknowledgement that he was not culpable.'[8]

Dark, as the ship's representative, was found negligent in the highest court in Australia by five distinguished judges. This appears extraordinary. The judgment has been examined subsequently and deemed legally sound. However, was it morally sound? The judgment upheld the 25% contribution of the Commonwealth of Australia, thus attributing some degree of negligence to the government.

Yet Dark, a highly decorated captain who represented the shipping line, was found negligent in failing to protect the stevedores and others who worked on the ship. He may have believed that the three RAF overseers, the RAAF specialist (overseeing the safe removal of the cargo <u>above</u> the mustard) and the existence of a security regulation relating to the mustard gas had relieved him of some of the responsibility. But the law disagreed.

The reality was that Dark, short of overriding a military decree during a war, did all he could to prevent the tragedy. No ship's captain would have disobeyed military advice. While the stevedores justly received their compensation, the Blue Funnel Line and Dark in particular should not have been branded with the stain of negligence.

There is no denying that Eynon's patently false court declaration was damaging. Doubtless he was attempting to protect the Blue Funnel Line, however through faulty memory or otherwise his testimony had the reverse effect. Even had a declaration been read to the stevedores, by being specific in the number of gas masks available — stating that there were seven, when in fact there were eight stevedores working below — he had demonstrated that the shipping company had not protected all the workers. This quickly became a key point in the case.

Nonetheless, Le Fèvre remained entirely responsible for his actions. The chemical weapons were the responsibility of the RAF and RAAF. They never assumed this responsibility or any other for that matter, apart from responsibility for the eye injuries to their staff. The RAAF personnel involved, including Les Parsons, were never informed that a Court of Inquiry had concluded that these injuries had been caused by the RAAF. As the labourers had not reached the drums in the course of their unloading, they denied that they had control of the cargo. They fell back on the national security order which admitted only to the care of the military cargo. This was despite Le Fèvre's assertion that his duties extended to the safe unloading of the cargo above — the soda ash and commercial cargo. They admitted no responsibility in court and justified their actions in a RAAF folio: 'The wharf labourers in SYDNEY would not properly use the respirators provided by the ship. This necessitates the RAAF taking over this job.'[9] This statement was nothing short of self-justification. However the RAAF eventually reneged and paid some compensation, largely in an indirect manner, admitting a role, albeit not publicly.

Why did Le Fèvre deny that the injuries had been caused by mustard gas? This case shows no evidence of direct political interference. That is not to say that the importation had no political implications — clearly there were serious implications. Had there been a belief within government circles that such importation was contrary to the Geneva Protocol, this disclosure would have been considered internationally embarrassing. However, Le Fèvre made his decision on the ground as events unfolded.

Chemical Weapon found on the Atherton Tablelands
Defence

Was Le Fèvre a victim of the system, essentially an academic caught up in a military system? He is described by various people who worked with him, particularly as a lecturer, as a warm, compassionate and caring man, which doesn't fit comfortably with the decision to allow people to be exposed to a deadly gas. Perhaps he was simply a 'nice guy' doing the wrong job at the wrong time. In his case his background in lecturing in organic chemistry did not translate into a successful career as a RAF wing commander or military leader. The skill sets are quite different. The military is an intimidating environment and Le Fèvre seemed unprepared to challenge something he knew to be wrong. The events clearly troubled the wing commander's conscience as he revealed the truth within ten minutes of the commencement of the first trial. His statement was remarkable as the Australian military was not under trial and his admission was completely voluntary. He surprised those attending the trial, so much so that he was asked to repeat the admission. Having maintained this secrecy for so many years, his testimony bears evidence of relief, as if a weight has been lifted from his shoulders. The transcripts reveal a relief that was almost palpable.

Regardless, Le Fèvre was still ultimately responsible for his actions. Although he regarded himself simply as an advisor and not the officer in charge of the RAAF personnel and labourers during the unloading, he should have stepped in and taken control. Only Le Fèvre had the technical knowledge to know that the hold was contaminated with mustard gas and that the stevedores were operating in a highly toxic environment. Only Le Fèvre knew that the Sydney summer heat was compounding the effect of the mustard gas, increasing its impact many times over. He should have intervened and ensured that RAAF personnel with chemical weapons experience, dressed in protective gear and wearing gas masks, unloaded the hold. Although the 'Mustard Gas Men' unit was yet to be created (and would so after this tragedy), there were enough RAAF recruits such as Frank Burkin, Kevin Garr and Geoff Burn, amongst others, who had gained 'on the job' experience in handling mustard gas bombs, already in the Marrangaroo Tunnel. Le Fèvre was the highest ranking Air Force official on the ship and stated at one point that his role was to 'advise on the safety of the holds during the unloading of certain general cargo'. But while Le Fèvre failed all those who were gassed on the *Idomeneus*, he was strong enough to tell the truth seven years later. Was this because he was now outside a military culture where secrecy was paramount? Regardless, he should be commended as he was under no instruction to do so.

The story of the *Idomeneus* has continued into the twentieth century. Not all of its legacy is visible, some of it remains buried — literally. At Marrangaroo Army Base a proof test yard adjacent to the base was

DEATH BY MUSTARD GAS

Marrangaroo Chemical Weapons Extraction

CONCLUSION

135

available for the inspection of RAAF ammunition following its receipt. Geoff Burn, one of the original mustard gas men, recounted later that he knew of filled phosgene bombs that had been buried in the proof yard and was unaware of their fate.[10] Burns was in Cairns at the time and subsequently received a request to travel to Marrangaroo for a 'special project'. This project involved the location of a cache of buried 250 lb bombs. He found them buried in a trench, although he was unsure what happened to them next. When this information was related to Dave Humphreys, a chemical UXO specialist, he visited Burn and they identified the site on an old map. Scans of the site revealed the bombs still in place in their underground tomb. The Department of Defence immediately acted to have the bombs removed.

Thousands of chemical weapons passed through Marrangaroo on their way to the nearby tunnel. As many of the phosgene bombs were leaking, a quick fix was necessary — burial. Some of these were from the *Idomeneus*, buried after their arrival at the siding. In 2008 and 2009 the bombs were extracted under the auspices of the Chemical Weapons

Idomeneus Veteran Stuart Glover at the Unveiling of the Chemical Warfare Armourers Plaque at Glenbrook

CONCLUSION

Convention, a treaty that Australia pushed hard to have ratified. A total of 281 bombs — 250 lb and 30 lb — were retrieved.

Over many decades wharf labourers have often received bad press, reputedly overpaid, under-motivated and too powerful in the union world. But in the case of the *Idomeneus* in 1943 they were simply performing a job vital to the war effort. In fact such was their dedication that many of the men in Melbourne returned to work, even after vomiting. They had a job to do. That was their commitment to the nation's war effort.

On 6 April 1962 the *Idomeneus* arrived in Genoa where she was to end her days as scrap. In 2015 the few survivors live on, coping with the health and personal legacy of over 70 years ago.

Nandor Somogyi
National Archives of Australia

Chapter 13

Nandor Somogyi

At the end of World War II the Australian government faced the considerable dilemma of disposing of its stock of 1,000,000 chemical weapons. Some of these were burnt, others dumped at sea or, in the case of phosgene stocks, vented into the atmosphere. Some were simply forgotten and one of these was a mustard gas-filled 6 lb ground bomb that lay abandoned at the end of an airstrip on Mount Bundy Station near Adelaide River in the Northern Territory.[1]

The body of the bomb consisted of a light steel cylindrical case, painted grey, with a metal lid fastened to the body by adhesive tape. When the lid was removed the charge was visible, consisting of gunpowder connected by a fuse almost three feet long. The long fuse gave a delay of two minutes, enough time to clear the area after it was thrown or ignited on the ground. The bomb was sizeable, measuring 9 inches by 3.75 inches, and held 3.5 lbs of the toxic agent. It was ideally suited to military use — small and easily transported, safe to handle and required very little training to operate. It was not, however, safe in the hands of a novice — in fact it was to prove lethal.

The 6 lb ground bomb was an Army weapon and, by February 1945, there were 19,489 of these bombs filled with three mustard gas variants, two of them with benzene added. The bombs were boxed in lots of 10. How a metal box found its way to Mount Bundy is unclear but there is sufficient information available to make an informed guess. The most credible source is one of the two Army ammunition depots in the vicinity. The closest was 51 Forward Ammunition Depot (FAD) which was located at Mount Bundy Station itself. Another was the ammunition depot maintained by 5 Advanced Ammunition Depot (5AAD) at Mataranka, 300 kilometres south of Adelaide River. Both of these depots stored chemical weapons that originated from the Army's central repository of chemical weapons at Albury (1 Base Ammunition Depot).[2] All the 6 lb bombs were originally stored at Albury.

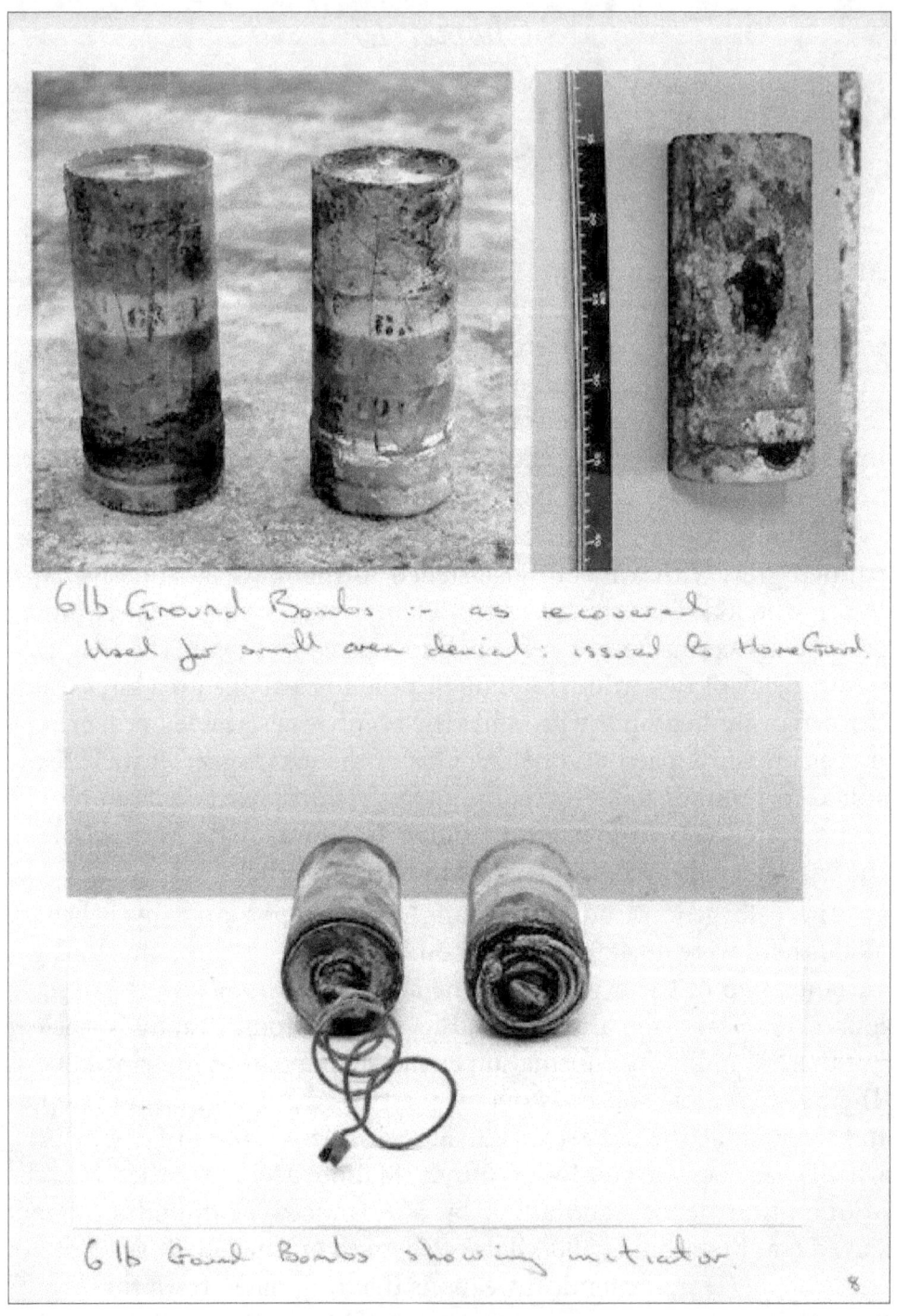

6 lb Mustard Gas Bomb
Major Keith Parker

There are two scenarios which could explain how the box was then relocated to where it was eventually discovered.[3] The first relates to its location next to a Relief Landing Ground (RLG). RLGs were airstrips acquired in the early months of World War II to act as overflows for flight training schools.[4] These were usually open areas of ground close to the parent station with a single landing strip which could be used as a practice strip by pupils. Most had only a grass surface and none had any permanent buildings. There were two RLGs in the vicinity of the bomb, although which of these the bomb was located next to is uncertain. The nearest was a proposed RLG named Brooks followed by Payne, which lay just to the south-east. Regardless of which it might be, those investigating the find were able to identify the remnants of a runway.

Two Views of the Mt Bundy Homestead
Doug Tilley

An intriguing possibility was that the bombs were pre-positioned next to the RLG ready to use if the Japanese used it as a forward landing area. The bombs would have been activated on the runway prior to an invasion with the resultant contamination making the strip unusable for landing aircraft.[5] In this case the bomb would have been used as what the military refers to as an 'area denial weapon'. A search of the RLG revealed nine other empty bomb casings within an area of around four square yards. An imprint in the hardened mud showed where the culprit bomb had been and also indicated that a whole box of bombs had once been located here.[6] It was clear that an attempt had been made to destroy the ten bombs by demolition with high explosives.

A more extensive search revealed a separate cache of 6 lb mustard bombs less than one kilometre from the Mount Bundy homestead. This was described as a major demolition area and lay just to the south of the road leading to Mount Bundy Station. The area had been used extensively for the destruction of smoke grenades[7] and, 15 yards north-east of an ant hill, there was 'considerable evidence of destruction of bombs ground 6 lb'.[8] In this case the destruction with high explosive had been complete, as no intact cylinders were found in or around the resulting pit. One bomb was found 50 to 60 yards away from the main group, having been 'kicked out' during the detonation, although it, too, was empty.

A P-40 Kittyhawk on a Mt Bundy Station Airfield
Doug Tilley

So how do these fit in with the 'area denial' hypothesis? They may have been part of a central cache (or commander's reserve) ready for deployment to airfields when a Japanese attack was imminent. Notably, there were other airstrips on the station including one a kilometre south of the main cache of weapons. While these were constructed for the RAAF, they were also used by the US Army Air Force's 49th Fighter Pursuit Group Squadron which flew Kittyhawks into the base. Mount Bundy was operational from 1940 to 1942[9] and, assuming the bombs were in place by August 1942 (when the Army chemical weapons started to arrive in Australia), they may have been available for deployment to this site. It must be remembered that the threat of invasion was palpable, nearby Darwin having been bombed in February 1942. Having a means to deny Japanese access to an airfield is a logical scenario.

Another explanation could lie in their use as a training aid. Although there was a training variant of the weapon which housed a mustard substitute, the mustard gas-filled bomb was declared an obsolete item in early 1944 and redesignated as a training item only. It is believed that 6 lb ground bombs filled with mustard were used in demonstration training so perhaps they were housed at Mount Bundy for this reason. Support for this hypothesis comes from records of the Army Mobile

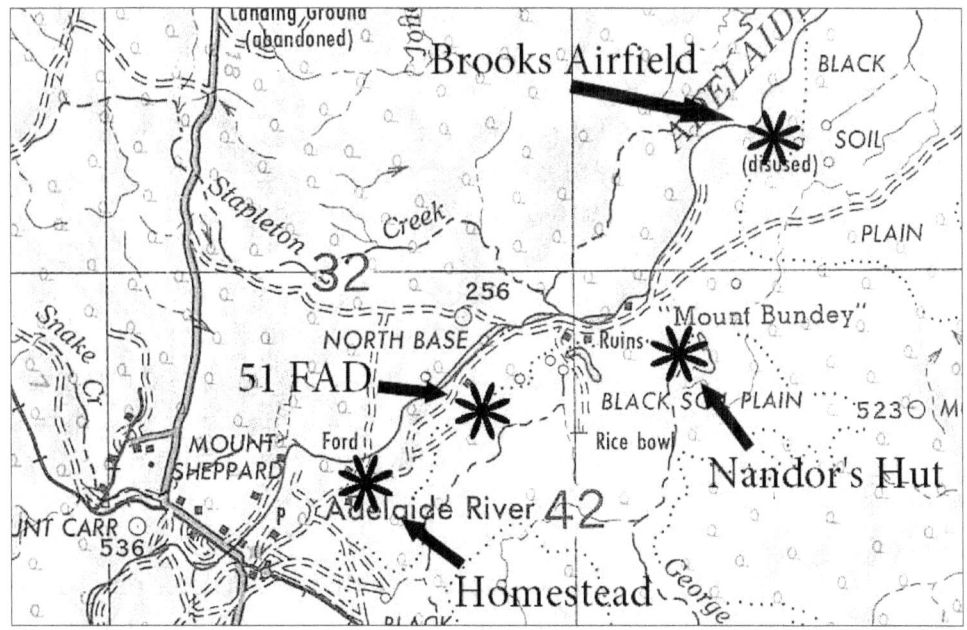

Map of Mt Bundy Station

United States Base Section 1 Motor Pool on Mt Bundy Station
Doug Tilley

Gas Training Wing which was based at Cabarlah (Queensland) at the time. On 21 February 1944 the mobile wing left Townsville for Port Moresby, New Guinea, and returned on 25 June 1944 after a stay of four months conducting gas courses for service personnel.[10] It then spent two months attached to the Northern Territory Force, training personnel in the Darwin area.[11] A staggering 150 units were camped in the Adelaide River area including the Royal Australian Engineers and a cavalry regiment. Perhaps some of these units completed a gas course. It is also possible that Mount Bundy, as isolated as it was, was chosen as a central training point with personnel moved there for gas training courses. This would explain a central cache — but not the box on the airstrip.

All the evidence pointed to the bombs having been issued at a 'unit' level rather than being stocks from a storage depot.[12] An area denial hypothesis would fit an earlier deployment of the bombs sometime around 1942 because, as the war progressed, the threat of invasion diminished. A training scenario is more likely late in the war.

Whatever its origin an intact bomb sat there and deteriorated for almost 20 years until 29 September 1964 when a curious passer-by picked it up.

NANDOR SOMOGYI

Nandor Somogyi picked up the unmarked cylinder and could feel the liquid sloshing inside. Curious, he took it back to the makeshift shack that he called home. He picked up his .22 rifle and loaded it with a cartridge. He was very proud of his ability with small arms. Using home-made equipment he had made the bullet himself — moulded the casing, inserted a primer and added the propellant, scavenged from larger calibres that were scattered liberally around the area in which he lived.[13] A hermit, he had learned to be self-sufficient and live off the land — apart from the gun and a broken down bicycle he had absolutely nothing.

Somogyi raised the weapon, took aim at the cylinder and pulled the trigger. The round made a clean hole. He picked up the container and put his nose to the hole. The smell was hard to pin down but was strangely redolent. It was worth further investigation.

He collected two cordial bottles and decanted the mystery liquid. It was black and oily, very much like dirty car oil, but different in a way that was hard to define. And there was that smell again — unusual but now with a definite garlicky element. And it was then that he made

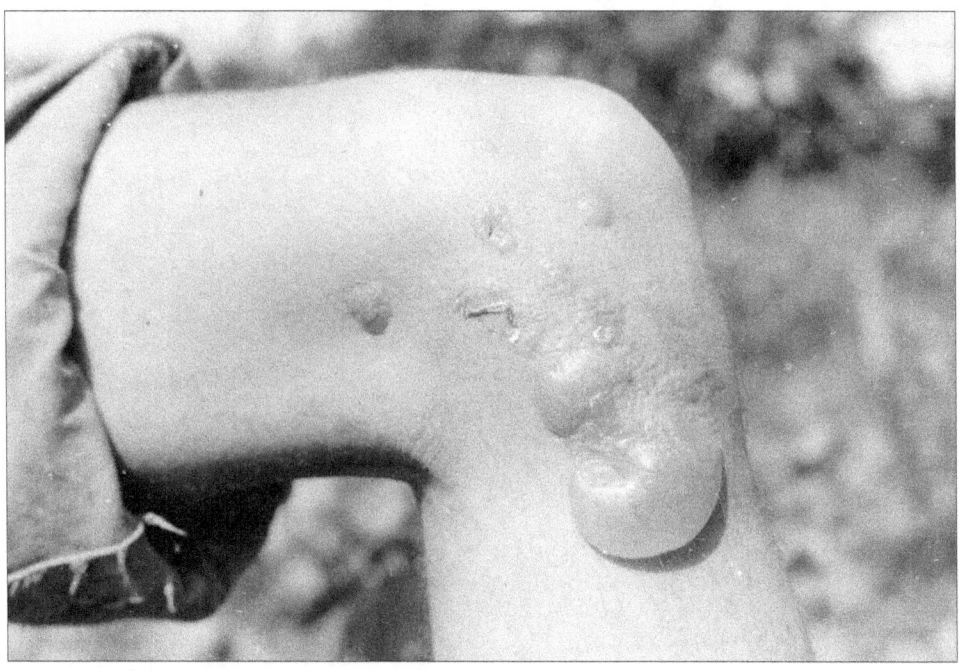

Mustard Gas Blisters

DEATH BY MUSTARD GAS

This margin is for Official use only	**COMMONWEALTH OF AUSTRALIA**
	INCOMING PASSENGER CARD (SURFACE VESSELS)

NOTE.—THE INFORMATION GIVEN HEREON IS REQUIRED UNDER THE AUTHORITY OF THE IMMIGRATION ACT AND REGULATIONS

1. Name of Ship MS/ Nelly
2. Full Name of Passenger S O M O G Y I, Nandor
   (Underline Surname. Print in Block Letters)
3. Permanent Address IRO Camp Bagnoli
4. Country of Last Permanent Residence Italy
5. Occupation Mech/
6. Date of Birth 21.10.1929
7. Sex (Male or Female) M.
8. Place of Birth Erzsi, Hungary
9. Nationality (as shown in Passport) Hungarian
10. If Naturalized—Place .... Date ....
11. Passport No. 173215 Issued at .... Date 23.9.1950
12. Date of Disembarkation 30 DEC 1950
13. Port of Embarkation Nordenham, Germany
14. Class Travelled (1st, 2nd, or 3rd) D.P.
15. Port of Disembarkation Sydney
16. Conjugal Condition (Married, Widowed, Single, Divorced) S.
17. Racial Origin (European, Asiatic, African, Polynesian) European
18. Proposed Length of Stay in Australia Indefinte
19. Purpose of Stay Emigration
20. Does Passenger Hold Authority to Enter Australia for an Unlimited Period of Residence (Yes or No)? No.
    (Europeans of British Nationality not required to answer)
21. Whether Passage Money Provided—
    (a) By Self.
    (b) Under United Kingdom Free Passage Scheme.
    (c) Under United Kingdom Assisted Passage Scheme.
    (d) Under Ex-servicemen's Assisted Passage Schemes from Countries other than United Kingdom.
    Place X against appropriate Sub-heading
22. Intended Address in Australia RECEPTION AND TRAINING CENTRE BATHURST, N.S.W.
23. If Previously Resident in Australia state—
    (a) Whether Previously Registered (Yes or No) ....
    (b) Alien Registration Certificate No. ....
24. Personal Description—
    Height 5 Ft. 4 Ins. Colour of Eyes grey
    Colour of Hair brown Notable Marks ....

.... Signature of Passenger

To be answered only by Aliens

CERTIFICATE OF EXEMPTION 24 MONTHS

the connection. It reminded him of a liniment used in Hungary, his birthplace, a potion used for arthritis and other ailments. Although only 35, it was precisely this complaint which afflicted him. He sized up the oil: surely it couldn't do any harm and, with a bit of luck, it might do some good. It was worth a try.

Using a rag he dabbed some on his hands and waited — there was no immediate reaction. He was unaware that the poison had a latency period. Convinced it was non-toxic he applied it to his shoulders, knees and other areas where the pain from arthritis was keenest. He sat back and waited for the elixir to work its magic.

After an hour his skin began to redden where he had applied the liquid. His eyes had also begun to smart. After two hours he felt tired and had developed a headache. He now decided that the lotion was producing some bad side-effects and he needed to remove it. Somogyi drenched the rag with water from his drum supply and splashed it over his shoulders and the rest of his body. The water-soluble poison spread all over his body.

After several hours his throat was sore, his eyes inflamed and he was in intense pain. At the nine-hour mark, fluid had begun to collect under the skin and blisters had developed, encasing a clear yellow fluid. The blisters resembled grapes hanging from his body. Unable to sleep that night, he paced around his hut as the pain increased.

Somogyi's condition was deteriorating by the minute and, although reclusive by choice, he knew he needed outside help. The next morning he mounted what remained of his bicycle and, in great pain, trying hard to avoid rubbing the huge blisters as best he could, he rode the few kilometres to the nearby settlement of Adelaide River, south of Darwin. Despite his best efforts his legs chafed on the seat causing excruciating pain. When he arrived at Adelaide River he staggered into Bill Hezle's general store. He would be dead in two weeks, killed by a chemical weapon in what must be the strangest and most bizarre death since the poison's introduction in 1917.[14]

Somogyi's pathway to the intact mustard bomb involved a long, often desperate and intriguing journey from Hungary to Adelaide River. Hermits leave few footprints but Somogyi left traces through his immigration records.[15] He was born on 21 October 1929 at Erzsi in Hungary. He had two brothers and a sister, had completed six years of primary school and then three years' training as a blacksmith. Efforts to track his surviving family are continuing, but thus far have been unsuccessful. His early years are unknown. But we do have a physical description. On arrival in Australia he was five foot four inches, of medium build, with piercing blue-grey eyes and brown hair. A good-looking man, his photo shows a striking 'James Dean' haircut and youthful look. In his last three years Somogyi wore a black beard and his outdoor living left him well tanned.

In April 1949 Somogyi fled his birth country. Soviet troops had occupied Hungary after the fall of Germany and installed an iron-fisted Stalinist regime. Somogyi told immigration authorities in Australia that he belonged to a Catholic organisation and disagreed with communism, although the religion entry on his immigration form was marked 'Protestant'. He made his way south to Yugoslavia and finally swung west, arriving in Italy on 27 September 1949.

The United Nations had created the International Refugee Organisation (IRO) to deal with the continuing refugee problem in Europe. In the period following the end of World War II a number of displaced person camps had been established in Europe to deal with the massive dislocation of the war-torn populace. Somogyi found his way to a successive number of Italian camps. Australia was one of 18 IRO member countries and he was selected as an émigré to Australia on 27 September 1950 as Displaced Person number 0023669.

Carrying a shipment of refugees, the Motor Ship Kelly left Nordenham, Germany, on 30 December 1950. Arriving in Sydney, Somogyi was put on a train, his destination the Kelso railway station from which he travelled by bus to the Reception and Training Centre in Bathurst, where the accommodation was basic Army fare.

Somogyi then made his way to Cooma to work on the massive Snowy Mountains Hydro Electric Scheme, the largest engineering project Australia has ever seen, responsible for the construction of 16 dams. He stayed there for nine months before moving to Sydney's 'inner west' for six years, his longest period in one location in Australia. He spent time in Brisbane and then travelled to Adelaide, living in the Salvation Army Men's House where he was listed as 'not working'. 'He was involved in a disturbance at the home and received minor injuries which resulted in him having to remain in bed for a week.' He then moved on. By now he had been in Australia for seven years.

Snowy Mountains Hydro Electric Scheme
National Archives of Australia

With his non-British background, Somogyi was automatically labelled an 'alien' by the Australian government. Between 1939 and 1971 this carried the tedious requirement to register any change of address with the local authorities. Somogyi was also required to carry an Alien Registration Card, No. 220736. The card included information on the ship and date of arrival, date and place of birth, occupation, marital status, a physical description and photograph. In registering changes of address, Somogyi was less assiduous than he should have been and eventually attracted the attention of the authorities.

Somogyi applied for a replacement Certificate of Registration while in Brisbane in 1957 and in Adelaide the following year. On his application he wrote that he had 'lost his memory'. He subsequently claimed that he had lost his all his papers at MacDonaldtown Station, Sydney, in 1954, and was asked to appear in person at the Commonwealth Migration office with two recent 'passport type' photographs. However he never appeared, leaving the Army home in Adelaide in mid-August 1958 apparently stating that he was going to Melbourne. He found his way to the Salvation Army in Perth and then to Carnarvon.

At Carnarvon, north of Perth in Western Australia, his now troubled existence continued — here he was convicted of vagrancy and sentenced to 14 days' hard labour. In the late 1950s the Commonwealth Immigration Department lost track of him and his card was placed on the 'missing index'. His peripatetic lifestyle was now entrenched.

Somogyi then reappeared in Darwin where he decided to leave his job at the Shell Company and continue his itinerant lifestyle. He bought his bicycle from Davies Sports Store, Darwin, in April 1960 for £42, a substantial sum for an itinerant whose employment history was fragmented at best. Presumably he had decided that this was to be his major form of transport and was thus worth committing a portion of his presumably meagre funds.

He next surfaced 1000 kilometres south-east of Darwin at Borroloola on the McArthur River. Known for its fishing and cattle stations, Borroloola had been a thriving town in the early 1900s when iron telegraph poles were landed and taken by horse and cart to lay the telegraph line. Once the line was completed, however, the township died, albeit not before it gained 'a fierce reputation as a frontier town of total disrepute' with 'criminals, murderers and alcoholics'. It was later described as an 'isolated township full of eccentric stories about its unusual residents'.[16] It is easy to imagine that Somogyi's presence would have raised few eyebrows.

Senior Constable Donald Honeysett, based at Tennant Creek, made his way to Borroloola for Somogyi's obligatory alien interview. He arrived in the town noting that there was 'nothing there aside from an old store and shell of the old thriving hotel'. McHolland, a fossicker,

A Bark Hut at Borroloola
Northern Territory Library

lived in the shell while an old timer, Roger Jose, lived in a couple of water tanks.[17]

Honeysett noted on his report that Somogyi was 'living in a bark hut with a layer of straw on the ground, and is neglecting his health by living on a diet of fish and rice. He appears to be mental, but not sufficient enough to be charged with being a mental defective <u>at large</u>.'[18] Honeysett was concerned that Somogyi had no passport or Alien card — in fact he had never had these replaced since losing them years before. He had been investigated as resembling a missing Englishman by the name of Edmonds, although this had clearly proven a case of mistaken identity. The bike was his only valuable possession and he had a total of £10 in his Commonwealth Bank account.

Somogyi returned to Darwin and was subsequently arrested and finger-printed on 27 September 1961 at Darwin police station.[19] While the reason is unclear, it is most likely to have been for vagrancy, which simply meant he had insufficient means of support.

Bill Ross was manager of Mount Bundy Station from 1957 to 1967. At that stage it was owned by Mr Perrett and Honour Burcher. Perrett had

Bill Ross at Mount Bundy Station
Bill Ross

bought the station in 1952 from Bill White who had co-owned it with Captain Gregory, a pearler. Measuring approximately 1250 square miles, the station ran 25,000 head of buffalo and 8000 cattle. While smaller, the station still operates, and lies 117 kilometres south of Darwin. Ross recalls seeing a sign in the Mount Bundy workshop, 'US Naval Reserve Transmitter Room', a legacy of the station's wartime role.[20]

Ross also vividly remembers the day in December 1963 when Somogyi was seen in the neighbourhood for the first time. He wandered into the Adelaide River General Store, a small corrugated iron Sydney Williams building, originally built by Mrs White and located only a few kilometres from Mount Bundy Station. Adelaide River at that time boasted a population of some 20 people and its heart was the General Store which was run by Bill Hezle and located close to the police station, where Somogyi was later to dramatically reappear.

Ross greeted Somogyi's first appearance at the store with a searching look. The stranger was around medium height and wore a black beard. He obviously lived rough, but then many did in this part of the world. In his broken English the stranger told him, 'I want to get to Finke Bay.' Ross replied, 'Well, it's due north of here but you've got buckleys of getting up there now. The wet season's almost here and all the rivers will

Adelaide River Police Station
Harold Darwen

be flooded. You won't reach there.' Ross knew anyone attempting the journey would have to wade through multiple creeks, rivers, swamps and flood plains which became virtual inland seas in the wet season. In any case, there was nothing at Finke Bay, 'no people, no nothing'.

The stranger was still keen on directions, so Ross obliged. 'Just head due north of here.' He made a mental note that no-one in his right mind would try riding there on a bike in the dry season, let alone the wet. Ross recalls, 'At this stage he simply disappeared and I didn't think too much about him.' However one day in March, when the country had begun to dry out, he was out driving in his truck and was intrigued to find some bicycle tracks on the property. He followed them to the banks of the Margaret River.

There he found makeshift accommodation which consisted of a simple lean-to and about two to three square metres of a vegetable garden which consisted of lettuces and cabbages which never would have grown in the conditions Ross found them. He was used to strange sights in the Northern Territory but this one turned his head. The site had been abandoned for some time. Ross knew whoever it was would have been stopped initially at the Margaret River because it would have been in flood, ten or more feet deep.

Ross then checked the nearby Margaret River hut, another Sydney Williams hut. Here he found a rifle and a few belongings. He had no idea who they belonged to, but noted that the fire had not been lit for some time. Assuming that the site was abandoned, he took the items into the Adelaide River Police Station where the gun was eventually gifted to an aboriginal tracker.

The police subsequently searched the area in an attempt to determine who owned the items that Ross had found. A police officer found a man in another hut who turned out to be the same man who had made enquiries at the shop. Ross was informed that he had a neighbour and recognised him as the man who had previously visited the Adelaide River store. Somogyi had completed his journey from Hungary.

The hut was on Block 111, in 'levee' country, on the silt-rich banks of the Adelaide River. In fact the neighbouring blocks 109 and 110 were capable of sustaining a market garden run by the Australian Army. The hut was already on the site when Somogyi took up squatting rights.

Blocks 108 to 111 measured 1000 acres each, having been surveyed for White Russians during World War I. Apart from the banks of the river they were never viable for farming and were abandoned in the late 1920s and reverted to the Crown. Block 111 was essentially undeveloped and had been previously occupied by an Austrian, Billy Binder. He worked in Darwin but came down to the property at weekends, using a tractor to clear the land, but abandoned the effort in the late 1950s. Somogyi's hut was some six kilometres from the Mount Bundy Station homestead.

Somogyi never called in at the homestead and appeared to avoid contact with others, including the inhabitants of the nearby aboriginal camp. Occasionally when driving past his hut Ross would see him peering out and, every so often, he was seen going to the store to buy odds and ends. He reflected later,

> *Essentially he was a squatter or what you might call a hippie today. This was the Northern Territory, you never asked a person a question about what they were doing, you would wait for them to tell you — it was the last refuge for rogues. He never worried anybody, he was not doing any harm so we let him be. All types of people floated around at that stage, even the ones you were employing — you couldn't be sure they were giving you the right name.[21]*

Harold Darwen (Left) at the Adelaide River Police Station
Harold Darwen

Tommy Faucett, a local man, was around 20 years old and used to see Somogyi occasionally. What he remembers most is the bike — an old bike with tyres fashioned from a garden hose. Tommy recalls that there were rumours about him — he believed he lived in a water tank and was a hermit who used mustard gas to get rid of mozzies. This is a rumour that has lasted to this day — that he covered himself with mustard as a mosquito repellent.[22]

Harold Darwen was the local Adelaide River policeman at this time.[23] He kept an eye on this stranger — this was his job. He noticed him occasionally coming into town to buy some essentials, but otherwise he had nothing to do with anyone else in the town. Darwen remembers, 'For a hermit he didn't dress too bad but you could tell he was living rough off the land. He caused no problems, minded his own business so I left him alone. There was no evidence he was a drinker.' Darwen briefed his relieving police officer, Bruce Mangleson, on the community, but didn't think it important enough to mention Somogyi. He was never a problem.

Ross later recalled, 'One day when I was back at Bill Hezle's store Somogyi turned up on his bike in obvious distress. I could see blisters all over his arms.'[24] Bruce Mangleson was relieving Harold Darwen for three months and, while out on a patrol, he was approached by a member of the public who told him that someone was injured.[25] By now Somogyi had left the Adelaide River store and Mangleson met him near the Adelaide River Hotel. He noted Somogyi's stature, slight build, and the burns on his hands and legs. Mangleson put him into the police 4WD vehicle and took him to the nearest hospital which was at Batchelor, a 30-minute drive away.

Batchelor was built around the nearby uranium mining town of Rum Jungle and was serviced by a very basic clinic, now replaced by a Health Centre. Grace Hutchings was a nursing sister employed by the Department of Health in Darwin. At 10.20 am on 30 September 1964 Mangleson brought Somogyi into the clinic. Hutchings observed large blisters on his lower legs, thighs, hands and shoulders.[26]

Somogyi told her, 'I found a lime bomb and I rubbed fluid on my knees,' adding, 'I have a sample of the fluid outside in a bag.' Nurse Hutchings went outside and fetched the sample. Somogyi warned her, 'Be careful as it's very dangerous.' He then explained that he had used the material in the bottle as a liniment to ease his arthritis. Hutchings

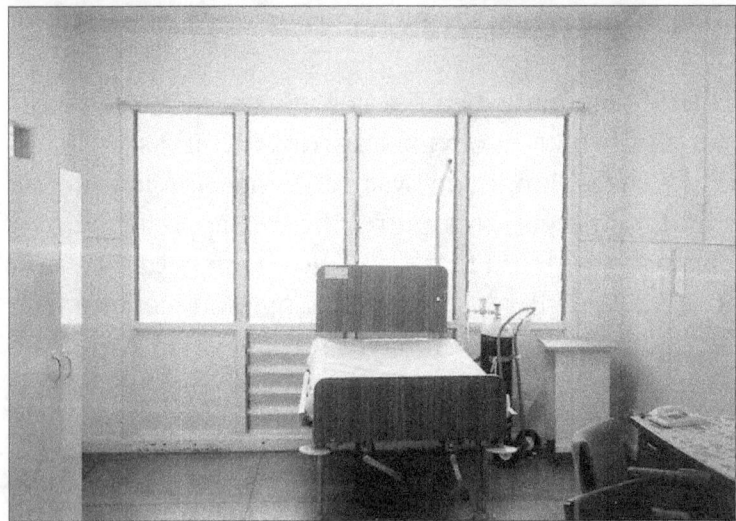

Batchelor Clinic
Ros Jones

took the bag and gingerly opened it up. She eased the bottle out of the bag and, as a precaution, placed paper towelling around it before carefully unscrewing the lid. She took a whiff and concluded that it was 'like garlic with an oily base'.[27] It was then that Les Cox, a student from Batchelor Higher Primary School, arrived at the hospital.[28]

Cox had come to the hospital because he had a cold. He recalled the nursing sister giving him 'the standard pink pills which you got at that time'. On the waiting room floor he saw a scruffy, dirty individual with long hair and a beard. He was doubled up, rolling around, moaning and clutching his stomach asking for help. Cox asked Nurse Hutchings, 'What on earth is up with him?' She said he had found a container in the bush, put a hole in it with a bullet and covered himself with the contents. She also said he had drunk some of the liquid. Cox saw him bursting his many blisters.

Nurse Hutchings told Cox that the man had brought in a sample and she had no idea what it was. She passed it to Cox — a small glass essence bottle with a screw lid, still in its wrapping — and asked, 'Do you know what this liquid is in the bottle?' Cox replied, 'It smells a bit like aniseed, otherwise I haven't any idea.' The

Les Cox

Les Cox

presence of a school student gave Nurse Hutchings an idea and she asked, 'Is there a science teacher at the school? Do they study chemistry?' 'Yes,' came the reply. 'Would you take this over to the school and see what it is?' Cox agreed and headed off with the bottle and the leaking chemical weapon, held in his bare hands.

Cox took the bottle across the road to the Batchelor school and gave it to Colin Raymond, who taught science among other subjects. Raymond had a sniff of the bottle's contents and then handed the lethal

Batchelor School. The Medical Clinic is Arrowed in the Top Photo. The Science Laboratory was to the Far right in the Photo Below.

Ros Jones

concoction to a Mr Harriss and other members of the school staff. They all smelt the mysterious liquid, but none could identify it. Mr Harriss' opinion was that the liquid was a mixture of petrol, oil and aniseed. Cox then followed teacher Raymond to the science laboratory which was an annex to the main building. He 'did a few litmus tests' and wrote down what it showed. Raymond, having concluded that the liquid was a harmless mixture of petrol, oil and acid, poured the samples down a science bench sink! Les Cox duly took the note and remaining sample back to the hospital.[29]

While Cox was at the school, Somogyi was observed removing a thumb tack from the wall to puncture the blisters. He told Nurse Hutchings, 'I feel very ill' and, as he lay on the waiting-room floor, he vomited into a bowl. Hutchings noted that 'the vomit smelt very strongly of the liquid' and, as he was 'talking strangely', she decided to telephone the local police station.[30] Kevin Smith, an ex-coal miner and the Officer in Charge, answered the call and listened to Hutchings' description of the 'mentally unbalanced' patient.[31] He had already been briefed on the badly burnt alien as Mangelson had arrived at the police station several minutes before. The two immediately 'patrolled' to the hospital.

They observed Somogyi on the outpatients' floor and Smith could see the burnt thighs, hands feet and chest and blisters six inches to a foot along his arms. Cox had arrived back with the sample and Nurse Hutchings handed it to Smith. Smith examined it, noting that the liquid was black in colour. He smelt the sample, but couldn't detect any odour. On a second smell he could make out a garlicky odour, as the others had. 'Where did you get it?' he asked. 'From a bomb,' Somogyi replied. He also explained that he had rubbed the liquid on his legs for arthritis. Smith was irate that Hutchings had handed a sample of dangerous liquid to others, putting them at risk.

As it happened, two weeks prior, Smith had read an article concerning a doctor, whom he remembered as from New York or Chicago, who had served in a medical capacity in World War I. A returned soldier had souvenired a mustard bomb from the Western Front and bought it home to the United States and had later become covered in the

Kevin Smith
Kevin Smith

mustard. The liquid from the bomb was described as black, with a smell similar to garlic, and had caused blisters. Smith pondered — it was one in a million, but could this be the same stuff?

From the hospital Smith rang Inspector Hook, who was in charge of the Northern Police Division. Smith described the liquid as 'dark, oily, the guy has burns and I think it might be mustard gas.' Hook responded in a lively manner: 'Oh shit! How the hell do you know it's mustard?' Hook, an ex-Army officer, knew Smith's background and that it didn't include any involvement with chemical weapons. Without waiting for an explanation from Smith, Hook instructed him, 'Get Mangleson and get him to take this man to Darwin Hospital with the sample. Be careful not to come into contact with him or the liquid.'

Smith decided to cover the patient with a sheet and Mangleson took him north to Darwin Hospital with the sample in tow. No medical treatment had been given to him during his stay at Bachelor. Hook immediately contacted the Army for assistance and, later that afternoon, sent Smith to inspect Somogyi's hut with some Army personnel.[32]

Army Major David Luke, an ammunition technical officer, received a call from Police Headquarters in Darwin alerting him that there had been an incident at Adelaide River.[33] As this was an emergency, he quickly made his way to the Adelaide River police station and met Constable Smith. Smith took Major Luke and Staff Sergeant Frank Holmes, who was Luke's ammunition technician, to the hut which, as they discovered, was more akin to a bush humpy. It had no door as such and had been constructed from abandoned Army materials which were scattered everywhere and included fibro cement, corrugated iron and some scavenged louvres.

They carefully examined both the inside and outside of Somogyi's hut and David Luke immediately picked up the smell of mustard gas and found the unmarked cylinder Somogyi had described to Smith. Using available manuals, the sense of smell and other professional expertise, Luke was quickly able to identify the offending item as a 6 lb mustard gas bomb. He later recalled, 'I had, during my ammunition training, quite considerable experience in the identification by odour of the war gases, the common ones by way of smelling bottles. Also, I had a drop of mustard gas put on the inside of my left arm so we could see the effects of mustard gas and I had the blister or the scar from the blister for some years after.'

Major Luke was regularly involved in searching the area around Adelaide River and beyond to ensure that no unexploded ammunition had surfaced as a result of the action of wind or water. Many armies had passed through the area and left a bewildering array of live and expended wartime ammunition. In fact the Adelaide River region was an Army disposal area and the problem of stray ordnance remains extant to this day.

In the hut they found some 500 rounds of assorted small arms ammunition, a reflection of the quantity of discarded ammunition that lay in the vicinity of Mount Bundy Station. It was obvious to the Army professionals that Somogyi had some knowledge of small arms ammunition. 'He was ingenious in this regard,' Luke recalls, 'he didn't have the correct tools but certainly had the knowhow — some of this ammo had been broken down, pulled apart and propellant placed in tobacco tins.' Somogyi confirmed his penchant for tinkering with ammunition to Luke when they later met in Darwin Hospital. Luke adds,

Major David Luke
David Luke

From the military small arms ammunition he'd discovered, the 50 calibre in particular, he had removed the projectiles and emptied out the propellant into a tobacco container so that he could then use the propellant in his .22 calibre rifle, which used a

modified .303 British cartridge case — how he capped them I can't remember. He was pressing his own bullets and fitting them into these cartridge cases. Making ammunition was part of the game in the Northern Territory. Wandering the countryside was a disease of the Darwinians.

Even young Les Cox had taken boxes of .303 ammunition home and made his own explosives using cordite. His brother had gone one step further and brought home an abandoned grenade.

Somogyi displayed other craftsmanship throughout the crude hut. He was well set-up and self-contained as a hunter, fisherman and fossicker cum prospector. He had a table and chair, both bush items. They found a lamp he had manufactured from an old jam tin and odds and ends, with a self-feeding apparatus. 'I distinctly remember he had a grinding wheel, chest height, which was ingeniously made out of bush timber and operated by a foot pedal,' recalls Luke. 'The bed was saplings and hessian. There were basic utensils, an open fire and he clearly fed on

6 lb Mustard Gas Bomb
Jeff Osbourne

wallabies; the remains and skins of a number of small native animals were scattered around the hut. He clearly lived off the land.'

Having searched for other canisters and found none, Luke carefully placed the cylinder in the back of his ute, surrounded by makeshift padding. They removed a number of articles which appeared to have come in contact with the mustard as well as the two filled cordial bottles and placed them in an isolated spot, away from the hut, for recovery the following day. It was too risky to remove the liquid mustard at this stage and take it back to Darwin.

Luke and Holmes proceeded back to the Army's Larrakeyah Barracks in Darwin, with Luke parking the explosives utility outside the office of the Commander, Northern Territory, Lieutenant Colonel Bob Millar. Luke went straight to Millar's office: 'He was very interested in what I had been up to and he wanted to know what I had done with the cylinder. I told him "It's in the utility just outside the door," which worried him not a little and I told him it was mustard gas of course. So he came out to have a look and he stretched his neck to get a view of the cylinder at the back of the utility, then told me to get the billy-o out of there.' Luke took the cylinder across to the ammunition sub-depot at Francis Bay, on the other side of Darwin. [34] The two cordial bottles and Somogyi's sample bottle were later recovered, placed in a padded cylinder and also taken the Francis Bay depot where they were destroyed by incineration in the demolition area on 21 October.

The next morning Luke visited Somogyi in hospital hoping to discover where he had found the bomb. 'He wasn't in a good way. According to the nursing staff he was refusing medication. I managed to speak to him well enough. I found out where he'd found the cylinder, what he'd done with it. There was a bit of doubt if he had actually taken a taste of the liquid. He had blisters around his face and nose but this could have been from an accidental large sniff or whatever,' relates Luke. When Somogyi pulled up his hospital gown sleeve Luke could see large blisters all over his arms. He adds, 'He was in great pain, there was no doubt about that.'

Somogyi told Luke that he had found the cylinder on the end of an emergency airstrip at Mount Bundy Station. There were emergency airstrips everywhere, particularly around the Adelaide River. Luke returned to Mount Bundy Station and, using Somogyi's description, went directly to the spot where the cylinder had been found. There was a mark in the earth where Somogyi had removed the bomb, with an imprint of a box and cylinder. Nine other empty casings were found nearby.[35]

The day after handling the sample, Les Cox noticed that he had a couple of blisters on his left wrist and red skin irritations on both thighs and the throat. Presumably there had been mustard around the lid of the bottle which had leaked onto his hand and he had then touched his thigh. Cox had not been told to clean his hands after the exposure. The Batchelor Hospital was usually manned only by a nurse, but on Mondays a doctor from Darwin Hospital would visit and see all the minors and mothers during the clinic. Cox went to see him when the blisters appeared and asked the doctor about them. He was disappointed with the response: 'I told him how they originated but he dismissed it and said "You must have got them gardening." As if a 16-year-old does gardening!' The burns persisted, so the following Monday he saw the next doctor on duty. 'It was déjà vu, he said it was caused by something else.'[36] Mr Harriss also developed several small blisters on his left index finger and an irritation under his nose. Nurse Hutchings had phoned Harriss asking, 'Have there been any side-effects from the liquid to anyone at the school?' Mr Harriss replied, 'Both myself and Les have received burns.' Hutchings discovered that penicillin was being used to treat Somogyi's burns so she gave Les Cox and Mr Harriss the same treatment.

Remarkably, Somogyi held on to life for two weeks, but was found dead in bed by Dr White on 13 October at 8.30 am. John Haywood, the Coroner's counsel, accepted the body at the morgue and recalls, 'His skin was hanging off him, he was a shocking sight. He lay in the fridge for 3 months while they were looking for next of kin. There was nobody to bury him.' Haywood believes he refused a blood transfusion and presumed this was on religious grounds. He was told they could have saved him if he had accepted the transfusion but this is very unlikely.[37]

A post-mortem was ordered and was conducted at 11.00 am on 20 October by Dr John Crotty. Crotty noted that there were burns over the whole of the trunk, all the limbs and neck. Internally, there was bleeding on the surface of the organs and an infarct (tissue death) in the right lung. The intestines showed evidence of paralytic ilius (blockage) and there was some bleeding on the brain. These appearances were compatible

Newspaper Headlines. Major Bill Lewis Examining the Killer Bomb.
Northern Territory News

with death due to mustard gas poisoning followed by pancytopaenia (a generalised reduction in the white and red blood cells which has been recorded in some of the gassed Iranian victims of the Iran/Iraq war). In summary there was a complete depletion of all the blood elements. Somogyi's immune system had been destroyed.[38]

Luke attended the autopsy and, as the main organs were uncovered, he tested for mustard by dabbing litmus paper on them. The litmus changed colour with mustard gas contact. 'They all tested positive. He was full of the stuff. All his main organs showed evidence of mustard which would have been absorbed through the system quite aside from the fact that he may have taken a sip of it.'

On 13 January, Constable Reed of Police Headquarters phoned Smith and requested that all people who had been in contact with the mustard bomb sample at Batchelor proceed to Darwin for a check-up as Somogyi had now died. Mr Harriss and Cox were sent immediately to the hospital. Cox recalls, 'The next thing that happened was that I was in school in class, when a police paddy wagon turned up with Kevin Smith. He said they were taking me to Darwin Hospital as the guy had died and I needed checking. Smith had obtained permission from my father. They duly took me to the hospital on the 13th, the day he died.'

At Darwin Hospital Cox was placed in an isolation ward which resembled 'a football field with a bed in the middle'. To Cox it seemed enormous. He was visited by his sister-in-law, Helen, but she had to leave as a group of Army and Air Force personnel arrived. They probed Cox concerning his involvement, 'Where did the bomb come from etc?' He explained that he had only carried a sample from the Bachelor Hospital to the school. It was at the hospital that he was given a more detailed picture of what had happened, how Somogyi had found the bomb, drained it and covered himself in the black liquid. He was also told that Somogyi had refused a blood transfusion.

After Cox was discharged from hospital, the incident became mired in mystery:

The strange thing was that, Colin [Raymond] denied that the incident had ever occurred. He was definitely burnt in two places, just below the hem of his shorts and on the eyebrows. This was because he had a nervous habit of twiddling his hairs in those two areas. I gathered they were trying to cover it up by pretending it never happened as it was never talked of again. This was made more awkward because, when my parents were away, my brother and me were invited over to the Raymonds' for dinner and we all just pretended the incident never occurred. It gave me the impression I was to shut up about it too and I did.[39]

Luke was told to have a blood test. 'The result of the blood test was that I had a low white cell count which is one of the symptoms that could come from mustard gas poisoning so they immediately sent me to the hospital — the very old Darwin Hospital where its isolation ward was little more than mosquito netting — fly wire type thing with multiple chambers. Leprosy was rampant at that time and I gathered these wards were their first point of call.'

He spent the night there and, while he was resting, Lieutenant Colonel Millar visited him in what he related as a very humorous incident. 'Bob [Millar] turned up at hospital. He had a full gown on, gloves and approached me with his arms stiffly outstretched holding on to a map. He said "mark the spot" where the item was found. It was as if I was a leper and it was so over the top and I burst out laughing. In fact I felt fine and didn't think there was anything wrong with me.' Millar retired later that year to take over the management of the famous Victoria River Downs property.

The next morning they repeated the blood test and declared Luke fit to return to duty. They decided that there must have been an anomaly in the first test. Harriss, Cox and Smith also had a low blood count. They were told that mustard could affect their white cell count.[40]

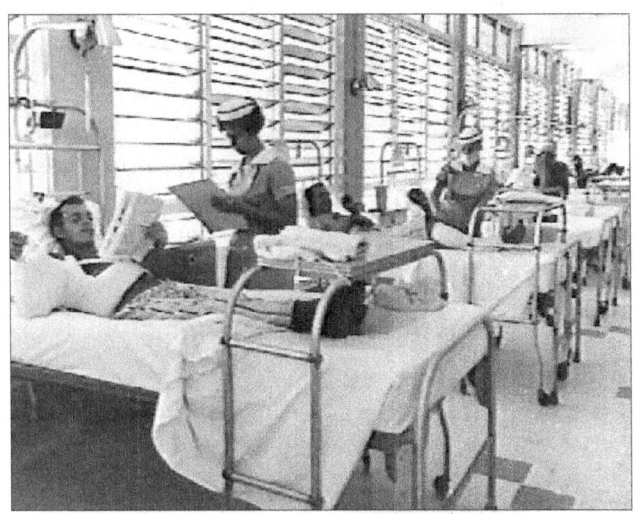

Darwin Hospital
Northern Territory Library

Major Bill Lewis in a 'Vapor Proof Suit'
Bill Lewis

Around this time Bill Lewis joined the fray. Lewis was a senior inspector of armaments at the Ordnance School in Bandiana, Victoria, and had been flown up to advise on the incident.[41] His sole safety gear was a Melbourne Fire Brigade vapour-proof suit. 'It was useless, I would have died of heat exhaustion before mustard gas poisoning.'

On 16 January, Smith travelled to the hut with Luke, Lewis and Darwen. With Somogyi now dead there was no argument over how to decontaminate the hut — it was torched along with all the contents and his bike and saddle bag, which had been neutralised with bleach paste before being recovered from Adelaide River. A search of Somogyi's belongings had been conducted in the vain hope that some personal papers would be recovered that would contain the identity of his next of kin. Some 50 years later, there are still no clues to Somogyi's next of kin. As no relative had been located, his cremation was paid for by the Welfare Department. Mustard gas warning signs were subsequently erected in the area.

An inquest was held into Somogyi's death at the Coroner's Court on 5 November 1964 led by Coroner Leeder. Major Luke proved a coy witness and revealed little. Luke recalled that a message had filtered down,

> ... through the appropriate army channels from Bob Menzies, the Prime Minister, of all people, that we didn't have chemical weapons in Australia. My impression was that I was being told that he didn't want it spoken of, that was to be kept hush-hush. This was reinforced by Neil Thomas at Army Headquarters who said to me, 'The PRIME MINISTER says the Australian Army never had any chemical weapons in Australia.' That was why I was a bit elusive at the inquest as to the source of the mustard gas bomb.

Luke stated that no mustard gas was used by Australian troops during World War II and that the origin of the mustard was a mystery.[42]

Whether the Prime Minister did in fact intervene or whether Luke's superiors were simply sending a message of their own is unclear. But what is clear it that, almost 20 years on from Andrew Williams' death, the climate of secrecy had remained and continued to remain until the early 1990s when the Australian government, like Wing Commander Le Fèvre in 1950, revealed the truth. That it took 50 years to acknowledge such a truth can be partially attributed to lost 'corporate knowledge'. The events were so far removed that the knowledge of their existence was buried in the archives or known only to the few survivors of Australia's chemical weapons past. The critical importance of revealing a truth such as this is clearly demonstrated in the tragic fate of those who died following exposure to these weapons (either because of military secrecy or abandonment). The careful treatment of such information — including its revelation if lives are at stake — is a critical lesson from history that Australia's military needs to learn, if only to ensure that these needless tragedies never recur.

Epilogue

The Idomeneus

(written by Ken Heydon in his mid-eighties)

They asked for volunteers, but for what they wouldn't say
But we'd be lined up against a brick wall if we gave the game away
We were just a lot of aircrew sprogs, still green behind the ears
But a change was like a holiday said I and all my peers
Anything was better than doing maths and sentry guard
So we swore to keep our traps shut, to this Wing Commander card
It seemed a ship called *Idomeneus* while full of poison gas
Had locked horns with some Stukers, and was in a frightful mess
She had mustard gas encased in drums and phosgene gas in shell
The top mustard drums were riddled, that ship was meant for hell
Some nose caps from artillery shell were loosened or astray
So the phosgene hold was reeking with the smell of musty hay
The wharfies had refused the job, both navy and army too
So they tried us poor air force sods, who hoped to make air crew
We were promised wharfies danger pay on top of our 5 bob
So with all that lovely brass in sight we were eager for the job
The top drums of mustard having dribbled down all the way
Meant us hosing down each layer before the slingmen had their say
So encased in total gas gear, down the ladder we would climb
To descend into that dungeon for just twenty minutes at a time
The air was full of mustard, mixed up with all the spray
That hold was like an oven, we could have been in Mandalay
Eight days passed, some lads badly gassed, the job was nearly done
When a break was called and we were told to gather in the sun
We stood there on the wharf that day to be told in good old strine
That our extra pays had been cancelled now, sorry boys don't whine

EPILOGUE

The unloading of *Idomeneus*, it really changed my life
For while I was on sick leave, it was when I met my wife
All that gas came up past Lithgow to near Marrangaroo
And as I pass it now I wonder, what and where and who
IF I HADN'T VOLUNTEERED THAT DAY WHERE WOULD I BE NOW
Driving my new Roller or behind a horse and plough

Ken Heydon Preparing for a Documentary Interview

Documentary Maker Jorge Farre (Left) with Chemical Warfare Armourer Frank Moran

Casualty Roll Call

Deceased

A Williams
O'Brien

Sydney Stevedores

English A
Flanagan J
Gillanders J
Horton F
Jones T
Kearney J
Minor E
Muggivan P
Roach W
Pearce W
Quentin
Shannon (Captain)
Smith A
Spiteri C
Swinton W
Wilson C
Whitton G

Melbourne Stevedores

Alexander C
Campbell J
Cook D
Dahlstedt F
Duck W
Mat(t)hews S
McDonald L
Prazenica (Prazenich?) F
Rowden J

Idomeneus Crew

Booth(by?) H *(Eye)*
Bradley A *(Eye)*
Blayney F *(Eye)*
Carton N
Dark W *(Eye)*
Eynon W *(Eye)*
Frankes W *(Neck, Arm)*
Goblowski O *(Eye, Hip)*
Kellock G *(Arm)*
Martin W *(Neck)*
Murphy A *(Chest)*
Pilcher W *(Eye, Larynx)*

Pilkington *(Eye)*
Triller A *(Eye)*
Williams J *(Hip, Thigh)*

RAAF

Bainbridge E
Bardsley G *(Eye)*
Begley G
Blake G *(Fatigue)*
Boase N *(Nausea)*
Bourke P
Boyland J
Bridgland A *(Burns)*
Broadhurst *(Eye)*
Brogan I *(Lost Smell)*
Brown W *(Face)*
Burke F *(Burns)*
(Bourke? 74132 FC)
Buttfield E *(Eye)*
Caller W *(Hand, Elbows)*
Cameron R *(Eye)*
Castle F *(Eye)*
Cohen G
Craig W
Craven A *(Eye)*
Daley A
Davies H *(Groin, Scrotum)*
Dixon R *(Burns)*

Dodd T
Donnellan
Dowes W
Dyett S *(Fatigue)*
Edwards S *(Nausea, Chest)*
Everett R *(Eye)*
Fairburn S
Finn M *(Fatigue)*
Finney B *(Burns)*
Fischer A
Fowles K
Freeman H *(Eye)*
Giddings A
Gilbert D *(Fatigue)*
Glasgow G
Goodyear E *(Headaches)*
Graham W
Gray J *(Eye)*
Grimble C
Halge L
Harper S
Harrison F
Hartley J
Hawkins C *(Face)*
Hembrough R
Heydon K
Humphreys J *(Fatigue)*
Johnson R *(Scrotum)*
Johns L *(Eye)*

Johnston E
Kellow J *(Eye)*
Kelly N *(Fear)*
Langer N *(Groin)*
Le Fèvre R
Linder A
McKenna J *(Eye, Gastritis)*
Mooney F
Morrow N
Muir W
Muldraney R *(Fatigue)*
Nadsen C *(Headache)*
Newbound S *(Weariness)*
Orchard S
Parsons G *(Burns)*
Parsons L *(Eye)*
Patfield R
Percival J
Perry H
Peterson E
Pickering A
Porter J *(Fatigue)*
Preston I *(Eye)*
Reynolds J
Reynolds J F
Ridgway G *(Vomiting)*
Roberts A
Russell L *(Eye)*
Russell R
Sellers C *(Fatigue)*

Sexton J
Sharp M *(Nausea)*
Shaw N *(Fatigue)*
Symons S *(Eye)*
Thomas R
Tonks R
Trewin A *(Weariness)*
Wallis *(Arm, Scrotum)*
Walsh J *(Nausea, Chest)*.
Waters G *(Burns)*
Wilkinson L
Willis
Wilson H *(Eye)*
Winter A

RPA Staff

Dr Ross *(From Williams)*

Chemist

McKenzie H

Guard Dogs (Marrangaroo Tunnel)

Gassed – 'Stood down'

Sources

This is a work of non fiction: The quoted conversations are taken verbatim from court records, coroners reports, interviews with participants and other archival material.

Andrew William Williams

Interviews were conducted with Iris Bourke, Geoff Burn, Arthur Dark, Harry Evans, Kevin Garr, Stuart Glover, Ken & Phyllis Heydon, Ron Hughes, Joan Hunt, Tim Miers, Beryl Miller, Margaret Miller, Ron Patfield, Les Parsons, Olive Tampe, Elizabeth Russ, Arthur Trewin and June Trewin.

Principal Primary Sources

Files marked Digitised are viewable online at http://naa.gov.au

Unless otherwise referenced the information for the book comes from;

- A1196 58/501/ PART 1 - Visit of M.Vs 'Idomeneus' and 'Birchbank' to Melbourne and Sydney Jan-Feb. 1943 (Compensation Claims etc.) Part 1 - National Archives of Australia (Canberra) – Digitised.

- A1196 58/501/ PART 2 - Visit of M.Vs 'Idomeneus' and 'Birchbank' to Melbourne and Sydney Jan-Feb. 1943 (Compensation Claims etc.) Part 2 - National Archives of Australia (Canberra) – Digitised.

- A462 379/5 - Defence. Claim by stevedores engaged on 'Idomeneus' (1943) - National Archives of Australia (Canberra) – Digitised.

Flanagan v. China Mutual Steam Navigation Co. Ltd. – Commonwealth of Australia – Third party – 26 June 1950 – State Records of NSW Court Reporting Office; NRS 13713; Transcripts of Evidence, 1900-1960; [6/2518] Causes, 1950, State Records Authority of New South Wales, Kingswood.

Pearce v. China Mutual Steam Navigation Co. Ltd. – Commonwealth of Australia – Third party – 1 August 1950 – State Records of NSW Court Reporting Office; NRS 13713; Transcripts of Evidence, 1900-1960; [6/2523] Causes, 1950, State Records Authority of New South Wales, Kingswood.

Swinton v. China Mutual Steam Navigation Co. Ltd. – Commonwealth of Australia – Third party – 6 August 1950 – State Records of NSW Court Reporting Office; NRS 13713; Transcripts of Evidence, 1900-1960; [6/2524] Causes, 1950, State Records Authority of New South Wales, Kingswood.

A10071, 1951/13 TRANSCRIPT -2 - SWINTON William Robert versus The China Mutual Steam Navigation Company Limited; Ocean Steamship Company Limited; Commonwealth of Australia [Transcript Recording of Proceedings - Original] - National Archives of Australia (Canberra) – Digitised.

A10071, 1951/13 TRANSCRIPT - 2 COPY - SWINTON William Robert versus The China Mutual Steam Navigation Company Limited; Ocean Steamship Company Limited; Commonwealth of Australia [Transcript Record of Proceedings] - National Archives of Australia (Canberra) – Digitised.

A10071, 1951/13 PART 2 COPY - SWINTON William Robert versus The China Mutual Steam Navigation Company Limited; Ocean Steamship Company Limited; Commonwealth of Australia - National Archives of Australia (Canberra) – Digitised.

A10071, 1951/13 PART 1 - SWINTON William Robert versus The China Mutual Steam Navigation Company Limited; Ocean

SOURCES

Steamship Company Limited; Commonwealth of Australia - National Archives of Australia (Canberra) – Digitised.

A10071, 1951/13 PART 2 - SWINTON William Robert versus The China Mutual Steam Navigation Company Limited; Ocean Steamship Company Limited; Commonwealth of Australia - National Archives of Australia (Canberra) – Digitised.

Swinton v. China Mutual Steam Navigation Co. Ltd. – The Australian Law Journal, Vol 25, pg 515 – 19 November 1951.

State Coroners; NRS 345, Coroners' inquest papers, 1851-1963; 22 February 1943. Inquest on Dead Body of Andrew William Williams, State Records Authority of New South Wales, Kingswood.

A1196 9/501/32 Gas Warfare - Medical Aspects of Policy - National Archives of Australia (Canberra) – Digitised.

A705 229/1/141 [Chemicals and Chemical Warfare - General] - Air Force Headquarters - AMEM [Air Member for Engineering and Maintenance] - DARM [Director of Armaments] - Transportation of CW [Chemical Warfare] weapons by road, rail and sea - Reports - National Archives of Australia (Canberra).

A9300 FREEMAN H B – FREEMAN HAROLD BRIAN: Service Number 264318: Date of Birth 27 Jul 1900 – National Archives of Australia (Canberra) – Digitised.

Nandor Somogyi

Interviews were conducted with Les Cox, John Crotty, Harold Darwen, Tommy Faucett, John Haywood, Donald Honeysett, Bill Lewis, David Luke, Bruce Mangleson, Denzel McManus, Bill Ross and Kevin Smith.

Principal Primary Sources

Northern Territory Archives Service – Coroner's Court, Darwin – F864 – 18/64 Inquest into the death of Nandor Somogyi – died on 13-10-1964 Inquest held 5-11-1964.

Northern Territory Archives Service – Police Station, Batchelor – F133 Correspondence Books – 1964 to 1976 [Vol 1].

Northern Territory Archives Service – Police Station, Batchelor – NTRS 2080 - Day Journals (Previously Registered as F1331) – 1954 to 1995 – Batchelor Day Journal 12/9/1964 to 6/3/1966.

National Archives of Australia – Somogyi, Nander (sic) [Alien Registration File] – E40 SOMOGYI N – 1964.

National Archives of Australia – Somogyi Nandor born 21 October 1929 – A12045 731 – 1950.

National Archives of Australia – Somogyi Nondor (sic) – Nationality: Hungarian – Arrived Sydney per Nelly 30 December 1950 – D4881 SOMOGYI NANDOR – 30 Dec 1950 to 31 Dec 1976.

'Killer Gas Bomb', Northern Territory News, 16 October 1964, p. 1.

'Died in Agony From Gas Bomb', Northern Territory News, 16 October 1964, p. 2.

'Wide Hunt for Mustard Gas Bombs: Mystery to Us how it Got There', Sun-Herald, 18 October 1964, p. 19.

SOURCES

'Tried to Get Relief with Mustard Gas: Coroner Hears How Man Died', Northern Territory News, 6 November 1964, p. 3.

Report of Major E.F. Lewis, Ordnance School Bandiana, Department of Defence.

Endnotes

Foreword

1   E.M. Spiers, *Chemical Warfare*, University of Illinois Press, Chicago, 1986.
2   R. Harris and J. Paxman, *A Higher Form Of Killing*, Noonday Press, New York, 1981.
3   Authors Note: On 13 October 1944, a secret memorandum to the Commonwealth of Australia read, 'I am to inform you that Their Lordships have had under consideration the report of a recent air raid on loss of life and injury due to poison gas. The gas was present as part of the cargo of a ship which was set on fire, exploded and sank in the harbour. It appears that the local Naval and Military Authorities had not been warned of the presence of this cargo and as a result no precautions were taken to warn personnel, nor were steps taken to treat casualties for gas poisoning. More than 800 casualties were admitted to hospital after the raid, 628 suffering from mustard exposure, and some 70 deaths occurred caused wholly or partly by mustard gas.' This referred to the Bari tragedy, one year after the *Idomeneus* death. MP1049/5 1830/2/150 – Regulations for ships carrying Poisonous Gas or Smoke Ammunition - National Archives of Australia (Melbourne).

Chapter 1

1   Malcolm Falkus, *The Blue Funnel Legend: A History of the Ocean Steam Company 1865 – 1973*, MacMillan Academic & Professional Ltd, London, 1990.
2   Stuart Glover commented that the Blue Funnel employees thought highly of the company and were 'glad they had their war with Blue Funnel'.
3   Walter Dark's life is described in Arthur Dark's 'Dark of Parkham' (CDROM), compiled in 2004, Chapter 6 'Instow Darks' refers. This copy kindly provided to me by Arthur Dark.
4   Description of the *Titan* torpedoing in *A Merchant Fleet in War. Alfred Holt & Co., 1939-1945*, by S.W. Roskill, Collins, 1962. Also see Record of Medal, 14 February 1941. Guildhall Library, London.
5   Interview with Stuart Glover, November 2005.

ENDNOTES

6 Email 9 January 2008, Arthur Dark to author.
7 Detail kindly provided by Stuart Glover.
8 Exhibit 2 in A10071, 1951/13 PART 2 - *SWINTON William Robert versus The China Mutual Steam Navigation Company Limited*; Ocean Steamship Company Limited; Commonwealth of Australia - National Archives of Australia (Canberra) – Digitised.
9 Filmed interview with Stuart Glover, March 2005.
10 http://en.wikipedia.org/wiki/Idomeneus
11 Technical details of the *Idomeneus* kindly provided by maritime historian Ron Parsons.
12 See Falkus, *The Blue Funnel Legend*, for a description of the process of the carriage of chilled beef.
13 Filmed interview with Stuart Glover, March 2005.
14 Ibid.
15 *A Merchant Fleet in War. Alfred Holt & Co., 1939-1945*, by S.W. Roskill, Collins, 1962.
16 *Comanchee* description from *Everyone Has 15 Minutes of Fame, and Other Stories* by Barry Ainsworth (WW2 People's War) http://www.bbc.co.uk/ww2peopleswar/stories/29/a6676329.shtml
17 Chief Officer Henderson's Report of Interview in *Empire Sailor of London* – 6,140 Gross Tons – Survivors' Report. Kindly provided by Ian Stockbridges. Thanks to International Maritime Research.
18 W.F. Dark in *Flanagan v. China Mutual Steam Navigation Co. Ltd.* – Commonwealth of Australia – Third party – 26 June 1950 – State Records of NSW Court Reporting Office; NRS 13713; Transcripts of Evidence, 1900-1960; [6/2518] Causes, 1950, State Records Authority of New South Wales, Kingswood.

Chapter 2

1 Exhibit 2 in A10071, 1951/13 PART 2 - *SWINTON William Robert versus The China Mutual Steam Navigation Company Limited*; Ocean Steamship Company Limited; Commonwealth of Australia - National Archives of Australia (Canberra) – Digitised.
2 Minute Sheet, 13 January 1943 in A1196 58/501/102 PART 1 - Visit of M.V.s 'Idomeneus' and 'Birchbank' to Melbourne and Sydney Jan-Feb. 1943 (Compensation Claims etc.) Part 1 - National Archives of Australia (Canberra).

3   MP1049/5 1830/2/150 – Regulations for ships carrying Poisonous Gas or Smoke Ammunition - National Archives of Australia (Melbourne).

4   *Empire Sailor of London – 6,140 Gross Tons* – Survivors' Report. International Maritime Research.

5   W.F. Dark in *Flanagan v. China Mutual Steam Navigation Co. Ltd. – Commonwealth of Australia – Third party – 26 June 1950* – State Records of NSW Court Reporting Office; NRS 13713; Transcripts of Evidence, 1900-1960; [6/2518] Causes, 1950, State Records Authority of New South Wales, Kingswood.

6   M.J. Aroney and A.D. Buckingham, *Raymond James Wood Le Fèvre 1905-1986*, Historical Records of Australian Science, Vol. 7, No. 3, 1988 available at: http://www.science.org.au/fellows/memoirs/leFèvre.html

Le Fèvre was also interviewed for *The Gillis Report, Australian field trial with mustard gas, 1942-1945*. Report edited by R.G. Gillis and published in 1992 with a foreword by Shirley Freeman.

7   Indeed one of Le Fèvre's notes was written in a RAAF file was on Methodist Church of Australasia writing paper.

8   Letter to Geoff Plunkett, 13 July 2007.

9   Discussions with Arthur and June Trewin; http://cas.awm.gov.au/item/P05255.001

10 Minute Sheet, ? January 1943 in A1196 58/501/102 PART 1 - Visit of M.V.s 'Idomeneus' and 'Birchbank' to Melbourne and Sydney Jan-Feb. 1943 (Compensation Claims etc.) Part 1 - National Archives of Australia (Canberra).

11 P.C. Alexander in *Flanagan v. China Mutual Steam Navigation Co. Ltd. – Commonwealth of Australia – Third party – 26 June 1950* – State Records of NSW Court Reporting Office; NRS 13713; Transcripts of Evidence, 1900-1960; [6/2518] Causes, 1950, State Records Authority of New South Wales, Kingswood.

12 W. Duck in *Flanagan v. China Mutual Steam Navigation Co. Ltd. – Commonwealth of Australia – Third party – 26 June 1950* – State Records of NSW Court Reporting Office; NRS 13713; Transcripts of Evidence, 1900-1960; [6/2518] Causes, 1950, State Records Authority of New South Wales, Kingswood.

13 Reports re Handling of Poison Gas Cargo, SS *Idomeneus*, Melbourne, 8.1.43 in A1196 58/501/102 PART 1 - Visit of M.V.s 'Idomeneus' and 'Birchbank' to Melbourne and Sydney Jan-Feb. 1943 (Compensation Claims etc.) Part 1 - National Archives of Australia (Canberra).

14 Ibid.

ENDNOTES

15 D.W. Cook in *Flanagan v. China Mutual Steam Navigation Co. Ltd. – Commonwealth of Australia – Third party* – 26 June 1950 – State Records of NSW Court Reporting Office; NRS 13713; Transcripts of Evidence, 1900-1960; [6/2518] Causes, 1950, State Records Authority of New South Wales, Kingswood.

16 Ibid.

17 SS *Idomeneus* Victoria Dock Melbourne 8-10 Jan 1943, 18 January 1943 in A1196 58/501/102 PART 1 - Visit of M.V.s 'Idomeneus' and 'Birchbank' to Melbourne and Sydney Jan-Feb. 1943 (Compensation Claims etc.) Part 1 - National Archives of Australia (Canberra).

18 Ibid.

19 W. Duck in *Flanagan v. China Mutual Steam Navigation Co. Ltd. – Commonwealth of Australia – Third party* – 26 June 1950 – State Records of NSW Court Reporting Office; NRS 13713; Transcripts of Evidence, 1900-1960; [6/2518] Causes, 1950, State Records Authority of New South Wales, Kingswood.

20 P.C. Alexander in *Flanagan v. China Mutual Steam Navigation Co. Ltd. – Commonwealth of Australia – Third party* – 26 June 1950 – State Records of NSW Court Reporting Office; NRS 13713; Transcripts of Evidence, 1900-1960; [6/2518] Causes, 1950, State Records Authority of New South Wales, Kingswood.

21 SS *Idomeneus* Victoria Dock Melbourne 8-10 Jan 1943, 18 January 1943 in A1196 58/501/102 PART 1 - Visit of M.V.s 'Idomeneus' and 'Birchbank' to Melbourne and Sydney Jan-Feb. 1943 (Compensation Claims etc.) Part 1 - National Archives of Australia (Canberra).

22 Ibid.

23 Ibid.

24 W.F. Dark in *Swinton v. China Mutual Steam Navigation Co. Ltd. – Commonwealth of Australia – Third party* – 8 August 1950 – State Records of NSW Court Reporting Office; NRS 13713; Transcripts of Evidence, 1900-1960; [6/2524] Causes, 1950, State Records Authority of New South Wales, Kingswood.

25 Copies of certificates issued to Captain Dark, MV *Idomeneus*, in Sydney by Wing Commander Le Fevre in A1196 58/501/102 PART 1 - Visit of M.V.s 'Idomeneus' and 'Birchbank' to Melbourne and Sydney Jan-Feb. 1943 (Compensation Claims etc.) Part 1 - National Archives of Australia (Canberra).

26 A1196 58/501/102 PART 1 - Visit of M.V.s 'Idomeneus' and 'Birchbank' to Melbourne and Sydney Jan-Feb. 1943 (Compensation Claims etc.) Part 1 - National Archives of Australia (Canberra).

27 A1196 58/501/102 PART 1 - Visit of M.V.s 'Idomeneus' and 'Birchbank' to Melbourne and Sydney Jan-Feb. 1943 (Compensation Claims etc.) Part 1 - National Archives of Australia (Canberra).
28 Reports re handling of poison gas cargo, SS *Idomeneus*, Melbourne, 8.1.43 in A1196 58/501/102 PART 1 - Visit of M.V.s 'Idomeneus' and 'Birchbank' to Melbourne and Sydney Jan-Feb. 1943 (Compensation Claims etc.) Part 1 - National Archives of Australia (Canberra).

Chapter 3

1 Interview with Stuart Glover, November 2005.
2 W.F. Dark in *Flanagan v. China Mutual Steam Navigation Co. Ltd.* – Commonwealth of Australia – Third party – 26 June 1950 – State Records of NSW Court Reporting Office; NRS 13713; Transcripts of Evidence, 1900-1960; [6/2518] Causes, 1950, State Records Authority of New South Wales, Kingswood.
3 W.F. Dark in *Swinton v. China Mutual Steam Navigation Co. Ltd.* – Commonwealth of Australia – Third party – 8 August 1950 – State Records of NSW Court Reporting Office; NRS 13713; Transcripts of Evidence, 1900-1960; [6/2524] Causes, 1950, State Records Authority of New South Wales, Kingswood.
4 Ibid.
5 H.F. McKenzie in *Flanagan v. China Mutual Steam Navigation Co. Ltd.* – Commonwealth of Australia – Third party – 26 June 1950 – State Records of NSW Court Reporting Office; NRS 13713; Transcripts of Evidence, 1900-1960; [6/2518] Causes, 1950, State Records Authority of New South Wales, Kingswood.
6 Ibid.
7 A.W. English in *Flanagan v. China Mutual Steam Navigation Co. Ltd.* – Commonwealth of Australia – Third party – 26 June 1950 – State Records of NSW Court Reporting Office; NRS 13713; Transcripts of Evidence, 1900-1960; [6/2518] Causes, 1950, State Records Authority of New South Wales, Kingswood.
8 R.J.W. Le Fevre in *Flanagan v. China Mutual Steam Navigation Co. Ltd.* – Commonwealth of Australia – Third party – 26 June 1950 – State Records of NSW Court Reporting Office; NRS 13713; Transcripts of Evidence, 1900-1960; [6/2518] Causes, 1950, State Records Authority of New South Wales, Kingswood.

ENDNOTES

9   Exhibit 5 in *SWINTON William Robert versus The China Mutual Steam Navigation Company Limited*; Ocean Steamship Company Limited; Commonwealth of Australia. AA(ACT) A10071 1951/13 PART 2.

10   W.R. Swinton in *Flanagan v. China Mutual Steam Navigation Co. Ltd. - Commonwealth of Australia - Third party - 26 June 1950* - State Records of NSW Court Reporting Office; NRS 13713; Transcripts of Evidence, 1900-1960; [6/2518] Causes, 1950, State Records Authority of New South Wales, Kingswood.

11   Report re Handling of Poison Gas Cargoes, SS *Idomeneus* at Sydney on 15.1.43 in A1196 58/501/102 PART 1 - Visit of M.Vs "Idomeneus" and "Birchbank" to Melbourne and Sydney Jan-Feb. 1943 (Compensation Claims etc.) Part 1 - National Archives of Australia (Canberra).

12   H.F. McKenzie in *Flanagan v. China Mutual Steam Navigation Co. Ltd. - Commonwealth of Australia - Third party - 26 June 1950* - State Records of NSW Court Reporting Office; NRS 13713; Transcripts of Evidence, 1900-1960; [6/2518] Causes, 1950, State Records Authority of New South Wales, Kingswood.

13   State Coroners; NRS 345, Coroners' inquest papers, 1851-1963; 22 February 1943; Inquest on Dead Body of Andrew William Williams; State Records Authority of New South Wales, Kingswood.

14   W.R. Swinton in *Flanagan v. China Mutual Steam Navigation Co. Ltd. - Commonwealth of Australia - Third party - 26 June 1950* - State Records of NSW Court Reporting Office; NRS 13713; Transcripts of Evidence, 1900-1960; [6/2518] Causes, 1950, State Records Authority of New South Wales, Kingswood.

15   Interview with Stuart Glover, November 2005.

16   A.W. English in *Flanagan v. China Mutual Steam Navigation Co. Ltd. - Commonwealth of Australia - Third party - 26 June 1950* - State Records of NSW Court Reporting Office; NRS 13713; Transcripts of Evidence, 1900-1960; [6/2518] Causes, 1950, State Records Authority of New South Wales, Kingswood.

17   A.W. English in *Pearce v. China Mutual Steam Navigation Co. Ltd. - Commonwealth of Australia - Third party - 1 August 1950* - State Records of NSW Court Reporting Office; NRS 13713; Transcripts of Evidence, 1900-1960; [6/2523] Causes, 1950, State Records Authority of New South Wales, Kingswood.

18   Ibid.

19   G.W. Whitton in *Flanagan v. China Mutual Steam Navigation Co. Ltd. - Commonwealth of Australia - Third party - 26 June 1950* - State Records of NSW Court Reporting Office; NRS 13713; Transcripts of Evidence,

1900-1960; [6/2518] Causes, 1950, State Records Authority of New South Wales, Kingswood.

Chapter 4

1   G.W. Whitton in *Swinton v. China Mutual Steam Navigation Co. Ltd.* – Commonwealth of Australia – Third party – 6 August 1950 – State Records of NSW Court Reporting Office; NRS 13713; Transcripts of Evidence, 1900-1960; [6/2524] Causes, 1950, State Records Authority of New South Wales, Kingswood.

2   W. Pearce in *Pearce v. China Mutual Steam Navigation Co. Ltd.* – Commonwealth of Australia – Third party – 1 August 1950 – State Records of NSW Court Reporting Office; NRS 13713; Transcripts of Evidence, 1900-1960; [6/2523] Causes, 1950, State Records Authority of New South Wales, Kingswood.

3   G.W. Whitton in *Swinton v. China Mutual Steam Navigation Co. Ltd.* – Commonwealth of Australia – Third party – 6 August 1950 – State Records of NSW Court Reporting Office; NRS 13713; Transcripts of Evidence, 1900-1960; [6/2524] Causes, 1950, State Records Authority of New South Wales, Kingswood.

4   Ibid.

5   E.M. Williams in State Coroners; NRS 345, Coroners' inquest papers, 1851-1963; 22 February 1943; Inquest on Dead Body of Andrew William Williams, State Records Authority of New South Wales, Kingswood.

6   A.W. English in *Flanagan v. China Mutual Steam Navigation Co. Ltd.* – Commonwealth of Australia – Third party – 26 June 1950 – State Records of NSW Court Reporting Office; NRS 13713; Transcripts of Evidence, 1900-1960; [6/2518] Causes, 1950, State Records Authority of New South Wales, Kingswood.

7   G.W. Whitton in *Swinton v. China Mutual Steam Navigation Co. Ltd.* – Commonwealth of Australia – Third party – 6 August 1950 – State Records of NSW Court Reporting Office; NRS 13713; Transcripts of Evidence, 1900-1960; [6/2524] Causes, 1950, State Records Authority of New South Wales, Kingswood.

8   A.W. English in *Flanagan v. China Mutual Steam Navigation Co. Ltd.* – Commonwealth of Australia – Third party – 26 June 1950 – State Records of NSW Court Reporting Office; NRS 13713; Transcripts of Evidence, 1900-1960; [6/2518] Causes, 1950, State Records Authority of New South Wales, Kingswood.

ENDNOTES

9   W.R. Swinton in *Flanagan v. China Mutual Steam Navigation Co. Ltd. – Commonwealth of Australia – Third party* – 26 June 1950 – State Records of NSW Court Reporting Office; NRS 13713; Transcripts of Evidence, 1900-1960; [6/2518] Causes, 1950, State Records Authority of New South Wales, Kingswood.

10 W. Pearce in *Pearce v. China Mutual Steam Navigation Co. Ltd. – Commonwealth of Australia – Third party* – 1 August 1950 – State Records of NSW Court Reporting Office; NRS 13713; Transcripts of Evidence, 1900-1960; [6/2523] Causes, 1950, State Records Authority of New South Wales, Kingswood.

11 E.M. Williams in State Coroners; NRS 345, Coroners' inquest papers, 1851-1963; 22 February 1943. Inquest on Dead Body of Andrew William Williams, State Records Authority of New South Wales, Kingswood.

12 G.A. Williams in State Coroners, NRS 345, Coroners' inquest papers, 1851-1963, 22 February 1943, Inquest on Dead Body of Andrew William Williams, State Records Authority of New South Wales, Kingswood.

13 C.C. Ross in State Coroners; NRS 345, Coroners' inquest papers, 1851-1963; 22 February 1943; Inquest on Dead Body of Andrew William Williams, State Records Authority of New South Wales, Kingswood.

14 Filmed interview with Les Parsons, March 2005.

15 J.T. Flanagan in *Flanagan v. China Mutual Steam Navigation Co. Ltd. – Commonwealth of Australia – Third party* – 26 June 1950 – State Records of NSW Court Reporting Office; NRS 13713; Transcripts of Evidence, 1900-1960; [6/2518] Causes, 1950, State Records Authority of New South Wales, Kingswood.

16 R.J.W. Le Fevre in Royal Australian Air Force Court of Inquiry, 21 January 1943; A1196 58/501/102 PART 1 - Visit of M.V.s 'Idomeneus' and 'Birchbank' to Melbourne and Sydney Jan-Feb. 1943 (Compensation Claims etc.) Part 1 - National Archives of Australia (Canberra)..

17 Filmed interview with Les Parsons, March 2005.

18 Filmed interview with Stuart Glover, March 2005.

19 *Idomeneus* casualties are listed in Official Log-Book – A Foreign-Going or a Home-Trade Ship – Official No. 149597, Port Liverpool 9 November 1942. My thanks to Roger Hollywood from: http://www.mercantilemarine.org

20 Report re Handling of Poison Gas Cargoes, SS *Idomeneus* at Sydney on 15.1.43 in A1196 58/501/102 PART 1 - Visit of M.V.s 'Idomeneus' and 'Birchbank' to Melbourne and Sydney Jan-Feb. 1943 (Compensation Claims etc.) Part 1 - National Archives of Australia (Canberra).

21 D.M. Flanagan in *Flanagan v. China Mutual Steam Navigation Co. Ltd. – Commonwealth of Australia – Third party – 26 June 1950 – State Records of NSW Court Reporting Office; NRS 13713; Transcripts of Evidence, 1900-1960; [6/2518] Causes, 1950, State Records Authority of New South Wales, Kingswood.

22 Filmed interview with Stuart Glover, March 2005.

Chapter 5

1 R.L. Harris in State Coroners NRS 345, Coroners' inquest papers, 1851-1963, 22 February 1943, Inquest on Dead Body of Andrew William Williams, State Records Authority of New South Wales, Kingswood.

2 G.A. Williams in State Coroners, NRS 345, Coroners' inquest papers, 1851-1963, 22 February 1943, Inquest on Dead Body of Andrew William Williams, State Records Authority of New South Wales, Kingswood.

3 J.T. Flanagan in *Flanagan v. China Mutual Steam Navigation Co. Ltd. – Commonwealth of Australia – Third party – 26 June 1950 – State Records of NSW Court Reporting Office, NRS 13713, Transcripts of Evidence, 1900-1960 [6/2518], Causes, 1950, State Records Authority of New South Wales, Kingswood.

4 Margaret Miller, neé McMullen.

5 Recorded interview with Margaret Miller, March 2005.

6 Filmed interview with Phyllis Heydon, March 2005.

7 J.T. Flanagan in *Flanagan v. China Mutual Steam Navigation Co. Ltd. – Commonwealth of Australia – Third party – 26 June 1950 – State Records of NSW Court Reporting Office, NRS 13713, Transcripts of Evidence, 1900-1960 [6/2518], Causes, 1950, State Records Authority of New South Wales, Kingswood.

8 Ibid.

9 H.B. Harwood in *Flanagan v. China Mutual Steam Navigation Co. Ltd. – Commonwealth of Australia – Third party – 26 June 1950 – State Records of NSW Court Reporting Office, NRS 13713, Transcripts of Evidence, 1900-1960 [6/2518], Causes, 1950, State Records Authority of New South Wales, Kingswood.

10 Filmed interview with Phyllis Heydon, March 2005.

11 Ibid.

12 E.M. Williams in State Coroners, NRS 345, Coroners' inquest papers, 1851-1963, 22 February 1943, Inquest on Dead Body of Andrew William Williams, State Records Authority of New South Wales, Kingswood.

ENDNOTES

13 J.F. Williams in State Coroners, NRS 345, Coroners' inquest papers, 1851-1963, 22 February 1943, Inquest on Dead Body of Andrew William Williams, State Records Authority of New South Wales, Kingswood.

14 C.C. Ross in State Coroners, NRS 345, Coroners' inquest papers, 1851-1963, 22 February 1943, Inquest on Dead Body of Andrew William Williams, State Records Authority of New South Wales, Kingswood.

15 J. Rablah in State Coroners, NRS 345, Coroners' inquest papers, 1851-1963, 22 February 1943, Inquest on Dead Body of Andrew William Williams, State Records Authority of New South Wales, Kingswood.

16 Interview with Olive Tampe, May 2008.

17 E.M. Williams in State Coroners, NRS 345, Coroners' inquest papers, 1851-1963, 22 February 1943, Inquest on Dead Body of Andrew William Williams, State Records Authority of New South Wales, Kingswood.

18 C.C. Ross in State Coroners, NRS 345, Coroners' inquest papers, 1851-1963, 22 February 1943, Inquest on Dead Body of Andrew William Williams, State Records Authority of New South Wales, Kingswood.

19 J.F. Williams in State Coroners, NRS 345, Coroners' inquest papers, 1851-1963, 22 February 1943, Inquest on Dead Body of Andrew William Williams, State Records Authority of New South Wales, Kingswood.

20 J. Rablah in State Coroners, NRS 345, Coroners' inquest papers, 1851-1963, 22 February 1943, Inquest on Dead Body of Andrew William Williams, State Records Authority of New South Wales, Kingswood.

21 Ibid.

22 Ibid.

23 Interview with Elizabeth Russ, March 2012.

24 Ibid.

25 H.R. Kelly in State Coroners, NRS 345, Coroners' inquest papers, 1851-1963, 22 February 1943, Inquest on Dead Body of Andrew William Williams, State Records Authority of New South Wales, Kingswood.

26 Visit of *Idomeneus* to Sydney 13th January 1943 in A1196 58/501/102 PART 1 - Visit of M.V.s 'Idomeneus' and 'Birchbank' to Melbourne and Sydney Jan-Feb. 1943 (Compensation Claims etc.) Part 1 - National Archives of Australia (Canberra).

27 Filmed interview with Beryl Miller, March 2005.

28 Visit of *Idomeneus* to Sydney 13th January 1943 in A1196 58/501/102 PART 1 - Visit of M.V.s 'Idomeneus' and 'Birchbank' to Melbourne and Sydney Jan-Feb. 1943 (Compensation Claims etc.) Part 1 - National Archives of Australia (Canberra).

Chapter 6

1. Filmed interview with Stuart Glover, March 2005.
2. Filmed interview with Geoff Burn, March 2005.
3. Filmed interview with Kevin Garr, March 2005.
4. The reason blisters were usually left intact was that the fluid contents were believed to be toxic and would contaminate new areas of skin if they ran. Recent research has shown the fluid is, in fact, non-toxic, and current practice is to lance all blisters over one centimetre.
5. Which measured about 12x12 feet.
6. Filmed interview with Ken Heydon, March 2005.
7. Filmed interview with Phyllis Heydon, March 2005.
8. Filmed interview with Ken Heydon, March 2005.
9. Visit of *Idomeneus* to Sydney, 13 January 1943 in A1196 58/501/102 PART 1 - Visit of M.V.s 'Idomeneus' and 'Birchbank' to Melbourne and Sydney Jan-Feb. 1943 (Compensation Claims etc.) Part 1 - National Archives of Australia (Canberra).
10. Ibid.

Chapter 7

1. Offloading of Chemical Cargoes from MV *Idomeneus* in A1196 58/501/102 PART 1 - Visit of M.V.s 'Idomeneus' and 'Birchbank' to Melbourne and Sydney Jan-Feb. 1943 (Compensation Claims etc.) Part 1 - National Archives of Australia (Canberra).
2. Interview with Tim Miers, 2010.
3. Filmed interview with Harry Evans, March 2005.
4. RAAF Explosives Depot: Use of Railway Tunnel RAAF Hiring No. 708 in A705 171/1/805 - DWB [Director of Works and Buildings] – Property – Glenbrook NSW – Hiring of railway tunnel - [Hiring of] Campsite – National Archives of Australia (Canberra) – Digitised.
5. Gwen Rowe's hand written recollections held by Tim Miers.
6. Report Hirings Service Serial No E C (RAAFH) 893 in A705 171/1/805. DWB [Director of Works and Buildings] - Property - Glenbrook NSW - Hiring of railway tunnel - [Hiring of] Campsite - National Archives of Australia (Canberra).

ENDNOTES

7 Untitled memo in A705 171/1/805 DWB [Director of Works and Buildings] - Property - Glenbrook NSW - Hiring of railway tunnel - [Hiring of] Campsite - National Archives of Australia (Canberra).

8 Interview with Ron Hughes, 2010.

9 A705 12/4/530 – Special bomb storage – National Archives of Australia (Canberra) – Digitised.

10 Agenda No 4109/1942 in A705 171/1/1023 - RAAF No 1 Sub Depot Marrangaroo Tunnel Buildings and Services - National Archives of Australia (Canberra).

11 Report (Ctd.) Casualties From CG Poisoning No 1 CR RAAF Lithgow in A1196 58/501/102 PART 1 - Visit of M.V.s 'Idomeneus' and 'Birchbank' to Melbourne and Sydney Jan-Feb. 1943 (Compensation Claims etc.) Part 1 - National Archives of Australia (Canberra).

12 Storage of 250 lb LC Bombs in Mark II filled CG at No 1 Central Reserve RAAF Lithgow in A1196 58/501/102 PART 1 - Visit of M.V.s 'Idomeneus' and 'Birchbank' to Melbourne and Sydney Jan-Feb. 1943 (Compensation Claims etc.) Part 1 - National Archives of Australia (Canberra).

13 Report (Ctd.) Casualties From CG Poisoning No 1 CR RAAF Lithgow in A1196 58/501/102 PART 1 - Visit of M.V.s 'Idomeneus' and 'Birchbank' to Melbourne and Sydney Jan-Feb. 1943 (Compensation Claims etc.) Part 1 - National Archives of Australia (Canberra).

14 These should be preserved. Along the concrete igloos at Talmoi, Richmond (Queensland) and the 100 m^2 capacity gas chamber from Innisfail, they are the only remnants of Australia's extensive World War II chemical warfare presence.

15 Report (Ctd.) Casualties From CG Poisoning No 1 CR RAAF Lithgow in A1196 58/501/102 PART 1 - Visit of M.V.s 'Idomeneus' and 'Birchbank' to Melbourne and Sydney Jan-Feb. 1943 (Compensation Claims etc.) Part 1 - National Archives of Australia (Canberra).

16 Ibid.

Chapter 8

1 Exhibit 2 in *Swinton in Flanagan v. China Mutual Steam Navigation Co. Ltd.* – Commonwealth of Australia – Third party – 26 June 1950 – State Records of NSW Court Reporting Office; NRS 13713; Transcripts of Evidence, 1900-1960; [6/2518] Causes, 1950, State Records Authority of New South Wales, Kingswood.

2   Filmed interview with Stuart Glover, March 2005.

3   W.F. Dark in *Flanagan v. China Mutual Steam Navigation Co. Ltd.* – Commonwealth of Australia – Third party – 26 June 1950 – State Records of NSW Court Reporting Office; NRS 13713; Transcripts of Evidence, 1900-1960; [6/2518] Causes, 1950, State Records Authority of New South Wales, Kingswood.

4   R.J.W. Le Fevre in *Swinton v. China Mutual Steam Navigation Co. Ltd.* – Commonwealth of Australia – Third party – 26 June 1950 – State Records of NSW Court Reporting Office; NRS 13713; Transcripts of Evidence, 1900-1960; [6/2518] Causes, 1950, State Records Authority of New South Wales, Kingswood.

5   R.J.W. Le Fevre in *Flanagan v. China Mutual Steam Navigation Co. Ltd.* – Commonwealth of Australia – Third party – 26 June 1950 – State Records of NSW Court Reporting Office; NRS 13713; Transcripts of Evidence, 1900-1960; [6/2518] Causes, 1950, State Records Authority of New South Wales, Kingswood.

6   Visit of *Idomeneus* to Sydney 13 January 1943 in A1196 58/501/102 PART 1 - Visit of M.Vs 'Idomeneus' and 'Birchbank' to Melbourne and Sydney Jan-Feb. 1943 (Compensation Claims etc.) - National Archives of Australia (Canberra).

7   Filmed interview with Stuart Glover, March 2005.

8   Report of the decontamination processes carried out by Flight Lieutenant A.H. Trewin on No. 1 Hold of M/V Idomeneus from 20th – 31st January 1943 Inclusive in A1196 58/501/102 PART 1 - Visit of M.V.s 'Idomeneus' and 'Birchbank' to Melbourne and Sydney Jan-Feb. 1943 (Compensation Claims etc.) Part 1 - National Archives of Australia (Canberra).

9   Interview with Ron Patfield, October 2012.

10 Interview with Iris Bourke, October 2012.

11 Ibid.

12 Ibid.

13 Ibid.

14 Report on the casualties produced and protective measures taken during the unloading of the MV Idomeneus and the MV Birchbank in A1196 9/501/32 Gas Warfare – Medical Aspects of Policy.

15 Flight Lieutenant T. Conlon Testimony, Court of Inquiry in A1196 58/501/102 PART 1 - Visit of M.V.s 'Idomeneus' and 'Birchbank' to Melbourne and Sydney Jan-Feb. 1943 (Compensation Claims etc.) Part 1 - National Archives of Australia (Canberra).

16 Official Log-Book – A Foreign-Going or a Home-Trade Ship – Official No. 149597, Port Liverpool 9 November 1942.
17 Minute Sheet 23 ; 5A in A1196 58/501/102 PART 1 - Visit of M.V.s 'Idomeneus' and 'Birchbank' to Melbourne and Sydney Jan-Feb. 1943 (Compensation Claims etc.) Part 1 - National Archives of Australia (Canberra).

Chapter 9

1 Court of Inquiry, 21 January 1943 in A1196 58/501/102 PART 1 - Visit of M.V.s 'Idomeneus' and 'Birchbank' to Melbourne and Sydney Jan-Feb. 1943 (Compensation Claims etc.) Part 1 - National Archives of Australia (Canberra).
2 R.J.W. Le Fèvre in *Pearce v. China Mutual Steam Navigation Co. Ltd.* – Commonwealth of Australia – Third party – 1 August 1950 – State Records of NSW Court Reporting Office; NRS 13713; Transcripts of Evidence, 1900-1960; [6/2523] Causes, 1950, State Records Authority of New South Wales, Kingswood.
3 R.J.W. Le Fevre in Court of Inquiry, 21 January 1943 in A1196 58/501/102 PART 1 - Visit of M.Vs 'Idomeneus' and 'Birchbank' to Melbourne and Sydney Jan-Feb. 1943 (Compensation Claims etc.) - National Archives of Australia (Canberra).
4 Ibid.
5 H.B. Freeman in Court of Inquiry, 21 January 1943 in A1196 58/501/102 PART 1 - Visit of M.Vs 'Idomeneus' and 'Birchbank' to Melbourne and Sydney Jan-Feb. 1943 (Compensation Claims etc.) - National Archives of Australia (Canberra).
6 H.F. McKenzie in Court of Inquiry, 21 January 1943 in A1196 58/501/102 PART 1 - Visit of M.Vs 'Idomeneus' and 'Birchbank' to Melbourne and Sydney Jan-Feb. 1943 (Compensation Claims etc.) - National Archives of Australia (Canberra).
7 W.F. Dark in Court of Inquiry, 21 January 1943 in A1196 58/501/102 PART 1 - Visit of M.Vs 'Idomeneus' and 'Birchbank' to Melbourne and Sydney Jan-Feb. 1943 (Compensation Claims etc.) - National Archives of Australia (Canberra).
8 Court of Inquiry, 21 January 1943 in A1196 58/501/102 PART 1 - Visit of M.Vs 'Idomeneus' and 'Birchbank' to Melbourne and Sydney Jan-Feb. 1943 (Compensation Claims etc.) - National Archives of Australia (Canberra).
9 Ibid.

10 Visit of *Idomeneus* to Sydney 13 January 1943 in A1196 58/501/102 PART 1 - Visit of M.V.s 'Idomeneus' and 'Birchbank' to Melbourne and Sydney Jan-Feb. 1943 (Compensation Claims etc.) Part 1 - National Archives of Australia (Canberra).

11 Injuries to Workmen – MV Idomeneus in A1196 58/501/102 PART 1 - Visit of M.V.s 'Idomeneus' and 'Birchbank' to Melbourne and Sydney Jan-Feb. 1943 (Compensation Claims etc.) Part 1 - National Archives of Australia (Canberra).

12 Interview with Joan Hunt, June 2010.

13 G.A. Williams in State Coroner's NRS 345, Coroners' inquest papers, 1851-1963; 22 February 1943. Inquest on Dead Body of Andrew William Williams, State Records Authority of New South Wales, Kingswood.

14 S. Sheldon in State Coroner's NRS 345, Coroners' inquest papers, 1851-1963; 22 February 1943. Inquest on Dead Body of Andrew William Williams, State Records Authority of New South Wales, Kingswood.

15 Coronial Inquiry into the Death of Andrew William Williams following his Employment as Wharf Labourer in Unloading Chemical from MV Idomeneus. 1 March 1943 in A1196 58/501/102 PART 1 - Visit of M.Vs 'Idomeneus' and 'Birchbank' to Melbourne and Sydney Jan-Feb. 1943 (Compensation Claims etc.) - National Archives of Australia (Canberra).

16 Untitled D Arm notes, 8 March 1943 in A1196 58/501/102 PART 1 - Visit of M.V.s 'Idomeneus' and 'Birchbank' to Melbourne and Sydney Jan-Feb. 1943 (Compensation Claims etc.) Part 1 - National Archives of Australia (Canberra).

17 Assessment of Andrew's mental state was also assisted by Dr Matthew Friedman.

Chapter 10

1 Description of the *Idomeneus*' return journey in *A Merchant Fleet in War. Alfred Holt & Co., 1939-1945*, by S.W. Roskill, Collins, 1962.

2 Filmed interview with Stuart Glover, March 2005.

3 There are many articles on the effects of mustard on the health. One recent example is 'Review – Chronic health effects of sulphur mustard exposure with special reference to Iranian veterans', *Emerging Health Threats Journal*, Vol. 1, 2008, p. 7, at: http://www.eht-forum.org/ehtj/journal/v1/pdf/ehtj08007a.pdf

Dr Andy Robertson pointed me to Edward Lucci's 'Vesicants', Chapter 20 in *Physician's Guide to Terrorist Attack*, Michael Roy (ed), Springer-Verlag Press, New York, 2003. This is a useful guide presenting the latest research on the medical effects of mustard. See also C. Pechura and D. Rall (eds.), *Veterans at risk – The Health Effects of Mustard Gas and Lewisite*, National Academy Press, Washington, 1993.

4 J.T. Flanagan in *Flanagan v. China Mutual Steam Navigation Co. Ltd.* – Commonwealth of Australia – Third party – 26 June 1950 – State Records of NSW Court Reporting Office; NRS 13713; Transcripts of Evidence, 1900-1960; [6/2518] Causes, 1950, State Records Authority of New South Wales, Kingswood.

5 W.R. Swinton in *Swinton v. China Mutual Steam Navigation Co. Ltd.* – Commonwealth of Australia – Third party – 8 August 1950 – State Records of NSW Court Reporting Office; NRS 13713; Transcripts of Evidence, 1900-1960; [6/2524] Causes, 1950, State Records Authority of New South Wales, Kingswood.

6 Escape of Mustard Gas on MV Idomeneus in January, 1943 – Claim by H.F. McKenzie in A1196 58/501/102 PART 1 - Visit of M.V.s 'Idomeneus' and 'Birchbank' to Melbourne and Sydney Jan-Feb. 1943 (Compensation Claims etc.) Part 1 - National Archives of Australia (Canberra).

7 My thanks to Les Parsons' daughter, Eileen Kaye Charushenko, for providing access to Les' medical records. Also filmed interview with Les Parsons.

8 Les Parsons' medical records.

9 A casualty list is included at the back of the book which lists only those identified as poisoned by mustard gas.

10 R.J.W. Le Fèvre, Notes, Folio 34, 17 March 1943 in A1196 58/501/102 PART 1 - Visit of M.V.s 'Idomeneus' and 'Birchbank' to Melbourne and Sydney Jan-Feb. 1943 (Compensation Claims etc.) Part 1 - National Archives of Australia (Canberra).

11 Minute by Defence Committee at Meeting held on Thursday, 29th April 1943. No. 72/1743 – Discharge From Ships of Chemical Warfare Ammunition. A816 9/301/93 -Discharge from ships of chemical warfare ammunition at Australian wharves - National Archives of Australia (Canberra).

Chapter 11

1 Unless otherwise stated the court extracts are sourced from *Flanagan v. China Mutual Steam Navigation Co. Ltd.* – Commonwealth of Australia – Third party – 26 June 1950 – State Records of NSW Court Reporting Office; NRS 13713; Transcripts of Evidence, 1900-1960; [6/2518] Causes, 1950, State Records Authority of New South Wales, Kingswood; *Pearce v.*

China Mutual Steam Navigation Co. Ltd. – Commonwealth of Australia – Third party – 1 August 1950 – State Records of NSW Court Reporting Office; NRS 13713; Transcripts of Evidence, 1900-1960; [6/2523] Causes, 1950, State Records Authority of New South Wales, Kingswood; *Swinton v. China Mutual Steam Navigation Co. Ltd.* – Commonwealth of Australia – Third party – 8 August 1950 – State Records of NSW Court Reporting Office; NRS 13713; Transcripts of Evidence, 1900-1960; [6/2524] Causes, 1950, State Records Authority of New South Wales, Kingswood. Legal interpretation assisted (considerably) by my brother David.

2. Visit of *Idomeneus* to Sydney 13 January 1943 in A1196 58/501/102 PART 1 - Visit of M.V.s 'Idomeneus' and 'Birchbank' to Melbourne and Sydney Jan-Feb. 1943 (Compensation Claims etc.) Part 1 - National Archives of Australia (Canberra).

3. Ibid.

4. He actually means the MV (motor vessel) *Idomeneus*, not SS (steam ship).

5. Defence – Claim by Stevedores Engaged on Idomeneus 1943 in A462 379/5 - National Archives of Australia (Canberra).

6. Ibid.

7. Unsigned. Defence – Claim by Stevedores Engaged on Idomeneus 1943 in A462 379/5 - National Archives of Australia (Canberra).

8. Re MV *Idomeneus* in A1196 58/501/102 PART 1 - Visit of M.V.s 'Idomeneus' and 'Birchbank' to Melbourne and Sydney Jan-Feb. 1943 (Compensation Claims etc.) Part 1 - National Archives of Australia (Canberra).

9. *Swinton v China Mutual Steam Navigation Company Limited and the Ocean Steamship Company Limited*: Commonwealth of Australia Third Party, Judgement in A1196 58/501/102 PART 1 - Visit of M.V.s 'Idomeneus' and 'Birchbank' to Melbourne and Sydney Jan-Feb. 1943 (Compensation Claims etc.) Part 1 - National Archives of Australia (Canberra). Reproduced in *The Australian Law Journal*, Vol. 25, November 1951, p. 515.

10. Escape of Mustard Gas on MV Idomeneus in January 1943: Claim by H.F. McKenzie in A1196 58/501/102 PART 1 - Visit of M.V.s 'Idomeneus' and 'Birchbank' to Melbourne and Sydney Jan-Feb. 1943 (Compensation Claims etc.) Part 1 - National Archives of Australia (Canberra).

11. Untitled Memorandum for The Official Secretary, Office of the High Commissioner for Australia, London, England in A1196 58/501/102 PART 1 - Visit of M.V.s 'Idomeneus' and 'Birchbank' to Melbourne and Sydney Jan-Feb. 1943 (Compensation Claims etc.) Part 1 - National Archives of Australia (Canberra).

ENDNOTES

12 Supreme Court Action: *Minor v China Mutual Steam Navigation Co Ltd & ORS*: The Commonwealth Third Party, 21 August 1952 in A1196 58/501/102 PART 1 - Visit of M.Vs 'Idomeneus' and 'Birchbank' to Melbourne and Sydney Jan-Feb. 1943 (Compensation Claims etc.) - National Archives of Australia (Canberra).

13 *Flanagan v The China Mutual Steam Navigation Co Ltd* and Others – Claim For Ex Gratia Payment. A1196 58/501/102 PART 1 - Visit of M.V.s 'Idomeneus' and 'Birchbank' to Melbourne and Sydney Jan-Feb. 1943 (Compensation Claims etc.) Part 1 - National Archives of Australia (Canberra)..

14 SS *Idomeneus*, 17 February 1955 in A462 379/5 - Defence. Claim by stevedores engaged on 'Idomeneus' (1943) - National Archives of Australia (Canberra) – Digitised.

15 Whose symptoms included vomiting, conjunctivitis, burns to the throat, skin and larynx in A462 379/5 - Defence. Claim by stevedores engaged on 'Idomeneus' (1943) - National Archives of Australia (Canberra) – Digitised.

16 SS *Idomeneus*: Claim by South British Insurance Co Ltd for Compensation Paid to O'Brien and Williams, 14 December 1953 in A462 379/5 - Defence. Claim by stevedores engaged on 'Idomeneus' (1943) - National Archives of Australia (Canberra) – Digitised.

17 Claim by Leo Joseph McDonald – Injuries Due to Mustard Gas on MV Idomeneus, Melbourne 1943, 4 September 1943 in A462 379/5 - Defence. Claim by stevedores engaged on 'Idomeneus' (1943) - National Archives of Australia (Canberra) – Digitised.

18 *Idomeneus* January 1943. Mr L.J. McDonald – Claim for Compensation, 12 May 1953 n A462 379/5 - Defence. Claim by stevedores engaged on 'Idomeneus' (1943) - National Archives of Australia (Canberra) – Digitised.

19 Re *Idomeneus* Claims, 2 February 1953 in A462 379/5 - Defence. Claim by stevedores engaged on 'Idomeneus' (1943) - National Archives of Australia (Canberra) – Digitised.

20 SS *Idomeneus*: Claim by South British Insurance Co Ltd for Compensation Paid to O'Brien and Williams, 14 December 1953 in A462 379/5 - Defence. Claim by stevedores engaged on 'Idomeneus' (1943) - National Archives of Australia (Canberra) – Digitised.

Chapter 12

1. Exhibit 2 in A10071, 1951/13 PART 2 - *SWINTON William Robert versus The China Mutual Steam Navigation Company Limited*; Ocean Steamship Company Limited; Commonwealth of Australia - National Archives of Australia (Canberra) – Digitised.

2. Letter to Mr Menzies from Ministry of Transport, London, 9 January 1951 in A1196 58/501/102 PART 1 - Visit of M.V.s 'Idomeneus' and 'Birchbank' to Melbourne and Sydney Jan-Feb. 1943 (Compensation Claims etc.) Part 1 - National Archives of Australia (Canberra).

3. R.J.W. Le Fevre in *Swinton v. China Mutual Steam Navigation Co. Ltd.* – Commonwealth of Australia – Third party – 8 August 1950 – State Records of NSW Court Reporting Office; NRS 13713; Transcripts of Evidence, 1900-1960; [6/2524] Causes, 1950, State Records Authority of New South Wales, Kingswood.

4. Filmed interview with Les Parsons, March 2005.

5. H.F. McKenzie in *Flanagan v. China Mutual Steam Navigation Co. Ltd.* – Commonwealth of Australia – Third party – 26 June 1950 – State Records of NSW Court Reporting Office; NRS 13713; Transcripts of Evidence, 1900-1960; [6/2518] Causes, 1950, State Records Authority of New South Wales, Kingswood.

6. R.J.W. Le Fèvre in *Pearce v. China Mutual Steam Navigation Co. Ltd.* – Commonwealth of Australia – Third party – 1 August 1950 – State Records of NSW Court Reporting Office; NRS 13713; Transcripts of Evidence, 1900-1960; [6/2523] Causes, 1950, State Records Authority of New South Wales, Kingswood.

7. H.F. McKenzie in *Flanagan v. China Mutual Steam Navigation Co. Ltd.* – Commonwealth of Australia – Third party – 26 June 1950 – State Records of NSW Court Reporting Office; NRS 13713; Transcripts of Evidence, 1900-1960; [6/2518] Causes, 1950, State Records Authority of New South Wales, Kingswood.

8. Email, 9 January 2008, Arthur Dark to author.

9. Minute Sheet. Folio 23, 2 (b) in A1196 58/501/102 PART 1 - Visit of M.V.s 'Idomeneus' and 'Birchbank' to Melbourne and Sydney Jan-Feb. 1943 (Compensation Claims etc.) Part 1 - National Archives of Australia (Canberra).

10. Filmed interview with Geoff Burn, March 2005.

ENDNOTES

Chapter 13

1. Mount Bundy is also spelled Mount Bundey.
2. Another possibility is it came from the nearby dedicated chemical weapons RAAF depot known as '88 Mile' which was just over 30 kilometres south of where the bomb was found. However, Army weapons were not stored there. This has been confirmed by the chemical warfare armourers who worked at the depot as well as by archival records which contain an inventory of the site. The former ammunition depot at Snake Creek is also worth considering. Established in 1943 by the Royal Australian Navy it was unknown as a chemical weapons storage area until 2006 when a routine inspection revealed a number of rusted drums suspected to be mustard gas storage containers. How these came to be here is unclear but, given its location as only two kilometres north-west of Adelaide River, it is in close proximity to the scene of the fatality. The last option relates to the US Navy which occupied Mount Bundy Station from 20 December 1944 to 30 September 1945. The US Navy used Mount Bundy as a transmitting station, with an antennae erected for the 'Fleet Radio'. There was no logical reason this unit would have housed any American let alone Australian chemical weapons.
3. A third, that the weapons were destined for the use in trials is theoretically possible, but less likely than the two scenarios discussed.
4. Information kindly provided by Stuart Hadaway at the Air Historical Branch (RAF).
5. Suggested to the author by Major Keith Parker. Thanks to Major Parker and Major Kevin O'Rourke for their many discussions on how the bomb came to be at Mount Bundy.
6. Report by Major E.F. Lewis, Ordnance School Bandiana, 1964. Excavation at the end of the imprint resulted in the recovery of an unfired fuse tube.
7. ASA grenades 63 smoke. A number of 30 lb mustard bombs have been recovered from Mount Bundy Station with 88 Mile the most likely point of origin.
8. Report by Major E.F. Lewis, Ordnance School Bandiana, 1964.
9. Information from the very helpful Doug Tilley who 'lives and breathes' Mount Bundy Station.
10. N. Carter, History of Directorate of Military Operations (Chemical Warfare Section) Land Headquarters in AWM54 179/1/1 Australian War Memorial.

11 A visit to 88 Mile by the gas wing could not be ruled out due its proximity to Mount Bundy Station.

12 On issue to any of the 150 units located in the Adelaide River area during World War II.

13 Given the availability of cartridge cases remaining from the war, it is likely that the .22 rifle was a wildcat version of the British .303 calibre.

14 Although the fact that Nandor covered himself ensured his demise, it was his curiosity and its accessibility that led him to examine it. Any inquisitive child or adult, on opening such a device, would be in grave, if not mortal danger.

15 Somogyi, Nander (sic) [Alien Registration File] – E40 SOMOGYI N – 1964, National Archives of Australia – Darwin; Somogyi Nandor born 21 October 1929 – A12045 731 – 1950 - National Archives of Australia – Canberra and Somogyi Nondor (sic) – Nationality: Hungarian – Arrived Sydney per *Nelly* 30 December 1950 – D4881 SOMOGYI NANDOR – 30 Dec 1950 to 31 Dec 1976, National Archives of Australia – Adelaide.

16 Interview with Donald Honeysett, December 2011.

17 Ibid.

18 Report of Donald Honeysett, 18 August 1960 in Somogyi, Nander (sic) [Alien Registration File] – E40 SOMOGYI N – 1964, National Archives of Australia – Darwin.

19 Ibid.

20 Interview with Bill Ross, October 2011.

21 Ibid.

22 Interview with Tommy Faucett, October 2011.

23 Interview with Harold Darwen, October 2011.

24 Interview with Bill Ross, October 2011.

25 Interview with Bruce Mangleson, September 2011.

26 Testimony, G.E. Hutchings in Northern Territory Archives Service – Coroner's Court, Darwin – F864 – 18/64 Inquest into the death of Nandor Somogyi – died on 13-10-1964. Inquest held 5-11-1964.

27 Ibid.

28 Testimony, L.A. Cox in Northern Territory Archives Service – Coroner's Court, Darwin – F864 – 18/64 Inquest into the death of Nandor Somogyi – died on 13-10-1964. Inquest held 5-11-1964. Also numerous interviews with the author.

29 Ibid.

ENDNOTES

30 Testimony, G.E. Hutchings in Northern Territory Archives Service – Coroner's Court, Darwin – F864 – 18/64 Inquest into the death of Nandor Somogyi – died on 13-10-1964. Inquest held 5-11-1964.

31 Testimony, K.J. Smith in Northern Territory Archives Service – Coroner's Court, Darwin – F864 – 18/64 Inquest into the death of Nandor Somogyi – died on 13-10-1964. Inquest held 5-11-1964; Northern Territory Archives Service – Police Station, Batchelor – NTRS 2080 - Day Journals (Previously Registered as F1331) – 1954 to 1995 – Batchelor Day Journal 12/9/1964 to 6/3/1966. Also numerous interviews with author.

32 Ibid.

33 Testimony, D.A. Luke in Northern Territory Archives Service – Coroner's Court, Darwin – F864 – 18/64 Inquest into the death of Nandor Somogyi – died on 13-10-1964. Inquest held 5-11-1964. Filmed interview with David Luke, 2008.

34 According to John Killingley, a cylinder may have been examined at the Rum Jungle lab at some stage. Killingley relates, 'I believe the [Batchelor] Clinic asked the Principal at the school to take a look at it and he, apparently, sniffed it and got some of the liquid on his nose, resulting in a large blister. Realising that this was a dangerous substance they then sent the khaki canister (with black-stencilled numbers and letters) to our lab at Rum Jungle (I was a chemist there until late 1963) where we gingerly put in a fume-hood and did a literature search on mustard gas and other possibilities. A few careful physical measurements and tests by chief chemist Merv Allman and chemist Harry Stockley then confirmed it to be mustard gas (sadly Merv and Harry are no longer alive).'

35 Filmed interview with David Luke, 2008.

36 Interview with Les Cox, June 2010.

37 Testimony, J.R. Haywood in Northern Territory Archives Service – Coroner's Court, Darwin – F864 – 18/64. Inquest into the death of Nandor Somogyi – died on 13-10-1964. Inquest held 5-11-1964. Interview with John Haywood, June 2010.

38 Testimony, J.M. Crotty in Northern Territory Archives Service – Coroner's Court, Darwin – F864 – 18/64. Inquest into the death of Nandor Somogyi – died on 13-10-1964. Inquest held 5-11-1964. Interview with John Crotty, August 2010.

39 Interview with Les Cox, June 2010.

40 Filmed interview with David Luke, 2008.

41 Filmed interview with Bill Lewis, March 2005.

42 Filmed interview with David Luke, 2008.

Photographs and Maps

Cover: Observer examining a 25 lb gas shell at Singelton during a trial in 1943
Back cover: Phosgene bombs from the *Idomeneus* being destroyed at Long Airfield, Northern Territory, in 1946

1	Chemical Research Unit mascot card produced in Bowen in 1944. The Chemical Research Unit provided aerial support for chemical weapons field trials in Queensland	viii
2	Australian soldiers gassed by mustard gas lie in the open at an overcrowded aid post near Bois De l'Abbe, France, 27 May 1918. They were gassed during operations at Villers-Bretonneux. This direct experience of gas was to profoundly influence Australia's desire to procure a retaliatory stock of war gases during World War II. A note by Sergeant A. Brooksbank, Gas NCO, 10th Australian Infantry Brigade, indicates that this is an example of what should not be done. The casualties should have removed their contaminated garments as they are continually being exposed to mustard gas vapour impregnated in their clothing	x
3	Observers watching the conflagration at Bari in 1943	xii
4	Australian soldiers at the firing line during a practice range outside As Samawah, 2006	xv
5	250 lb phosgene cylinders recovered from the former RAAF storage depot at Talmoi in 1990	xvii
6	Phosgene gas venting from cylinders at Talmoi during disposal operations in 1946	xviii
7	Mustard gas burns on a human guinea pig in experiments undertaken in Queensland	xix
8	Gas mask drill in London	xx
9	Intelligence photo circulated in Australia showing alleged used use of chemical weapons in China by the Japanese	xxii
10	Intelligence photo circulated in Australia showing alleged used use of chemical weapons in China by the Japanese	xxii

PHOTOGRAPHS AND MAPS

11	Intelligence photo circulated in Australia showing alleged used use of chemical weapons in China by the Japanese	xxii
12	Gas mask captured at Milne Bay, Papua New Guinea in 1942	xxii
13	*Idomeneus*	xxv
14	Andrew Williams	xxvi
15	Blue Funnel Line postcard	1
16	*Titan*	2
17	Walter Francis Dark	3
18	*Ixion*	4
19	Stuart Glover	6
20	*Idomeneus*	7
21	Mustard gas drums piled at Talmoi awaiting disposal by fire in 1945	8
22	250 lb phosgene bomb	10
23	U boat U-518 under attack by Royal Air Force Squadron in 1943	11
24	*Empire Sailor*	12
25	A field trial with phosgene gas in Queensland	13
26	Wing Commander Raymond Le Fèvre	15
27	250 lb phosgene bombs from the *Idomeneus* await destruction after being recovered from Marrangaroo Army Base	17
28	Japanese prisoners of war carry crates of munitions from the Japanese ammunition store in the Batu caves. Before Japanese use it was a RAF chemical weapons store	18
29	Arthur Trewin	20
30	RAAF recuits undertaking a gas drill	23
31	HMAS *Australia*	24
32	'Gerry' Forsgate (*Idomeneus* 3rd Officer) & Wife Betty	26
33	Mustard gas burns sustained by a human guinea pig in experiments undertaken in Queensland	28
34	Stuart Glover	29
35	Two women war workers moving a bag of soda ash in a chemical factory at Norwich, Manchester	31
36	Anti-Gas Ointment	32
37	Harold Freeman	33

38	Central Wharf Stevedoring Company	34
39	A winchman taking a break, 1941	37
40	Andrew Williams' Residence	40
41	Clontarf Coal Lumpers Union Picnic, 30 October 1907	41
42	Elsie Williams	42
43	Gilbert Williams	44
44	Dr Colin Ross	45
45	Les Parsons	46
46	Richard Harris	49
47	Margaret Miller	51
48	D2 Block, Royal Prince Alfred Hospital	52
49	Royal Prince Alfred Hospital Ambulance	52
50	Jean Williams	54
51	Joy Rablah	55
52	Typical ward layout, Royal Prince Alfred Hospital	57
53	A Williams' picnic	58
54	Williams family members present on the day Andrew died	59
55	Geoff Burn with 250 lb bombs at Marrangaroo tunnel	63
56	Wrist blisters from mustard gas	64
57	Ken Heydon	65
58	Cranes used to hoist the mustard gas drums from No. 1 Hold on the *Idomeneus*	66
59	Mustard gas drums from the *Idomeneus* at Glenbrook tunnel	68
60	Tim Miers	69
61	Siding at Glenbrook station used to offload mustard gas.	71
62	Truck used by Harry Evans to deliver mustard gas from the siding to the Glenbrook tunnel	71
63	Glenbrook tunnel being used as a mushroom farm by the Rowes in 1940	71
64	Mustard gas in the east cutting at Glenbrook tunnel	73
65	Ron Hughes	75
66	Phosgene bombs from the *Idomeneus* at Marrangaroo tunnel	77
67	Phosgene shed foundations at Marrangaroo Tunnel today	77
68	No. 8/9 Pier at Glebe Island	80

PHOTOGRAPHS AND MAPS

69	A number of aid raid precaution items including bleaching powder in a bucket	81
70	Ron Patfield	84
71	Iris Bourke	85
72	Frank Bourke	85
73	Frank and Iris Bourke	87
74	The devastating effects of mustard gas on the penis and scrotum. These injuries were sustained by human guinea pigs in experiments undertaken in Queensland	88
75	The devastating effects of mustard gas on the penis and scrotum. These injuries were sustained by human guinea pigs in experiments undertaken in Queensland	88
76	The devastating effects of mustard gas on the penis and scrotum. These injuries were sustained by human guinea pigs in experiments undertaken in Queensland	88
77	Harold Freeman	92
78	The effect of mustard gas on the eyes - conjunctivitis	95
79	Former Coroner's Court at The Rocks, Sydney	97
80	Diagrams from Coroner's Inquest showing the path Andrew Williams took from the toilet window at Royal Prince Alfred hospital	99
81	The wall from which Andrew Williams fell	100
82	*Lakonikos*	103
83	Les Parsons cross eyed after being exposed to mustard gas on the *Idomeneus*	104
84	*Idomeneus* veterans Les Parsons and Geoff Burn being filmed at Glenbrook tunnel for an upcoming documentary	107
85	Former New South Wales Supreme Court	109
86	Professor Raymond Le Fèvre in his Sydney University days	111
87	Walter Francis Dark	113
88	Court testimony from Professor Raymond Le Fèvre	114
89	X-Ray at Royal Prince Alfred Hospital, circa 1936	117
90	Sir Robert Gordon Menzies	119
91	Group Captain C W Pearce	120
92	Sir Dudley Williams	123
93	Sir Wilfred Fullagar,	123

94	Sir William Webb	123
95	Sir Owen Dixon	123
96	Sir Frank Kitto	123
97	No. 8 pier, Walsh Bay	125
98	The now abandoned Marrangaroo tunnel	127
99	Glenbrook tunnel today	130
100	4.2 inch chemical weapon found on the Atherton Tablelands in 1990	132
101	Marrangaroo chemical weapons extraction (5 photos)	134
102	Idomeneus veteran Stuart Glover at the unveiling of the Chemical Warfare Armourer's plaque at the Glenbrook War Memorial on Remembrance Day 2009	136
103	Nandor Somogyi	138
104	6 lb mustard gas bomb	140
105	Mt Bundy homestead, distant view	141
106	Mt Bundy homestead, close up	141
107	A P-40 Kittyhawk on a Mt Bundy Station airfield	142
108	**Map** of Mt Bundy station, showing where the 6 lb bomb was found in relation to Nandor's hut	143
109	United States Base Section 1, Motor Pool on Mt Bundy. Station. One of many units based at this location	144
110	Mustard gas blisters sustained by a human guinea pig in experiments undertaken in Queensland	145
111	The passenger card of Nandor Somogyi	146
112	Snowy Mountains hydro electric scheme	149
113	A bark hut at Borroloola	150
114	Mount Bundy Station manager Bill Ross	151
115	Adelaide River Police Station	152
116	Harold Darwen at Adelaide River Police Station	154
117	Batchelor Clinic, external view	156
118	Batchelor Clinic, second consulting room	156
119	Les Cox	157
120	Batchelor School, 1960. The close-by medical clinic is indicated by the arrow. Head teacher Max Koehne and wife Joan (infant teacher) are present	158

PHOTOGRAPHS AND MAPS

121	Batchelor School, 1960. The science laboratory, where the mustard gas was analysed, is to the far right (louvre windows)	158
122	Kevin Smith	159
123	Major David Luke	161
124	6 lb Mustard Gas Bomb	162
125	Newspaper headlines. Major Bill Lewis examining the killer bomb	165
126	Darwin Hospital, ward view.	167
127	Major Bill Lewis in a 'Vapor Proof Suit', supplied by the Melbourne Fire Brigade	168
128	Ken Heydon	171
129	Documentary maker Jorge Farre with Chemical Warfare Armourer Frank Moran	171
130	Phosgene Bombs from the Idomeneus Being Destroyed at Long Airfield in 1946	207

Phosgene Bombs from the Idomeneus Being
Destroyed at Long Airfield in 1946
Chemical Warfare Armourers

Acknowledgements

Thank you to;

Those who were there, this is your story; Iris Bourke, Frank Burkin, Geoff Burn, Les Cox, John Crotty, Harold Darwen, Harry Evans, Tommy Faucett, Kevin Garr, Stuart Glover, John Haywood, Ken Heydon, Phyllis Heydon, Donald Honeysett, Ron Hughes, Joan Hunt, Bill Lewis, David Luke, Bruce Mangleson, Denzel McManus, Tim Miers, Margaret Miller, Ron Patfield, Les Parsons, Coilin Raymond, Bill Ross, Kevin Smith, Olive Tampe and Arthur Trewin

The relatives of the players; Jane Campbell Allan, Eileen Kaye Charushenko, Arthur Dark, Brian Forsgate, Justine Glover, Nick Glover, Sue Lockett, Beryl Miller, Elizabeth Russ, June Trewin and Tracy Wales.

The staff at the Royal Prince Alfred Museum and Archives; Helen Croll, Kathryn Hillier and Vanessa Witton.

Graham Rees for assisting in tracking the retired Northern Territory police.

Andy Robertson for the foreword. Army Historian Roger Lee, Cathy McCullagh for editing (again) and Dr Andrew Richardson at the Army History Unit.

Mr Brian Barkworth, Major Kevin O'Rourke and Major Keith Parker.

My brothers; David for help in understanding the trials and Alan for locating the Dark medal folios at Guildhall.

Doug Tilley and Ros Jones.

The staff at National Archives of Australia, State Records Authority of New South Wales and Northern Territory Archives Service.

All those who supplied photos.

Jorge Farre for filming Australia's chemical warfare veterans for the upcoming documentary.

Index

A

Adelaide River 139, 144, 147, 153, 155, 160-161, 163, 168
    Police Station *152*, 153, *154*, 155, 160
Ainsworth, Merchantman Barry 12
Albury Ammunition Depot 139
Alexander, Percy 21-23, 25, 110, 124
Alfred Holt & Co 109
anti-gas ointment *32*, 33, 39
Armentières x
Ascot Vale 25, 28
atropine 25, 51, 83
Australia
    chemical weapons, and 19, 27, 83, 107-108, 116, 126, 133, 169
    Commonwealth *see* Commonwealth of Australia
    mustard gas in xv-xvi, xxi, 83, 89, 102, 113-115
    refugees 148
Australian Army x, xv
5 Advanced Ammunition Depot (5AAD) 139
51 Forward Ammunition Depot (FAD) 139

B

Bari xii
Batavia 21
Batchelor 155
    hospital 155-157, *156*, 164, 166
    school 157, *158*
Batu Caves 18, *18*, 74
Bavarian *11th Army* xi
Bell, Naval Gunner 13
Binder, Billy 154
Birkenhead Docks 7
Blakemore, Wing Commander George 46, 61
bleaching powder *81*
blindness xvii, 25, 42-43, 48-49, 51, 54, 56, 96, 100, 105-106
blistering x, xvii, *xix*, 51, *64*, 72, 74, 86, 106, 126, *145*, 155, 159, 164
Blue Funnel Line *1*, 1-2, 4, 8, 10, 21, 30, 34, 115, 118, 125, 130-131
Blue Star Line 9
Board of Reference 35
Borroloola 150-151, *150*
Bourke, Frank 85-87, *85*, *87*
Bourke, Iris 85-87, *85*, *87*
Bourke, Kathleen 85
Bourlon Wood x
Britain
    arming for war xx
    chemical weapons xi, xix-xxi
British Army
    15th Division x
    55th Division x
    mustard gas, use of xi, xvii
British Promise 11, 14
British Renown 12
Burcher, Honour 151
Burkin, Frank 85, 133
Burn, Geoff 62, *63*, *107*, 133, 136

burns xi, xvi, 25, 27, *28*, 50, 53, 61, *64*, 67, 72, 86, 89, 98, 105, 130, 155, 159-160, 164

C

Calverly, Mr 4
Cape Race 11
Carnarvon 149-150
Carter, Naval Gunner 13
Central Wharf Stevedoring Company 34
Chemical Research Unit
    A Nasty Brew - mascot card xviii
chemical weapons 128, *132*
    Australia, and xxi, xxiii, 19, 27, 83, 107-108, 116, 126-127, 133, 169
    banning xi, xix
    disposal 139, 142
    gas cylinders *xvii*, *xviii*
    sites xv-xvi, 133, 136, 139-143
    training 143-144
Chemical Weapons Convention 136-137
China
    Japanese in xi, xix-xx, xxiii, 19
China Mutual Steam Navigation Company Ltd 109
chlorine gas xvii-xviii
Clemens, Mr 110, 120
coal lumping 40
Collins, Dr 97
Comanche 12
Commonwealth of Australia 16
    compensation, liability for 105, 109-110, 115, 119-120, 122-124, 131
Concord Repatriation Hospital 86
conjunctivitis x-xi, 25-26, 31, 47, 126
Coroner's Inquest
    Court *97*
    Somogyi's death 169
    Williams' death 95-101, 128
Court of Inquiry (RAAF) 91-95, 98, 112, 131
Cox, Les 156-159, *157*, 162, 164, 166-167
Crotty, Dr John 164

D

Dark, Arthur 130
Dark, Captain Walter Francis xxiv, 2-7, *3*, 11, 14, 47, 91, 102, *113*, 118, 128-131
    character 2-3, 19, 130-131
    decontamination of *Idomeneus* 79-82, 89
    internal RAAF inquiry 94
    Melbourne, in 15, 24, 27
    Sydney, in 29-35, 39
Dark, Victor 130
Darwen, Harold *154*, 155, 168
Darwin 150-152 163,
    bombing 143
    Hospital 160-161, 164, 166-167, *167*
decontamination 32, 79-90-91, 126-127, 129
delirium 100-101
Dixon, Sir Owen 121, *121*
Duck, William 22, 25, 110, 124

INDEX

E

Egypt viii, 18
Einstein, Albert 125
Empire Sailor 12, 12-13, 16
English, Arthur 33-37, 42
Ethiopia xx
Evans, Harry 70
Eynon, William James Stewart 37, 39, 47
   legal action 118-119, 122, 131

F

Farre, Jorge *171*
Faucett, Tommy 155
Ferguson, Mr 110, 112, 114-115, 118-119
Finke Bay 152-153
Flanagan, Stevedore J 34, 45, 47-48,
   compensation 123
   illness, continuing 103-104
   legal action 109-110, 115, 118
Forsgate, Betty *26*
Forsgate, Hugh 'Gerry' 25, *26*, 65, 102
France
   chemical weapons xi
Freeman, Flying Officer Harold 32-33, *33*, 37, 39, 44, *92*,
internal RAAF inquiry 91, 93-94
Fullagar, Sir Wilfred 121, *121*

G

G1 phosgene bombs *see* phosgene

Garr, Kevin 63, 133
gas drill *xx*
gas masks xx, xxiv, 16, 22, *23*, 30-32, 36, 37, 45, 70, 91-92, 94, 98, 110, 114, 118-119, 122, 129-130
Geneva Protocol 1925 xi, xix, xxiii, 126, 132
German Army *see also* Bavarian Army x, xvii
   mustard gas, use of
Germany
   chemical weapons xi, xxi
Gillanders, Stevedore J 34, 123
Glenbrook 69-70, *71*, 72, 92
   tunnel 68, *71*, 72-74, *73*, *130*
Glover, Stuart xviii, 2, 6-7, *6*, 10, 29, *29*, 37, 47-48, 62, 79-80, 83, 102-103, *136*
Gorrill, Major 115-116
Gregory, Captain 152
Grose, Captain 17, 21-22, 24, 114
Group 13 cargo 5
Guthrie, Frederick xi

H

Hamilton, Flight Lieutenant 89
Harding, Flight Lieutenant 91
Harris, Richard 49, *49*, 57
Harriss, Mr 158, 164, 166-167
Haywood, John 164
Heatherington, Matron 96
Henderson, Chief Officer 12-14, 16-17
Herron, Justice 115, 118
Heydon, Ken 63-67, *65*, *171*

'The *Idomeneus*' 170
Heydon, Phyllis 50-51, 53, 67
Hezle, Bill 147, 152, 155
Hindenburg Line xi
HMAS *Australia* 24, *24*
Holmes, Sergeant Frank 160, 163
Holt, Alfred 1, 160, 163
Honeysett, Senior Constable Donald 150-151
Hook, Inspector 160
Horton, Stevedore F 34, 123,
House, Professor Dr Philip 106
Hughes, Ron 74-75, *75*
Humphreys, Dave 136
Hungary 147-148
Hunt, Joan 96
Hutchings, Grace 155, 157, 159, 164

I

Idomeneus xvi, xviii, xxiv, *xxv*, 4-11, *8*, 14, 53, 95, 110, 133, 136, 170
  cargo 16, 67-68, 102, 136
  decontamination 20, 33, 79-99, 105, 126
  Glebe Island, at 62, 79, 112
  Melbourne, in 14, 20-28, 30, 102, 123, 125-126
  Sydney, in 27, 29, 34, 37-39, 46-47, 126
  torpedoes 102-103
Innisfail xii, 116
Instow 2-3
Iraq xiii, xiv, *xiv*, 166
Italy xii, xx
Ixion 4, *4*

J

Japan
  chemical weapons xi, xix-xx, *xxii*, xxiii, 19
  China, and xi, xx, xxii, 19
Jones, Abel Seaman 102
Jones, Stevedore T 34
Jones, Steward 14
Jose, Roger 151

K

Kearney, Stevedore J 34
Kelly, Sergeant Hilton 58-59, 95-96
Kitto, Sir Frank 121, *121*
Kittyhawk *142*, 143
Kuala Lumpur 18

L

Lakonikos 102-103, *103*
Le Fèvre, Wing Commander Raymond xxiv, *15*, 15-17, 22, 24, 31-32, 61, 68, 94, 107-108, *111*, 125-126, 169
  background 17-20
  certificate, issue of 35, 122, 129
  character 19, 132-133
  chemical test 35
  Coroner's Inquest 95
  decontamination and clean up 80-83, 105
  hospitalised men, visiting 26
  Idomeneus, inspection of 20-21, 25, 32, 39, 44-45
  illness, continuing 105

INDEX

internal RAAF inquiry 91-93, 98-100
legal action, during 110-118
Marrangaroo, at 75-76
moral responsibility 128-129, 32-133
Singapore, in 18
statements to police 26, 59
League of Nations xi
legal action 109-124
Lewis, Major Bill 168, *168*
Lightfoot, Wing Commander 27-28
Lithgow xvi
hospital 78
Liverpool Holt Company 1
Luke, Major David 160-164, *161*, 167-169

M

McDonald, Stevedore L 123
McFarlane, Professor Sandy 100
McKenzie, Harold 30-32, 34, 36-37, 39, 44, 113, 126, 129-130
illness, continuing 104
internal RAAF inquiry 93-94
Manchuria 19
Mangleson, Bruce 155, 160
Margaret River 153
Marrangaroo 20, 33, *63*, 75-77, *127*, 133, 136-137
chemical weapons extraction *134-135*
Martin, Squadron Leader 91
Mataranka 139

Menzies, Sir Robert Gordon 119-120, *119*, 169
Miers, Tim 69-70, *69*
Millar, Lieutenant Colonel Bob 163, 167
Miller, Beryl 59-61
Miller, Margaret 49-50, *51*
Miller, Naval Gunner 13
Minor, Stevedore E 34, 123
Moran, Frank *171*
Mount Bundy Station 139-144, *141*, 151-154, 161, 163-164
Muggivan, Stevedore P 34, 120
mustard gas (Y) xi, xvii-xviii, 5, 8-9, 16, 22-23, 30, 45, 81-82, 92, 97, 112-113, 115-116, 128, 160, 166, 168-169
bomb *140*, *162*
cancer and 106-107
casualties x, xi-xii, 46-47, 82-83, 89, 93-94, *95*, 98, 100-101, 107, 172-174
delayed effect 147
disposal 139, 142, 163
drums 8
first use x
heat, and 115-116, 126
smell 8-9, 20, 22, 25, 27, 32, 35-39, 70, 82, 91-92, 110, 116-117, 160

N

Nigerstrrom 76

O

Ocean Steam Ship Company Ltd 109

Oram, Mr 96

P

Palembang 18
Parsons, Les 44-46, *46*, 89, 95, *104*, *107*, 129, 131
    illness, continuing 105-106
Patfield, Ron 84-85, *84*
Pearce, Stevedore C W 34, 39, 43, 120
    illness, continuing 106
    legal action 113, 118-120
Pearl Harbour xxi
Perrett, Mr 151-152
phosgene xvii, *13*, 16, 31, 78-79, 107, 128
    bombs 5, 10, *10*, *17*, 37, 66, 75-77, *77*, 136-137
    delayed effects 14
    disposal 139
    exertion, and 14
photophobia 51, 83
pneumonia 106
Polydorus 11
Post Traumatic Stress Disorder (PTSD) 86, 100-101
Proserpine xii

Q

Quentin, Stevedore 34

R

Rablah, Joy 54-58, *55*, 96

Raymond, Colin 157-158, 166-167
Read, Flight Lieutenant 91
Reed, Constable 166
Relief Landing Ground (RLG) 141-142
respiratory distress xi, xviii, 25, 42, 51, 53, 56, 85, 97-98, 100, 106, 118, 124, 126
Roach, Stevedore W 34, 123
Ross, Bill 151-155, *151*
Ross, Dr Colin 43-44, *45*, 47-48, 54, 56
Rowe, Fanny 72, 74
Rowe, Gwen 72
Rowe, Herbert 72, 74
Royal Australian Air Force (RAAF) 19-20, 27, 30, 32, 37, 39, 46, 89, 131-133
    Ascot Vale hospital 25-26, 28
    Chemical Warfare Section 20,
    Glebe Island base 62, 69
    Glenbrook tunnel 72-74, 92
    internal inquiry 91-95, 98, 112
    Marrangaroo *63*, 75-77
    secrecy over chemical weapons xiv, 30, 55-56, 58-59, 61, 63, 66-67, 82, 96, 112-113, 125-128, 169
Royal Melbourne Hospital 27, 115, 126
Royal Prince Alfred Hospital xiv, 44, 46-47, 49-50, 53, 55, 58
    ambulance *52*
    D Block 50, *52*
    ward *57*
    x-ray *117*
Russ, Elizabeth 58

INDEX

Russell, Bill *59*
Russia xi

S

St Vincent's Hospital 47
Sheldon, Stratford 97-98
Shields, Security Officer 95-96
Sierra Leone 11
Silver Larch 18
Singapore, fall of xxi, 18
Sino-Japanese War xix
Smith, Dr Gordon 47
Smith, Kevin 159-160, *159*, 166
Smith, Stevedore A 34, 123
Smithers, Sammy, 34, 37, 39
Snowy Mountains Hydro Electric Scheme 148, *149*
soda ash 30, *31*, 35, 38, 40, 43, 91-93, 113, 132
Somogyi, Nandor xvi, 139, 145-169
    background 147-149
    passenger card *146*
South British Insurance Company Limited 124
Spiteri, Stevedore C 34, 123
SS *John Harvey* xii, *xii*
Swinton, Stevedore W 34, 36, 42, 46
    illness, continuing 104
    legal action 114, 121-122

T

Talmoi *xvii, xviii*
Tampe, Olive 55
Tasman Sea 14
Tennant Creek 150
testicles 51, 64-65, *88*
Thomas, Neil 169
Titan 3, *3*
Trewin, Flying Officer 19-20, *20*, 22-23, 26, 30, 116-117, 126
    decontamination of Idomeneus 92, 84, 89, 116
    illness, continuing 105
    internal RAAF inquiry 92
    Marrangaroo, at 76-78
Tung Song 18-19

U

U-boats 11-15,
    U-47 2
    U-518 11, *11*
United States xxi
    Army Air Force 49th Fighter Pursuit Group Squadron 143
    chemical weapons xi, xviii-xxi

W

Walsh Bay 27, 29, 40, 96, 125
    No. 8 Pier 29, *125*
Webb, Sir William 121, *121*
Welbourn, Mr 35, 47
White, Bill 152
white blood cell count 105, 166-167
Whitton, Stevedore G 34, 38, 39-40, 123
Williams, Andrew xiv, xvi, xviii, xxiii, *xxvi*, 34, 40, *41*, 43, 58-59, *58*, 169
    death 56-61, 69, 95-101

home *40*
   hospital, in 49-50, 53-56
   injuries 96-97
   insurance 124
   mental condition 100-101
Williams, Elsie *41, 42,* 43, 53-56, *58, 59,* 60
   Coroner's Inquest 96
Williams, Elsie (daughter) *59*
Williams, Gilbert 43, *44,* 49, 58, *59*
   Coroner's Inquest 96
Williams, Gwen *59*
Williams, Jean 53, *54,* 56
Williams, John 60
Williams, Sir Dudley 121, *121*
Wilson, Stevedore C 34, 123
winchman *37*

Y

Y3 *see* mustard gas (Y3)
Ypres x, xvii

www.ingramcontent.com/pod-product-compliance
Lightning Source LLC
Chambersburg PA
CBHW060510300426
44112CB00017B/2617